The Biblical Coun:

"*The Biblical Counseling Guide for Women* is a well-written, well-documented book. Dr. Street and his wife Janie have done a tremendous work for those desiring to counsel others. Each chapter is grounded in the Word of God, which is sufficient and authoritative. They also do a great job of explaining medical terms along with contrasting biblical terms with psychologized terms. An added bonus is the thought-provoking questions at the end of each chapter. This book is a must for every biblical counselor and a great help for training those who desire to counsel biblically. I look forward to having it as a resource!"

Susan Heck
ACBC-certified biblical counselor and author

"The Streets have written a very important book that will benefit those who counsel. Two unique aspects of this book: the amount of Scripture given for each challenging issue, and the case study format to which both counselors and counselees can relate. Helpful lists and descriptions are woven into the text. This book is a valuable resource for the Christian community."

Caroline Newheiser
ACBC-certified biblical counselor

"*The Biblical Counseling Guide for Women* is a most valuable resource for women counselors. Written in a counseling-case format, it lends a good picture of the sufficiency of God's Word and how to specifically apply it in a relative manner. The cases that the Streets unfold address some critical issues that women face today. They have taken a bold step to create biblical discussion around them."

Zondra Scott
ACBC-certified biblical counselor and author

"This is an important book that is enjoyable to read about a woman's faith and her God. Each engaging narrative discusses different kinds of personal struggles we women face, isolating the underlying core issue in our hearts along with the corresponding wisdom and insight from God's Word. This *targeted truth* enables every woman to know and trust her Savior and Lord in greater ways as well as build a bridge from the perception of arresting helplessness to sanctifying purposefulness. The result is pure joy and worship-enlarging faith as we repeatedly see our Creator, Savior, and Sustaining God as our loving Helper! Along with the Bible it will amply supply any Christian woman with a volume of material for personal worship time, parenting or discipleship relationship, or counseling opportunity. I guarantee it will ignite a well-worn path to the cross for all who bend its covers."

Donna Shannon
Elder's wife and discipler of women at
Grace Community Church, Sun Valley, CA

"John and Janie Street have filled this book with wise counsel. They tackle hard subjects and give light where there is often darkness. I would encourage every woman who counsels to get a copy."

Amy Baker
ACBC-certified biblical counselor and speaker

" *The Biblical Counseling Guide for Women* is an invaluable resource for any Christian who disciples women. This very readable book allows the reader to "listen in" on decades of ministry and learn from gifted and godly counselors who point the reader to the hope and help in God's inerrant Word. Through case studies of common difficulties with which women struggle, John and Janie Street give the counselor wisdom from God's Word and practical action steps that will serve as a helpful guide for anyone seeking to minister the Word to hurting women."

Lauren Lambert
Pastor's wife and discipler of women at
First Baptist Church, Jacksonville, FL

THE BIBLICAL COUNSELING GUIDE FOR *W*OMEN

John D. Street & Janie Street

HARVEST HOUSE PUBLISHERS
EUGENE, OREGON

Italicized text in Scripture quotations indicates authors' emphasis.

Cover by Dugan Design Group

Cover Image @ kupicoo / Getty Images

The characters in each chapter are fictitious yet represent a composite of many actual counselees. The story lines are not written to present the account of any one particular person. If some of the details of a chapter remind you of a situation with which you are familiar, this is purely coincidental.

Because the counseling scenarios in this book are composites, the actual specifics you find necessary for addressing individual counselees may vary depending on the factors involved in their cases.

THE BIBLICAL COUNSELING GUIDE FOR WOMEN

Copyright © 2016 John D. Street and Janie Street
Published by Harvest House Publishers
Eugene, Oregon 97408
www.harvesthousepublishers.com

ISBN 978-0-7369-6451-7 (pbk.)
ISBN 978-0-7369-6452-4 (eBook)

Library of Congress Cataloging-in-Publication Data
Names: Street,, John D., 1952- author. | Street, Janie, author.
Title: The biblical counseling guide for women / John D. Street, Jr. and
    Janie Street.
Description: Eugene, Oregon : Harvest House Publishers, 2016.
Identifiers: LCCN 2016023339 (print) | LCCN 2016025622 (ebook) | ISBN
    9780736964517 (pbk.) | ISBN 9780736964524 ()
Subjects: LCSH: Women—Pastoral counseling of. | Bible—Psychology. |
    Bible—Use. | Christian life—Biblical teaching. | Church work with women.
Classification: LCC BV4445 .S76 2016 (print) | LCC BV4445 (ebook) | DDC
    259.082—dc23
LC record available at https://lccn.loc.gov/2016023339

Printed in the United States of America

20 21 22 23 24 25 / BP-CD / 10 9 8 7 6 5 4 3 2

To Joan L. Street-Entingh and Carol J. Neely,
our mothers who introduced us to the sufficiency of Jesus Christ
through their lives and their gospel counsel.
To Jesus Christ belongs all the glory and honor,
both now and forever.
Amen!

Acknowledgments

There is a deep sense of gratitude we have to our Lord Jesus Christ for His sustaining grace over a two-year period as this book was being produced. We are grateful to our son, Jay Street, who did a significant amount of background research for each chapter while pursuing a Master's of Theology degree (ThM) and facing some physical challenges of his own. Then there was a time when all writing stopped. Janie was diagnosed with cancer, had surgery, and was eventually declared to be cancer-free. This has truly been a family effort: Jay doing the background research, myself writing the chapters, and my wife functioning as an editor. For months we have told her that she is the one who has helped to "feminize" each chapter.

We are also grateful for the unusually rich experience in supervising counselors seeking certification through the Association of Certified Biblical Counselors (ACBC), as well as opportunities to teach so many wonderful graduate students at The Master's University and Seminary. In many ways it is because of the sharpening interaction with these counselors and students that these chapters contain the practical help they do.

Finally, we are grateful to Harvest House Publishers and their willingness to publish this book. We want to especially thank Bob Hawkins and Steve Miller for their patience as we have encountered delays due to the challenges mentioned above. They have been a joy to work with.

Contents

Foreword

Have you ever had a problem you could not solve? Or a friend whom you could not help? In this book, John and Janie Street have made it abundantly clear that there is great hope no matter the kinds of problems women struggle with. They have laid out clear, biblical plans of action for issues that women face today. And through compelling stories, they have shown how women can help women to respond so that by the grace of God and obedience to His Word, they can help others to turn from the misery they find themselves in.

God's Word *is* "living and active" and sufficient to help us "in times of need" (Hebrews 4:12, 16). He has, in fact, "granted to us all things pertaining to life and godliness" (2 Peter 1:3). There is no need to embrace man-made ideas about what will help someone stuck in the midst of difficult emotional problems. Our Lord Jesus expressed it this way when He prayed to the Father in John 17: "Sanctify them in the truth; Your word is truth" (John 17:17).

This book points you to God's truth. It is full of hope and practical biblical guidance. My prayer is that God will use this book to bless those who read it for themselves or to help others.

To God alone be the glory.

Martha Peace
Biblical counselor and author
of *The Excellent Wife*

Seeking God's Wisdom for Real Hope and Change

A woman was the crowning point of God's original creation. In the first chapter of Genesis, at the end of each day of creation, God characterized what He had made as "good," but not until He created the woman did He pronounce "everything that he made" to be "very good" (Genesis 1:31). Our great God who made woman is also her Helper. This book is written to assist Christian women who possess a high view of the sufficiency of God's Word and its ability to adequately address the most serious personal struggles women will face. Women who trust His Word will benefit greatly from its narrative. You will need a Bible close at hand as you read each chapter, because this book is full of carefully selected Scripture references that should be consulted as you read.

Women have been sufferers ever since the entrance of sin into the human condition. Some of the chapters in this book are written for the woman who is suffering because she lives in this sin-cursed world. Because "all have sinned and fall short of the glory of God" (Romans 3:23), everyone around her is a sinner and she will often be sinned against. The Bible speaks to those who suffer, and its truth is especially powerful for those who suffer unjustly. Study Psalms 55, 56, and 57, and you will find help if you suffer from betrayal. Examine Psalms 37 and 73 if you struggle while watching the wicked prosper. Consider Hebrews 2:14-18 and 4:15-16 for a look at your Savior, who suffered unjustly in order to sympathize with your plight. How should a woman respond to unjust suffering? This book provides help!

This book is also about a woman's suffering as a result of her own sin (Romans 3:23). Scripture is clear that a woman's ungodly attitudes, thoughts, and behaviors will have consequences. Life will be difficult and adversity will dog her steps when a woman walks foolishly (Proverbs 13:15, 21). There are chapters in this book that are written to help women with this type of suffering as well. It will be particularly helpful to the woman who has lost hope of ever changing. The practical value of biblical counsel is unmatched.

In the Bible, God is revealed as creator of the world, sustainer of His creation, and gracious redeemer of His people. As the King above all earthy kings, He is absolutely sovereign in all the affairs of life (Romans 9:15-23; 1 Timothy 6:15; Revelation 4:11). God has chosen to reveal some of His purposes and plans in the Bible, but He has also sovereignly chosen to keep secret many of the things He is doing and intends to bring to pass for our good and His glory (Deuteronomy 29:29). You can be sure that whatever happens is the outworking of God's perfect blueprint for your life; and because He is a holy, good, just, and wise God, you can trust Him. Ecclesiastes 7:14 declares, "In the day of prosperity be joyful, and in the day of adversity consider: God has made the one as well as the other, so that man may not find out anything that will be after him." In other words, God expects you to trust Him by following what He has revealed to you in His Word and not expect to be told all of His reasons behind every providential detail of your life. This book is all about learning the rich insights that God's Word has for your life, and then understanding how to trust it enough to live by it— regardless of the details or difficulty of your circumstances.

Because the Bible is the very Word of God, it stands uniquely alone in its precision and comprehensiveness. Having originated with God, it is inerrant (without error) and sufficient (2 Peter 1:3; 2 Timothy 3:16-17). Both inerrancy and sufficiency are established upon the very nature and character of God; being absolutely perfect in His divine nature, His written revelation, the Bible, is absolute perfection (2 Samuel 22:31; Psalm 19:7). There is nothing unrevealed that is important or necessary for the welfare of the souls of His people. Furthermore, because your Bible preserves the very words of the King, it is absolutely authoritative. This authority surpasses and exceeds any and all theory or counsel that mere man can construct for dealing with the turmoil or difficulties of the soul (Proverbs 30:5). Not only does it possess remedies for the cure of the soul, it also possesses the diagnostic criteria. With inerrancy, sufficiency, and authority as its foundation, this book takes several contemporary problems that women face and shows how thoroughly and practically the Word of God speaks to each issue.

This book is based on real-life case studies of women who have faced formidable personal struggles and hardship, but have learned how to face them with competent biblical counsel. Although the characters in each chapter are fictitious, they represent a composite of many counselees that we have encountered in more than 35 years of biblical counseling—both through the hours we have spent in counseling and a vast amount of time supervising counselors-in-training as they opened their Bibles to counsel others. The story lines are not written to present the account of any one particular person. If some of the details of a chapter remind you of a situation with which you are familiar, this is purely coincidental.

However, the fact that these chapters draw upon actual counseling situations should enable you to see their practicality and usefulness in handling even the most severe mental, emotional, and spiritual problems. This book is written for the purpose of providing insightful practical answers from Scripture, and is not intended to be a scholastic review of various theoretical approaches to a particular problem, even though the authors are aware of such views. There are solid academic theses and manuscripts that support the counsel in each chapter, but it is not the purpose of this book to review such research. The chapters within address various problems of the soul. They are not comprehensive guides to each problem; instead, they are intended to address the most common features that each difficulty of the soul presents and point the reader to biblical help in finding practical and authoritative answers to their problems.

It is vital to the biblical counseling process for the reader/counselee to have a saving relationship with Jesus Christ. She must fully trust the Lord and His revealed will for this book to be of any substantial benefit. For the unbeliever, at best, the Bible is a set of suggestions. For the believer, it is her final authority for faith and practice. Biblical counseling is effective when the counselee is a Christian and fully trusts the inspiration of the 66 canonical books of the Bible. Change can be difficult for believers, but real change that God counts as righteousness is impossible for an unbeliever. That is because biblical change occurs at the heart level and is not merely behavioral or external. Only Christians, with the help of the indwelling Holy Spirit, can experience true change in the heart. For a clear explanation of saving faith in Jesus Christ, see Appendix A.

What is the goal of biblical counseling? In short, it is to help a counselee live a life of obedience and faith, and thus to be more Christlike (John 6:35-40). This is accomplished by living out the implications of the gospel in the midst of your problems, seeking to bring all of your life under the authority of the Lord Jesus Christ and His Word. The goal is not simply a short-sighted attempt to get a woman out of her problems, even though, when a person follows Christ's admonitions, her problems will often eventually be resolved.

However, some problems will not go away, even after you have faithfully obeyed Christ. Some of life's difficulties may even get worse (see, for example, Genesis 39:7-20). Consider the practical example of a Christian wife living out her Christianity in front of her unbelieving husband, which only serves to make him angrier (1 Peter 3:1-6). Regardless of his growing anger she remains faithful to Christ; the Lord uses her faithfulness to build her endurance, which, in turn, strengthens her godly character, thereby deepening her hope (Romans 5:3-5). The difficulty with her husband does not go away, but she is able to produce righteous fruit in the midst of her storm (Psalm 1; James 1:2-4). How can you, as a godly woman, learn to please God in the midst of your problems? This must be the pursuit of a woman who is a committed Christian (2 Corinthians 5:9; Colossians 1:9-10).

It is our hope that as you read and reflect on the topics and discussion questions at the end of each chapter that your love for the Lord and His Word will increase. It will be vital that, as you use your Bible and look up the textual references in each chapter, you not take verses out of context, unwittingly distorting their intended meaning. Read the surrounding context of the verse to ensure you are reading and understanding it properly. As you read, ask yourself: What did the original author of those words intend for them to mean to the original audience? Great care has been taken to place these counseling narratives into helpful biblical texts that either directly or indirectly match the original intent of the biblical author, but you will need to do careful studies of Scripture passages in order to properly understand them. Often the biblical reference provided will illustrate a theological truth referred to in the content of the story.

Remember, God's Word is your final authority, but the reference verse you are looking up must be understood within the context of the broader passage of Scripture from which it has been taken.

May the truths of Scripture bring lasting change and growth in your life as you seek practical answers for the problems you face—to the honor and glory of the Lord Jesus Christ.

Soli Deo Gloria
John and Janie Street
December 2016

1

Anger

Be not quick in your spirit to become angry,
for anger lodges in the heart of fools.

ECCLESIASTES 7:9

"Stop asking me stupid questions. Can't you see I'm trying to get dinner ready before soccer practice? You're going to make us late again!" Melinda heard her own voice raised once again in angry impatience with her children. She cringed inwardly as she recalled multiple times that she had responded similarly within the past week. An ugly, habitual pattern of angry outbursts was becoming obvious to her.

Like many busy moms, Melinda tries hard to remain calm and controlled in the face of mountains of laundry, tight schedules, and fatigue from insufficient sleep. But lately she senses a new intensity to her anger—which frightens her. After such a display of anger, she is overcome with remorse. This is not the way a godly woman should respond to her family. She realizes things must change, and yet, after months of wishing and praying for that change, she seems even further mired in her ungodly ways.

Her mind keeps running over and over again the disturbing words of Proverbs 14:1: "The wisest of women builds her house, but folly with her own hands tears it down." Would her next eruption be in public, perhaps ruining her husband's reputation at a company dinner? In a careless moment, will she explode and destroy a close friendship? During an angry outburst, might she wreck the car and cause bodily harm to some stranger? Or even worse, would she do something stupid and hurt her own children? She knows this is not the way a Christian is supposed to live. What is going on in her angry heart? Her ability to remain composed and self-controlled seems to slip away as her passion increases.

Frequently upset and frustrated, Melinda is beginning to think that perhaps she has a hormonal problem. This is just not like her— allowing little things to irritate her and losing her temper so quickly. Some of her friends had similar experiences and were diagnosed with physiological problems—hormonal imbalances and tumors. Maybe a simple hormonal treatment or vitamin supplements would be the answer. Or might she require a surgical procedure?

Resigning herself to these possibilities, Melinda went to see her doctor. But after several medical tests, all her reports were negative. "There is nothing physically wrong with you," her physician explained. "However, there are other explanations for what you are experiencing." He proceeded to describe how anger can be a symptom of recurring psychological problems, like attention deficit/hyperactivity disorder (ADD/ADHD), obsessive compulsive disorder (OCD), oppositional defiant disorder (ODD), paranoid personality disorder (paranoia), antisocial personality disorder (sociopathy), borderline personality disorder, or narcissism.

Melinda's mind raced, *Could this be true? Do I have some deeply embedded psychological problem that is the source of my anger? Do I need to see a psychologist or psychiatrist? Am I mentally disturbed and not recognizing it?* She had heard of some people who spent many years in psychotherapy sessions, paying thousands of dollars that ultimately depleted their insurance coverage, and yet their problems were never resolved. Was this in her future?

One day a close Christian friend suggested Melinda consider seeing a well-trained biblical counselor about her anger. "Biblical answers are always the best answers," her friend remarked with confidence. After thinking about this for a while, Melinda decided she really didn't need to talk to a counselor. She was quite sure that she didn't have a psychological disorder, as the doctor had suggested. And besides, her anger problems were normal, something every wife and mother goes through. She decided instead to memorize a few verses from the Bible and try to keep calm. "Keep calm and carry on—isn't that what everyone says these days?" James 1:19-20 seemed just right for her: "Know this, my beloved brothers: let every person be quick to hear, slow to speak, slow to anger; for the anger of man does not produce the righteousness of God." Feeling better already, Melinda read these verses over and over on her iPhone until James and Katherine came running toward the car after soccer practice was over.

For about a week, Melinda was on cloud nine. Several times, she had been tempted to blow up. But she had worked hard on being "slow to speak." James and Katherine seemed to be bickering less with each other, and they were more responsive to her as well. Even her husband, Doug, noticed a difference. Returning home early from work one day, he remarked at how cooperative the children seemed. He also complimented her, "It's good to see my beautiful wife looking so happy these days."

It was the phone call that started it all up again. Melinda's mother called to say that they were not going to visit at Christmas like they had promised. "It's your sister's fault, you know. She has such a hard life being a single mom, and your dad and I are trying to do everything we can to make her life easier. You understand, don't you, dear?

I know it's been a long time since we've had Christmas together, but you are the stronger daughter. I'm sure you and your family will have a nice time together. Maybe you can visit Doug's folks again."

At first Melinda was silent. Then she managed to say, "It's okay, Mom. Don't worry. We'll be fine." When the call ended, the raging thoughts began. *Why does my sister have to ruin everything? She's so controlling—always wanting her own way! She wouldn't have such a hard life if she hadn't married such a jerk. She makes all the bad choices and gets all the good stuff—Mom and Dad at the holidays, loads of sympathy, and no accountability. She never says, "I'm sorry." She just keeps taking and taking and taking. Well, I've had it with her!*

Before she could change her mind, Melinda picked up the phone and punched in her sister's cell number—not caring that she would interrupt her at work. When Jenna answered, she was surprised to hear from Melinda, but even more shocked to hear her pent-up anger erupt over the phone. She sat at her desk, stunned and silent, waiting for Melinda to finish her bitter tirade. Phrases like "you always," "you never," "you're so selfish," and "you never think of anyone but yourself" were ringing in her ears as she hung up the phone. Turning back to her computer in an attempt to focus on her work, tears threatened to spill out of her eyes.

Afterward, Melinda felt relieved of the weight of her bitterness, but that sense of relief was quickly replaced with the oh-so-familiar remorse. She had done it again, only this time worse than ever. Those awful things she had said to her sister! Why had she done that? Why hadn't her memory verses kept her from exploding in anger? Now things were much worse than before. Jenna would go crying to their mother, Doug would eventually find out, and Melinda felt full of guilt and shame once again.

Sobbing in distress, Melinda knew that her friend was right. It was time to get some help. Before she could talk herself out of it, she called the church office and set an appointment with an older woman who was trained to help people with their difficulties.

Melinda had always wanted to be a godly woman, wife, and mother, but she never considered that the Bible would have anything to do with her "emotional" problems. Happily, Melinda found out her assumptions were wrong! She was soon to discover that the Bible indeed had answers for the difficulties she faced, and that learning how God wanted her to handle her sinful anger was about to transform her life.

"Not all anger is sinful. Did you know that?" her counselor asked. Melinda had never heard this before. Her frequent outbursts of anger brought so much guilt and shame that she had never taken the time to look at anger from a biblical viewpoint. Helen, her biblical counselor, continued. "Psalm 7:11 says that God gets angry every day. The phrase 'every day' is a Hebrew idiom meaning all the time, or 'all day, every day.' In a display of righteous anger, Jesus drove the greedy money-changers out of the courtyard in the Jerusalem temple because zeal for the proper treatment of His Father's house overwhelmed Him (John 2:14-17). Like God and Jesus Christ, you have the capacity to become angry, which you are well aware of. This is what theologians call one aspect of the communicable attributes of God to His human beings who bear His image."

Melinda found out that there were two aspects to her capacity for anger: one good and one sinful. Everyone has the potential to become angry when observing an injustice, an act of wanton violence, or cruelty. This is a form of *righteous* anger; it is not sinful anger.

In writing to the Ephesian Christians concerning their interpersonal conduct with one another, the apostle Paul commented, "Be angry and do not sin; do not let the sun go down on your anger" (Ephesians 4:26). In this verse, Paul referenced Psalm 4:4, where the Old Testament word translated "anger" is a clear Hebrew imperative, while the Greek word used in Ephesians 4:26 can be taken as an indicative (statement of fact) *or* imperative (expressing a command). A good interpretation leads us to the indicative translation: Paul was not commanding Christians to be angry, which would be an imperative; rather, he assumed that there will be times in your life when you would be angry with good reason—an indicative, or a statement of fact. He conceded that anger will be a part of your life as you live in a sin-cursed world.

But then Paul proceeded to warn, presumably because of our sinful nature, that even righteous anger can quickly turn into wicked anger. "Do not let the sun go down on your anger." Some people have unwisely taken this to mean that Paul was giving permission to hold onto anger until a few minutes before sunset. On the contrary, this is an ancient first-century expression that means you must deal with your anger as quickly as possible. No one should remain angry for a long period of time, because even righteous anger can become unrighteous when left unresolved. Even your most positive human emotions can easily and quickly become tainted because of depravity.

While this information about anger was informative, Melinda wasn't sure her anger could be called *righteous*. How could it, since it brought such shame upon her? Helen then began to describe the sinful aspect of anger. The Bible calls this *unrighteous* anger. The essential difference between the two is that righteous anger always seeks God's goals. It always desires what God desires: justice, equity, goodness, and kindness. It is others-centered.

In contrast, unrighteous anger always seeks personal goals and rights. It is self-centered. It is consumed with being denied personal rights and is characterized by demanding attitudes. Unrighteous anger is seldom satisfied and most assuredly never *fully* satisfied. Ecclesiastes 7:9 indicates that anger or vexation resides in the bosom of fools. The unwise person will allow anger to fester and cultivate in the heart. The angry heart says, "I want what I want;" or "What I do have, I don't want." It refuses to be satisfied with anything short of its own selfish ambitions. Melinda began to cringe, as she felt this was describing her type of anger.

Helen illustrated it this way: If you were to observe someone violently abusing a small child, it *should* cause you to become angry. An injustice is being done, as well as a criminal act. God has created you with the ability to become passionately angry when you see such wicked behavior directed at a helpless child. When you are experiencing anger like this, it is righteous anger you are feeling.

However, when your friend does something you don't like, and perhaps you feel hurt and unloved because of it, and then you feel anger well up in your heart, it is often unrighteous. The source of your anger is your conclusion that your personal right was denied—your right to always be treated with loving respect by your friend. Your only thought in this moment is for yourself—what your friend has denied *you*, and how violated *you* feel by this unjust treatment. All you can think about is how badly she has hurt you. While there is no denying that friends and family members do hurt us at times, if your only thought is to get even—to make her suffer as she has made you suffer—then your anger is not righteous. It is not focused on how to be a blessing to your friend, but rather on yourself. You have plenty of pity for yourself; but in the anger of the moment, you have no pity for her. The Bible has the perfect prescription for times when we are hurt by others:

> Repay no one evil for evil, but give thought to do what is honorable in the sight of all. If possible, so far as it depends on you, live peaceably with all. Beloved, never avenge yourselves, but leave it to the wrath of God, for it is written, "Vengeance is mine, I will repay, says the Lord." To the contrary, "if your enemy is hungry, feed

him; if he is thirsty, give him something to drink…" Do
not be overcome by evil, but overcome evil with good
(Romans 12:17-21).

Melinda quickly saw the unrighteousness of her anger toward
Jenna. From her perspective, Jenna kept getting in the way of what
she wanted—a perfect Christmas with Mom and Dad; or better yet,
a world where Jenna's problems did not dominate and control everything. Her good desire for a loving Christmas with her parents had
become a self-centered desire because her heart not only desired it
but *demanded* it. And when she didn't get what she wanted, unrighteous anger was the result.

Even very good desires—like fun holiday times with family—
can turn into selfish and demanding ones. Melinda could tell that
her plan for Christmas was self-focused, because when it was denied,
she responded with an explosion of unrighteous anger. Perhaps what
Jenna did by dominating Mom and Dad was unjust; Melinda felt a
bit justified in her anger. But regardless of that justification, Melinda's angry reaction brought about "bitterness and wrath and anger
and clamor and slander"—all of which the Bible says we are to put
away from us (Ephesians 4:31). This indeed was unrighteous anger.

Anger is a volatile passion, and when it is ignited by unrighteous desires, it is destructive. If you permit it to rule your life, it
will destroy your closest relationships because no one wants to live
around an active volcano. Your family and friends will never be quite
sure when you are going to erupt. They will have been hurt too many
times from previous eruptions with your explosive words and abusive actions. If you allow angry outbursts to dominate your responses,
you will quickly find yourself isolated and alone as people begin to
avoid you. Even worse than these consequences, unrighteous anger
is sin against God.

"Let's look at the first chapter of James in the Bible to learn more about where sinful anger comes from and how deadly it is," instructed Helen. "In verse 20, James warns us 'the anger of man does not produce the righteousness of God.'" Helen then mentioned the tragedy of Cain and his brother Abel. The first murder recorded in the Bible was a result of anger! Helen and Melinda read together the ancient account of this violence.

> In the course of time Cain brought to the LORD an offering of the fruit of the ground, and Abel also brought of the firstborn of his flock and of their fat portions. And the LORD had regard for Abel and his offering, but for Cain and his offering he had no regard. So Cain was very angry, and his face fell. The LORD said to Cain, "Why are you angry, and why has your face fallen? If you do well, will you not be accepted? And if you do not do well, sin is crouching at the door. Its desire is for you, but you must rule over it." Cain spoke to Abel his brother. And when they were in the field, Cain rose up against his brother Abel and killed him (Genesis 4:3-8).

Clearly, from the beginning of mankind, unrighteous anger has brought about devastating results. Before Helen and Melinda studied the James 1 passage more thoroughly, they also looked at Jesus' words in His Sermon on the Mount:

> You have heard that it was said to those of old, "You shall not murder; and whoever murders will be liable to judgment." But I say to you that everyone who is angry with his brother will be liable to judgment; whoever insults his brother will be liable to the council; and whoever says, "You fool!" will be liable to the hell of fire (Matthew 5:21-22).

Jesus' association of anger with murder was a sobering consideration; it caused Melinda to take her anger problem much more seriously. As she thought about the reasons she had come to Helen for counseling, she realized that her initial motivation originated with embarrassment. Her angry outbursts were getting out of hand and causing her to look bad to her family and friends. She needed to show these loved ones that she was not a sinful person. If she could just stop blowing up, others would see her as a godly wife, mother, sister, and friend.

In addition to her anger, Melinda was suddenly ashamed of something else: Pride had motivated her to seek help. And in her pride, she had not thought about God's view of unrighteous anger—how serious a sin it was in His eyes. Her only thought had been to clean up the outside of her life—her behavior. But Jesus' words revealed that her angry heart was a murderous heart. How could this be? Never once had Melinda entertained even the thought of murder, but the connection between the two in Scripture was undeniable. Melinda's motivation for meeting with Helen about her anger was beginning to change. She was ready to see anger as God sees it, to call it what God calls it, and to humbly repent of it. Her heart became soft ground—fertile soil for learning God's ways and changing into the godly woman that she previously thought she already was.

Melinda was now eager to see what the book of James had to say about anger. It was written to Jewish Christians who were experiencing serious persecution for their faith in the Lord Jesus Christ. While this was not true of Melinda's life, nevertheless, she believed that all of God's Word was written to teach sincere Christians how to live in such a way that God would be honored (Romans 15:4-5). James charged these suffering Jewish readers to "count it all joy, my brothers, when you meet trials of various kinds" (James 1:2). While undergoing severe oppression, some were tempted to use their Jewish theology of God's sovereignty to blame Him for leading them into failure and tempting them to cave under the pressure (1:13).[1]

When disappointments and difficulties arise in your life, you may find yourself struggling with similar reactions. Stress and pain can make it easy for you to seek a nearby target on which to vent your frustrations—often those around you who are weak or the least threatening. Family members or friends who have loved you are the most common targets because you assume they will not retaliate, at least not in a way that will substantially hurt you.

Ultimately, however, your anger is against the One whom you believe permitted this unpleasant circumstance to occur. "How could God allow this to happen to me? He is the one who has backed me into a corner, and I have no choice but to respond the way I do." Melinda quickly recognized that she had responded in a similar way when disappointment (unrealized hopes for the holidays) and difficulties (dealing with a typical busy mom day) were a part of her life. Her sister had become her target for venting her anger when the disappointments increased; her children had borne the brunt of her irritation with the seemingly impossible task of managing a busy family schedule. She admitted that her anger was ultimately against God, just as happened with the Jewish believers James had written to centuries earlier.

James's readers felt the same way. They became offended with God, blaming Him for putting them into a situation in which they felt forced to respond in an angry way. In their view, not only was He at fault for the allowing the trial, but also for how they felt compelled to respond to the difficulty. James quickly corrected their wrong theology. In verses 14-15, he declared that God does not coerce His people to sin, and He Himself is never coerced to sin. Instead, each person sins because he is induced by his own lusts—sinful longings and desires. God is not the cause of you being dragged away in temptation; rather, your lust incites you to sin.

The word translated "lust" is predominantly used throughout

the New Testament to describe a strong internal passion. This kind of passion, in and of itself, is not wrong (for example, Paul used the word to speak of a person who *longs* to work in the Lord's service as an overseer—see 1 Timothy 3:1). But unbridled passion or lust that does not submit to the will of God is sinful lust. It is with this perspective that James targeted his readers' problem with their uncontrolled lusts, resulting in their anger against God. There was a raging passion warring within them that had resulted in their sinful zeal (James 4:1-3; see verse 2 for this same word "lust").

Next, James painted a portrait of how sin develops in your heart by using a familiar analogy of pregnancy and birth (verse 15). Lust is the starting point. It's what becomes conceived in the womb of the heart. Just like a baby develops and grows, this lust—this sinful longing or desire—if left unchecked, will mature and expand, often imperceptibly. Then, lust will give birth to sin. What was once a microscopic, secret heart issue has given birth to a full-blown sin (such as anger). Just as a baby cannot stay in his mother's womb forever, so the growing passion of lust will not be able to keep quiet. It will eventually come out for all to see in a clear presentation of wrath.

Finally, when this anger grows to full maturity, it brings forth death. In other words, a baby doesn't live as an infant forever. He will mature and become an adult. But even in his maturity, he is growing closer to the day of his death. Such is the case with sinful anger. It will only boil hotter when left to itself—uncontrolled and unrepented of—and will eventually lead to your demise.

Helen pointed out a couple of insightful truths from this short study in James.

- First, *anger always seeks a target*, perhaps directed toward a particular person or even a collective group of people. All sinful anger, however, is ultimately directed toward God.

- Second, *anger is in many ways an external manifestation of a larger problem going on inside the heart*—namely, there is something that you want ("lust") that you do not have (such as respect of others, material things), or something that you have that you do not want (such as persecution, disrespect of others, trial, etc.).[2]

Let's look at James's counsel starting in verse 21: "Therefore put away all filthiness and rampant wickedness and receive with meekness the implanted word, which is able to save your souls." The biblical command "put away" speaks of repentance. The Christian who has allowed desire to morph into sinful anger must repent of this sin. She must repent and turn away from it—"therefore put away all filthiness and rampant wickedness"—and turn toward being the kind of woman God wants her to be—"receive with meekness the implanted word." The key heart issue that needs to change is your view of yourself and the situation God has placed you in. Your attitude must be one of "meekness" or "gentleness." The word that James used can also be translated "humility." Developing a humble, submissive heart to the situation that God has placed you in is critical for your spiritual growth as it relates to your anger.

Furthermore, as you cultivate humility, you must receive the implanted Word. James is, of course, referring to the Word of God. The word he uses for "receive" carries the idea of welcoming the Word. Accept the Word that you already know comes from God. In fact, not only do you know it, but the apostle Peter explains that this Word was implanted in you as a seed that continues to grow in your heart and is producing fruit in your life (1 Peter 1:23). That is why James said this Word has already been implanted within you. So it is to your benefit to welcome the Word of truth, which is able to save your soul.

Melinda could see that this was the work that God's Word was doing in her own heart. It had revealed her "lust" (desires that she had allowed to become demands) and also her prideful heart. In repenting of her demanding heart and pride, she was able to begin to resist the temptations to become angry and verbally attack those closest to her. She began to trust that God knew what He was doing and had only good in mind when He placed her in the situations that previously had caused her such frustration. One of her new memory verses was Psalm 119:71: "It was good for me that I was afflicted, that I might learn your statutes." Meditating on that verse helped her to develop a thankful heart for everything in her day, even the stressful times with her children and the disappointments related to her extended family.

You see, when anger has stubbornly taken up residence in your heart, you well know that it is not always easy to simply welcome the Word of truth into your life. The truth of God's Word slices and dices your behavior and peers into the most shameful recesses of your heart (see Hebrews 4:12-13). Our hearts are resistant to this type of spiritual heart surgery. Thus we must pray that God will help us to humbly *repent* of this sin (Psalm 51:10).

That this was the case in Melinda's life was evident because the Word of God had not become sweet and attractive to her until she had repented of the sins of demanding her own way and the resulting anger that followed. The laying aside of all filthiness and the abundance of wickedness from you will require the work of the Spirit of God in your life (Galatians 5:16-26), and He *will* help you! He will do His part by helping you repent and live for Him, and you must also give all your effort to "receive with meekness the implanted Word." This is God's plan for change, and it will result in a gradual lessening of the control that anger has had in your life.

Furthermore, look at verses 19-20. James wrote, "Know this, my beloved brothers: let every person be quick to hear, slow to speak, slow to anger; for the anger of man does not produce the righteousness of God." Melinda was especially interested in these verses now, because she knew they would help her make a plan to stop responding in anger. Helen explained that for Melinda to make a commitment to deal with her anger with a self-willed determination was only the beginning. Many people who seek this kind of change fall prey to using human methods instead of God's method. For example, most secular counselors will urge you to find an inner strength and power, or to simply take out your anger on a substitute. In a psychotherapeutic way of thinking, anger is like a tea kettle of boiling water that will explode unless the steam is allowed to vent.

Some people try yelling into a pillow, hitting a punching bag, or releasing their frustration at a neutral object in order to vent their anger. But from a biblical standpoint, venting your anger does not get at the source. In fact, it is foolish to do this (Proverbs 29:11). Instead, you must turn off the heat under the kettle by approaching this problem as a struggle in your heart—dealing with your lusts before God. To do that, you must be ready and willing to listen, as our Scripture text says.

Listening is hard to do when you're angry, because true listening involves submission. This requires a silent, inward confession that your demands and anger are not right and that you need the correction and help of another. This is not listening for some audible voice from God, because He has already communicated to you everything you need in His Word. When you try to hear an audible voice, you betray your lack of trust in the sufficiency of His Word (2 Peter 1:3; 2 Timothy 3:16-17). Instead, listen to God through the truth of His Word—the Bible. It is vital that your heart is surrendered and submissive to His life-changing truth in the Scripture. This the picture-perfect portrayal of surrendering in war: You've lost and you need to listen carefully to God's terms of surrender, because He has won and He is always right.

But you must not stop with just listening. To listen carefully, *you must not continue to speak*. This is difficult for angry people to do, as they are continually engaged in spewing out their opinions and attacks. Oftentimes angry people say they are listening, but at the same time they persist in defending their viewpoint, often pointing out how another person also perceives the situation as unfair, jaded, or misconstrued—and it is clear that they are not really listening.

As Melinda thought back on recent episodes of anger, she found that to be true of herself as well. On one occasion, when she became angry with her husband about an investment he was considering, he asked her to hear him out—to listen fully to what he had to say. She responded, "I *am* listening! I always listen to you. You never want to hear *my* input. Why, Ellie's husband is always proposing these same kinds of things and never listens to her. She agrees that these investments are bad for the long term and wishes that her husband wouldn't keep bringing them up. I'm not the only one who thinks that!"

Melinda realized that she needed to begin to practice biblical listening—that is, listening to God's Word and to others. It is for reasons like this that James warned us to be slow to speak when we are angry. Speaking when you should be listening only interrupts the valuable insight that you are lacking. And what insight does James want you to gain? The implanted Word. You need to humbly submit by listening to and studying God's Word, asking God to soften your heart so that it is open to His work of conviction and growth. Otherwise, as verse 20 says, your anger will never work the righteousness of God.

Essentially, you yourself cannot produce the fruit of righteousness that God wants from you as a believer in Jesus Christ (Galatians

5:22-23). This fruit of righteousness comes from the Holy Spirit's sanctifying work in your life, and your anger will always seek to counteract His work. Immersing yourself in the careful study of God's Word—which is biblical listening—will allow God's Spirit to be at work in you, and will strengthen you as you pursue the eradication of unrighteous anger from your life.

Questions for Discussion

1. Read through James 4:1-3. What does James contend is the source of our fighting and anger?

2. According to verse 2, what kind of fruit does sinful anger produce in our lives? Look at verse 3. Why does God not always honor our prayers? What kind of heart does God seek from us in our prayer life?

3. Next, take a look at the earthly wisdom that James talks about in James 3:14-16. Do any of these characteristics define you? How is anger related to each of these?

4. Now look at James 3:17-18. Does anger fit in any of these descriptions?

5. James 1:19-21 and James 4:1-3 have a lot to say about the condition of our hearts. What can you do now to more actively cultivate the kind of heart God desires?

2

Anxiety

*Therefore do not be anxious about tomorrow, for tomorrow will
be anxious for itself. Sufficient for the day is its own trouble.*

MATTHEW 6:34

Sending Zach back into a war zone for the third time was more than
Audrey could take. He had survived two previous tours of duty in
that bloodthirsty place, but a third time was asking for more of a sacrifice than she was willing to make. His stories of IEDs exploding,
bullets whizzing past his helmet, watching his friends die—these
images raced through her mind.

Audrey remembered the day of Zach's birth as if it were yesterday.
His little round face, brown hair, and perfect fingers and toes made
him the cutest baby in the world. Today her baby boy is dressed up
in a military uniform awaiting his flight back to his unit. She noticed
how the first two deployments had aged him. No longer a boy, he
was in every way a man. But to her, he was still her baby. It had been
very hard to say good-bye on the first two deployments, but this was
beyond imaginable. An awful feeling of dread descended on her. She
felt her pulse quicken, and her breathing became shallow and rapid.
She had never had a panic attack before, but imagined this was what
it would feel like.

Bill and Audrey stayed at the airport and watched as their son's plane disappeared into the clouds. That's when the dam broke and her tear-filled eyes gushed. Convinced she would never see her boy again, a dark cloud of anxious dread settled around her. As days turned into weeks and weeks into months, Audrey's family and close friends observed changes in her that were concerning. She was not the cheerful Christian she used to be. Jumpy and preoccupied, every time the phone or doorbell rang she was startled, expecting news that Zach had been killed. In the past she had been a careful planner and a hard worker, but now she was falling behind on her responsibilities.

Bill was a patient husband, yet even he was nearing the end of his forbearance. He tried encouraging Audrey, praying with her, and even reading the Bible with her, but her anxiety only seemed to increase as each day passed. Her friends stopped calling, recognizing that this persistent problem was beyond their ability to solve. Those who loved her most were at a loss to know how to help her. It was as if she was trapped in a vortex of thoughts that would not let her go. *What is Zach doing today? Will this be his last day? How will I survive the crushing agony when that happens?* Audrey's increasing anxiousness and feelings of helplessness had a paralyzing effect on her, and as her neglected tasks piled up, so did her guilt.

Audrey never turned off her computer out of fear she might miss an email from her son. Television cable news was always on at home. When there were no reports from the war, she spent endless hours sitting—coffee cup in hand—staring into space, her mind far removed from what was going on around her. It became a ritual, staying up until 2:00 or 3:00 in the morning, watching the computer and every broadcast from the front lines. She would fall asleep only when she was totally exhausted, then sleep till mid-morning. Her eyes became dark and bloodshot, and her husband and children walked past her silently, doing their own laundry and preparing their own meals.

Audrey tried to convince herself that her vigilance in following the news was the proof she was a loving and faithful mother. Surely God would see her self-denial and diligence, and bring her son back alive. Yet in spite of the overwhelming fear of impending grief, she knew this was not the way that a Christian wife and mother should think and live. It slowly dawned on her that what began as simple apprehensiveness had turned into sinful anxiety. Anxiety was controlling her, and she didn't know how to stop it.

The next day, Audrey made plans for Bill and her to go out to dinner together. She prepared a casserole for the kids to heat up at home and made a reservation at a quiet restaurant just outside of town. Bill was surprised and a bit uncertain about what was up, given Audrey's state of mind. But he was very willing to spend some time alone with her.

After the waiter had served their entrees, Audrey looked directly at Bill and confessed, "I need help. I know I need help. I don't know what to do to get out from under my fears and anxiety. But I have seen how much control this fear has on me. I'm miserable. You're miserable. The kids are miserable. I'm ready to hear what you have to say. Please help me."

Tears had welled up in her eyes, and Bill was fighting back his own. To say he was relieved was an understatement. They talked at length during the dinner about the specific thoughts and feelings Audrey was struggling with. At the end of the meal, Bill recommended that they ask for help from their pastor. They both remembered a sermon series he had preached a few years back called "Facing Your Fears." Confident that he could help her, they both agreed to contact the church office for an appointment.

Pastor Andrew listened carefully to Bill and Audrey as they described the great difficulties of the past several months. He could relate well to their situation. His own son had served in the Gulf War a few decades back, so he knew what it meant to send his beloved child into harm's way and try not to fret about the possibilities. After hearing Audrey describe the control that anxiety had over her and how it had caused her to sin against her family, he knew she was ready for the first step. He read aloud to Audrey and Bill these comforting words:

> Blessed is the one whose transgression is forgiven, whose sin is covered. Blessed is the man against whom the Lord counts no iniquity, and in whose spirit there is no deceit. For when I kept silent, my bones wasted away through my groaning all day long. For day and night your hand was heavy upon me; my strength was dried up as by the heat of summer. I acknowledged my sin to you, and I did not cover my iniquity; I said, "I will confess my transgressions to the Lord," and you forgave the iniquity of my sin (Psalm 32:1-5).

Pastor Andrew then led Audrey to seek the Lord's forgiveness for her sins against her family as she had allowed anxiety to completely overwhelm her, causing her to neglect her loved ones. Many tears were shed, and the weight of depression began to lift. "Go home and do the same with your children," Pastor Andrew advised. "They need to hear your humble confession of sin and to see the work that God is doing in you to restore trust and hope in Him." With their children gathered around them, Bill and Audrey told them what the pastor had said and read Scripture to them. Audrey sought the forgiveness of her family and promised them she would be getting help to change and grow through this difficulty. Again, tears were shed, and there was also great rejoicing.

Pastor Andrew knew that it would take more than the initial confession of sin to bring about lasting change for Audrey, so he recommended that she meet with his wife, Dottie, who had recently been certified as a biblical counselor. Audrey agreed, and soon the two began to meet together. Before Audrey arrived at the first counseling session, she had already memorized a verse that she and Bill had talked about: "Casting all your anxieties on him, because he cares for you" (1 Peter 5:7). Dottie was pleased to see that Audrey was ready to work on her problem with anxiety with the help of God's Word.

"Fear and anxiety, while similar, are not the same thing," Dottie explained at their first session. "Fear is an emotional response directly related to an immediate, usually real, perceived threat or harm. Anxiety, on the other hand, is associated with the way you *anticipate* an expected threat. When you become anxious over some future event that has not occurred, your thinking becomes fixated on potential undesirable outcomes. Your imagination feeds these anxious thoughts with endless 'what ifs.' The more you dwell on these thoughts, the more your anxiousness grows. These thoughts are like quicksand. They seem to have their own gravitational attraction: The more you try to forget them. the more they seem to pull you in." Audrey listened carefully, taking notes on what she was hearing.

Dottie went on to illustrate the deceptive nature of anxiety. High blood pressure is a silent killer. Many who possess it do not think they have a problem until it is too late. Likewise, destructive anxiety silently overtakes the unaware because anxious people believe they are just trying to be cautious and thoughtful. Therein lies the deception. It is easy for you to deny you have a problem. In fact, Scripture does use the term that is often translated "anxiety" in a positive way when it speaks of deep concern and care for others (1 Corinthians 12:25; 2 Corinthians 11:28; Philippians 2:20). This concern is not sinful or destructive. However, there is a type of anxiety that *is* sinful and has the potential to destroy.

"Anxiety is a problem that has plagued Christians from the earliest days of the church, so you are not alone," Dottie reassured Audrey.

"It is possible, with the help of God's Word, to regain the peace that your soul desperately desires even though your present circumstances may not change." Turning to the promise of 1 Corinthians 10:13, together the women read: "No temptation has overtaken you that is not common to man. God is faithful, and he will not let you be tempted beyond your ability, but with the temptation he will also provide the way of escape, that you may be able to endure it."

Audrey realized that she was not facing anything unique. Others before her had faced a similar set of problems and faced them successfully—a comforting thought indeed. However, it seemed different in her situation. The anxious thoughts that persisted in regard to Zach's safety would not go away, even though she believed that God was in complete control of his circumstances. She knew that according to the truth of Scripture God would not allow anything to come into her life that would be more than she could bear—no matter how desperate the situation. She believed that those were true statements, but she wasn't sure they were true for her. "It's easy to quote those verses when it's someone else's son on the front lines. But every time I think of Zach, I cannot seem to believe that is true for me," she confessed to Dottie. "If my son were to be killed in battle, I know I could not bear it."

Dottie realized it was time to help Audrey examine her faith in God. What was it based on? What did she truly believe from the Bible, and what did she not believe? Could her underlying problem be one of *unbelief*? No true Christian wants to think they don't believe God, because in essence they would be calling Him a liar. And yet, this very fundamental belief in all of God's Word is often tested and proven in the fires of affliction and trials.

"God is faithful" (1 Corinthians 10:13). That's what His Word says about Him and that's who He is: faithful. Dottie assigned Audrey a bit of homework before their next session. She was to find ten passages of Scripture that either declared God's faithfulness (such as the one they just read) or that demonstrated His faithfulness to His loved ones (such as saving Lot and his family from destruction based on His faithfulness to His promise to Abraham in Genesis 19). As Audrey studied these passages during the week, she was to pray that God would help her *believe* this truth about Him, that He is faithful. This study proved to be a turning point for Audrey as the Spirit of God revealed her lack of faith—her unbelief—and brought her to repentance and a new confidence in the Most High God.

As the counseling sessions continued week by week, Dottie helped Audrey look at her anxiety from every angle possible, with the goal of truly putting this sin behind her completely. One of the things that had enabled Audrey to see her need for anxiety counseling was the effect that her sinful worry had on those around her. Centuries earlier, the Christians at Philippi were in danger of succumbing to this kind of harmful worry. They grieved over the fact that their spiritual mentor, Paul, had been imprisoned, and they had every reason to believe that they too might suffer for the gospel of Christ (Philippians 1:27-30). The potential for harm to Paul and themselves was very real.

But even when a person rightly anticipates future hardship, anxious worry about that reality still harms relationships, bringing about division and strife. Knowing this, Paul instructed the faithful believers in Philippi to maintain unity in Christ (Philippians 2:1–4:9). He directly addressed two women in the church, Euodia and Syntyche, whose disagreement was causing trouble (4:2-3). He then admonished the church, "Do not be anxious about anything, but in everything by prayer and supplication with thanksgiving let your requests be made known to God" (4:6).

It is important to see that part of the remedy for sinful anxiety—and the interpersonal problems it causes—is to bring God and His provision back to the forefront of your thinking. Christians *should* be deeply concerned about others and the future, but they must never lose sight of God's providential oversight. In fact, Paul mentions his gratitude for the Philippians' concern for him (Philippians 4:10), and yet the overall instruction of his letter to his dear friends is that they "rejoice in the Lord" (4:4) and "not be anxious about anything" (4:6).

As Audrey thinks of all the difficulties that might be in her future, she can begin to joyfully thank God for what He is doing, especially how He is providing "the peace of God, which surpasses all understanding" (4:7). She will not be able control the future, but if she is a Christian, she has a close relationship with the One who holds her future in His hands. This new peace will guard her heart and mind in Christ Jesus—a great promise from our great Savior!

Audrey pondered the implications of all she was learning. *Who is this great Savior in my time of great need? He is my faithful God! He is not thoughtless and forgetful* (Psalm 9:12; Isaiah 49:15). *He overflows with steadfast love and faithfulness to His children* (Psalm 86:5, 15). *In spite of the wickedness of my own heart, God went to great lengths to die for me, to satisfy His wrath through His Son, and He will not leave me to some arbitrary fate* (Ephesians 2:4-9).

You may be anxious like Audrey, even though your circumstances are different. Perhaps you are recently divorced, diagnosed with a life-threatening disease, grieving over the loss of a loved one, suffering from a significant financial loss, fearing the loss of your job, uncertain over the man you should marry, or simply concerned over losing your youthfulness as you grow older. Anxiety can take control of your life for many different reasons. If it is not handled properly, you will find yourself consumed by it, and it will radically change you when it does. It will be destructive to your health, your relationships, and especially your spiritual walk before God.

Anxiety is a frame of mind that is never constructive; it is always destructive. It is a deceptive thief that robs you of your joy, patience, profitable time, personal friends, family, peace, and health. But most of all, for you as a Christian, it casts doubt on the faithfulness of God to help you in your time of need. Without saying it, others around you will begin to wonder whether God can really do all that you have said He would. His reputation and good name suffers at the hand of your ongoing anxiety. Learning to put off anxiety and to rest confidently in His promises to you is what will bring honor and glory to your faithful God.

Another destructive result of anxiety is that you become consumed with yourself and your life. This self-centeredness only fuels more anxiety. The person consumed with herself believes that she deserves a problem-free future, but is anxious because she knows that this type of future is unlikely (Job 5:7; Ecclesiastes 7:14). Not only is increasing anxiety a destructive sin, but the self-deserving thoughts that accompany it have no place in a mind focused on the cross of Christ. The humble Christian will remember the death that Christ suffered to set her free from her sinful, selfish ways—leading her to live for Him. Gratitude floods her heart as she is reminded that she is the one who deserves to be hanging on the cross, and yet Jesus Christ was her substitute.

Once you establish this new mindset and your heart is set on serving and glorifying Him, then the anxious, self-deserving thoughts plaguing you will lose their grip. To help with this change, meditate on and memorize Romans 8:1-8. The mind that is set on the things of the flesh is a mind that is exalting the things of this world. It is a self-deserving mindset. But the mind that is set on the things of the Spirit has turned away from sin and self to the things of God. This is now a Christ-glorifying mindset that is full of "life and peace" (Romans 8:6).

Of course, it is far too common, even as a Christian, for you to find yourself worrying about the future instead of dealing with your anxiety in a biblical way. You know that you are becoming anxious and need biblical help when your anxiety enslaves you with automatic-like reactions and responses. Your concern has turned into sinful anxiety when

- your thoughts gravitate toward changing the future
- your thoughts are unproductive
- your concern controls you instead of you controlling it
- your concern causes you to neglect other responsibilities and relationships
- your concern alone starts damaging your body
- you lose hope instead finding answers
- you stop functioning in life

In other words, when your fears of the future control you and keep you from being a woman who honors the Lord, you have become sinfully anxious. When you are biblically motivated, you will find yourself focusing on God's glory and trusting Him with the welfare of yourself and others. But when you are sinfully worried, you will be focused on yourself and become unduly anxious over circumstances beyond your control.

A critical help in reversing sinful anxiety is proper prayer. Prayerlessness reveals your lack of trust in God's sovereignty and His goodness. The apostle Peter advises a humble response in 1 Peter 5:7: "casting all your anxieties on Him." Peter understood that when anxiety was on the increase, diligent prayer should increase as well. But you may say, "I *am* praying—all the time. And still I am overcome with anxiety." However, what you pray about is as important as your need to pray. Do your prayers sound like the following?

- "Lord, please make sure that nothing bad or hurtful ever happens to any of my family."
- "Lord, please make sure my daughter gets into the best medical school, because that will be the best thing for her!"
- "Lord, You must heal my husband of his cancer, or I will not make it through this trial!"

Do you see the anxiety and even arrogance in these types of prayers? God is not your "genie in a bottle" that you rub with prayer in order to get your wishes fulfilled. Look carefully at what Peter wrote to suffering Christians: "Humble yourselves therefore, under the mighty hand of God so that at the proper time he may exalt you, casting all your anxieties on him, because he cares for you" (1 Peter 5:6-7). You are to be humble, acknowledging that God's wisdom and knowledge concerning your future infinitely exceeds your own. He has a better future planned for you, although not likely a problem-free one.

Note that Peter did *not* say that you are to "inform and instruct" God about your anxieties. He said you are to cast your anxieties on Him. The word for "casting," in the original Greek text, means "to throw." And in order to throw something, you must let go of it. It is as if your anxieties are a heavy backpack that you need to take off and throw onto Him. Furthermore, this is not a burden you keep taking back from Him to carry once again. The tense of the original Greek text indicates a once-and-for-all removal from you and a final putting onto Him. This demonstrates your trust in God's ability to handle your future over your own ability to know what is best. You cannot truthfully say you have let go of your anxieties if you are continuing to worry about them. When you do that, it reveals that you do not believe that God actually cares for you, or that He is capable of handling your future. Your prayer must come instead from a humble heart and you must truly throw all your anxieties upon Him without any intention of taking them back. You are to make a once-for-all intentional commitment to your Lord!

• • • • •

What should you do if you have prayed a "humble-casting" type of prayer and yet find yourself unwittingly slipping back into your anxious frame of mind? Critical to your complete change is your agreement with God that anxious thoughts are sinful! You must see them as a cancerous toxin fully enveloping and choking out all your profitable thoughts and relationships. There are three actions steps you must take in order for true and complete change to take place.

Repentance

First, it is vital that you see your anxious thought-life as a habitual, life-dominating sin which requires proper repentance before God. Repentance, greatly misunderstood among many Christians, is a change of mind that is so complete that it leads to a change of life (James 4:6-10). In repentance you do not simply apologize to God, or merely say you are sorry. Genuine repentance accepts full responsibility for sin and seeks God's forgiveness, resisting the tendency to blame people or circumstances. Blaming others causes your prayer for repentance to fail because you have not owned up to your sin. Suppose Audrey had prayed, "Lord, I know I'm failing to trust You as my mind is consumed with anxious thoughts, but I can't help it when the military takes my boy from me for a third time." In essence she would be saying, "It's really not my fault!" Prayers like this are not real prayers of repentance. Instead, they are rationalized prayers of a heart not yet given over to humbly trusting God with the future.

True repentance fully accepts responsibility for personal sinful attitudes, actions, and reactions no matter what the circumstances and no matter how difficult the people.

When you are truly repentant, you will grieve over your sin instead of rationalizing it. You will see it as the great offense that it is against the Lord. The apostle Paul describes such grief that results in genuine repentance in 2 Corinthians 7:10: "Godly grief produces a repentance that leads to salvation without regret, whereas worldly grief produces death." This godly grief over your sinful and faithless anxiety must be present in your repentance—this repentance that frees you from the consequences of sin's judgment. If godly grief is lacking, then you are still somehow convinced of your right to be sinfully anxious, even when God has demonstrated that you can trust Him. It's like praying, "God, I'm sorry I'm anxious, but the reason I am still anxious is because I know You will not prevent these bad things from happening or even help me to stop being anxious!"

This kind of response is a worldly grief filled with "I'm sorry" and "I don't believe You anyway." Worldly grief is present in your life when you believe your way is better than God's. It results in death, which is God's warning about how sin—in this case, the sinfulness of persistent faithless anxiety—will destroy everything important in your life. While true repentance does not earn any favor with God (other than what has already been fully accomplished in Christ alone), it does show that the Holy Spirit is actively at work in your life as a believer. A real Christian will evidence this type of repentance in their life regardless of how stubborn their sin may be.

There are two more steps to take that will help you permanently overcome anxiety. They are the natural result of genuine repentance. In fact, these steps will be ineffective if repentance has not taken place.

Put Off

Read Ephesians chapters 1 through 3 carefully; then concentrate on 4:17-24. The changes you are instructed to make to finally resolve anxiety are only possible because of the enabling grace of the gospel (chapters 1–3). The gospel establishes that you are now "in Christ," anchoring your life in the overwhelming knowledge of the privileged life you enjoy because of the sacrificial atoning work of Jesus Christ. Knowing that Christ substituted His death for yours is a daily reminder that should invigorate your study and make this change a reality.

What really worries you? Write these things down and be specific. It is imperative your list is both explicit and exhaustive. These are the very things you must *put off*—stop doing, stop worrying about. Now take time to pray and ask the Lord to grant you the grace to remove each of these from your life. You may want to have a Christian friend or your husband join you in praying for their removal. As an example, in Audrey's case, she should put off her constant listening to the news reports from the front lines of the battle because this was providing fuel for her anxiety. Although it is not sinful to listen to newscasts, this activity had become sin for Audrey because she believed that if she listened without fail that her dedication would somehow prevent any harm coming to Zach. This was nothing but vain imaginations and falsehood and had to be removed from her life.

The exhortation to "put off" refers to a once-for-all action. In Ephesians 4:22, the Greek term translated "to put off" is an active, aorist infinitive, meaning you are to permanently "put off your old self" with all of its destructive practices because of who you are in Christ (see Colossians 3:5-10). This means you must be deliberately intentional about their removal from your life, never purposefully returning to them again. There is no place for half-heartedness here.

Consider this illustration: If you were to discover that your meal was laced with arsenic, you would immediately stop eating and refuse to put that poisonous food in your body ever again. This is the type of resolve you must have when putting off your anxious thoughts. You must be completely resolved not to focus on them ever again. Later, if you find yourself drifting back into your anxious thinking, it may be due to an ingrained habitual thought pattern. Confess this as sin and start again. The practice of putting off will require righteous persever-ance, and you may find yourself repeatedly confessing the same sin again and again. As Proverbs 24:16 confidently asserts, "For the righ-teous falls seven times and rises again." Your commitment to reengage the fight and remove those habituated anxious thoughts proves your original resolve to permanently purge them from your life. This type of deep resolve comes only from sincere godly repentance (Isaiah 1:16-18).

In the meantime, while you are at work, God is at work pro-viding you with a refreshing new outlook on your life and circum-stances. Ephesians 4:23 says you are to be "renewed in the spirit of your minds." Here the Greek infinitive, "to be renewed," changes to a present passive verb tense. You are no longer doing the action; God is the one who is at work. The passive tense indicates you are a passive recipient of God revitalizing your attitude and outlook. Your perspective is new, fresh, and filled with youthful exuberance—you are no longer negative, pessimistic, and apprehensive. Joy returns to your countenance. For the first time in a long time you are optimis-tic about the future instead of being fretful. Your attitude is confi-dent and calm. Your speech is full of trusting statements about how secure your future is in God's hands, even though your present cir-cumstances have not changed. It is *you* who has changed. Godly hope has finally quieted your restless thoughts.

Put On

Will the change last? This is a natural question for anyone who has been dogged by stubborn anxiety. Lasting change is a result of biblical replacement. If all you do is put off anxious thinking, you leave a vacuum that makes it easy for those vexing thoughts to return. Our next verse, Ephesians 4:24, continues the help by stating that you are "to *put on* the new self, created after the likeness of God in true righteousness and holiness."

Just as you made a list of your anxious thoughts to discontinue, now is the time to make a list of the thoughts you should be focusing on. These are truthful, God-honoring thoughts that demonstrate your complete faith in His sovereignty and trustworthiness. A good place to start finding thoughts for this list is by carefully reading and meditating on Bible passages such as Psalms 37 and 73. These psalms model the replacement of anxious thinking with hopeful thoughts. Make a list of at least 20 to 30 hopeful and thankful thoughts that should fill your mind (see Philippians 4:6-7). Keep this list with you at all times. Put those thoughts on small cards or on your cell phone to be carried everywhere. Each time you find yourself slipping back into an ungodly anxious frame of mind, pull out the list and focus your full attention on the replacement thoughts. Pray those thoughts back to God continually. The more you are faithful to do this, the less of a grip anxiety will have on your life. In fact, you have not really changed until this pattern of righteous thinking has occurred.

• • • • •

Applying the biblical counsel she had received, Audrey put off her practice of listening constantly to the newscasts, and replaced that with putting on right thoughts, such as, *My attentiveness to the newscasts does nothing to prove my love and dedication as a mother; it actually prevents me from loving and serving my family members who still live in the home. I cannot change any outcome by my obsessive listening, so instead, I will meditate on 1 Peter 5:6-7: "Humble yourselves, therefore, under the mighty hand of God so that at the proper time he may exalt you, casting all your anxieties on him, because he cares for you.*"

Audrey realized her apprehensiveness had turned to sinful anxiety. It was destroying her life and her family. The battle to change her thinking was not easy, but she was determined to apply the remedy in God's Word and defeat her sinful anxious thoughts.

Eventually Zach returned home from his deployment, but he came home to a different mother—one who had learned God's faithfulness through this difficulty and how life-changing biblical truth can be. As the psalmist so aptly states, "Before I was afflicted I went astray, but now I keep your word...It was good for me that I was afflicted, that I might learn your statutes" (119:67, 71).

Questions for Discussion

1. Many people make excuses for ongoing sin, saying that some sins cannot be overcome, that they are just a part of who we are. Read Philippians 4:4-9 and 2 Timothy 3:16-17. Write down the reasons why these excuses cannot be true.

2. What aspects of God's character are under attack when we fail to put off sinful anxiety?

3. Read 1 Samuel 30:1-6. When David found out his wives and children had been captured by the enemy, he could have become anxious. Instead, how did he respond (verse 6)?

4. Read Psalm 37 aloud. What specific declarations does the psalm writer make about his God?

5. Read Psalm 73. Write out a description of the psalm writer in his despair, and then write what happened after he went into the sanctuary of God.

3

Appearance

*Do not let your adorning be external—the braiding of
hair and the putting on of gold jewelry, or the clothing
you wear—but let your adorning be the hidden person
of the heart with the imperishable beauty of a gentle
and quiet spirit, which in God's sight is very precious.*

1 PETER 3:3-4

Allyssa stared at her image in the mirror. Not a hair out of place,
makeup perfectly applied, clothes in the latest style. She smiled at her
reflection, satisfied with the results of her efforts over the past two
hours. *Now* she was ready for the day—ready to have others see her
and talk with her. Picking up her purse, car keys, and cup of coffee,
she left her apartment. It was going to be a great day!

Allyssa was a gifted musician. In addition to being an accomplished pianist, she had an extraordinary voice. She was used to people noticing her and appreciating her exceptional talent. Whenever
she walked into a crowded room, her thoughts were consumed with
what others thought about her, especially her appearance. Always
"dressed to the hilt," her credit cards were charged to the limit due
to frequent shopping binges for new clothes and accessories. For as
long as she could remember, she had always enjoyed being the center of attention. Her friends jokingly called her a drama queen, but

Allyssa simply saw herself as full of life and interesting, even though she did acknowledge feeling down and a bit irritated when people were not focused on her.

As a Christian young woman, Allyssa was often asked to sing at church. She secretly relished being in the spotlight and having all the eyes in the congregation upon her. Thus she seldom turned down an opportunity for such "ministry." She found great joy in attending church and being around large groups of people. But, even there, she always worked her way to the center of the discussion group, sharing her views freely and openly to all who would listen. As long as she was receiving attention, Allyssa was happy.

Driving to the local university that morning, she thought back to last night's reading assignment for her morning class describing Histrionic Personality Disorder.

> The appearance and behavior of individuals with this disorder are often inappropriately sexually provocative or seductive…Individuals with this disorder consistently use physical appearance to draw attention to themselves…They are overly concerned with impressing others by their appearance and *expend an excessive amount of time, energy, and money on clothes and grooming.* They may "fish for compliments" regarding appearance and may be easily and excessively upset by a critical comment about how they look or by a photograph that they regard as unflattering.[3]

Allyssa wished she could get the words out of her mind. Despite her earlier feelings of satisfaction with her appearance, she couldn't help but wonder: *Could this be describing me? Is it possible that I am excessively preoccupied with what others think about me? Do I spend "an excessive amount of time, energy and money on clothes and grooming"? Is it possible that I suffer from this disorder?* Allyssa wanted to purge any such idea of having a mental disorder from her mind, but she was finding it difficult to do this. Feeling a bit uneasy, she tried to dismiss her concerns as she pulled into the parking lot, preparing her mind for the class before her.

After her behavioral psychology class was dismissed, Allyssa went to a quiet corner in the university library and sat down to wait until her next class began. Usually she hung out with other students in the café, sipping coffee and laughing the hour away. But today she had things to think about. All through her first class, she had not been able to shake the feeling that something was not quite right. Not only was she having difficulty putting that reading assignment out of her mind, but she kept thinking back to a recent conversation she had had with her parents.

Mike and Melanie had grown concerned of late as they noticed Allyssa's increasing obsession with her appearance. Although they recognized that it was characteristic for girls her age to be self-conscious, over the past several months they had observed a growing arrogance overtake their once sweet-natured daughter. As her parents, it was hard not to be pleased with her accomplishments and beauty, and yet they noticed a developing harshness in her personality along with an increasing tendency toward criticizing others. They were unsure how they should approach her about this, and yet they knew if they didn't help Allyssa to see these things about herself, life would begin to get more difficult for her. No one likes to be around someone who thinks about herself constantly, is arrogant and self-centered, fully focusing on her own appearance at the expense of having a genuine interest in others.

Two days earlier, while eating Sunday dinner together, Mike and Melanie had gently brought up their concerns. They had carefully pointed out the changes they were observing in Allyssa. She had immediately disagreed with their assessment: "How could you think such things about me, let alone say them to me? I have done nothing but work hard in school to excel in my studies and prepare myself for a productive life. And now you throw these accusations of arrogance and a critical spirit at me. What am I supposed to think, that you are saying these things in love? Well, I'm *really* feeling the love here," she retorted sarcastically.

As Allyssa sat quietly and mulled over what had happened, she knew her parents were right about her. She was ashamed of how she had treated them that day. After all, they had been gracious even as they shared their concern. Her arrogant response weighed heavily on her conscience—to the point that she realized she needed to talk with her mom and dad some more. They knew her well, and if they had noticed she had become more preoccupied with her appearance and that her attitudes had changed for the worse, then perhaps she needed to hear them out.

Allyssa, in addition to being a good student and exceptional musician, was also a regular church attender. Four years earlier, she had begun making a habit of reading her Bible, something her mother had always encouraged her to do. She loved the book of Psalms and chose Psalm 130 that day. Verses 3 and 4 caught her attention: "If you, O LORD, should mark iniquities, O LORD, who could stand? But with you there is forgiveness, that you may be feared."

Allyssa was struck with the realization that she stood under God's judgment for her iniquities—her sins—and that she would never be able to stand clean before the Most High God. Overcome with the guilt of her sins, she read the next words: "But with you there is forgiveness." Finding herself on her knees, Allyssa prayed, "Yes, Lord, that's what I need. My sins stand between me and You, and I know You do not look upon me with favor. Please forgive me! I want to fully repent of living for myself alone and cling to the cross of Your Son Jesus, who paid for all my sin with His great sacrifice. I don't deserve this gift of eternal life, but I receive it humbly from Your hand. Help me to love You and serve You all my days. Amen."

What a load of guilt was lifted off Allyssa's shoulders that moment! All the truths about Jesus Christ that she had said she believed as a girl, she now truly embraced as her only hope. She had stood in need of mercy, and God—in Christ—had given it to her. Joy now filled her heart and a new love for Christ had begun.

As Allyssa contemplated what had just happened in the quiet of the library that morning, she began to wonder about how she had become so caught up in herself and her appearance. Walking outside, she pulled her phone out of her purse and called her mother. She was ready to get some help.

Melanie was pleased to hear from Allyssa and was greatly encouraged by what her daughter had to say. Allyssa confessed her sinful anger and arrogance to her, and then asked for her forgiveness. Melanie was quick to forgive her and offered to help find someone who could provide Allyssa with the biblical guidance she needed. After a quick phone call to their church, Allyssa soon had an appointment with Jill, a woman they both knew who had taken biblical counseling training and was actively involved in helping women with their problems.

There was much for Allyssa to learn with regard to having a godly perspective on her appearance as a woman. She had never realized the Bible had so much to say about this area of her life. She listened intently as Jill gave a biblical overview of the subject first, and then proceeded to teach directly from God's Word.

Allyssa learned that although sinful concerns about one's appearance can emerge in both men and women, the battle is one predominantly experienced by women. What may seem to be an external matter—how one looks both to herself and to others—is in reality a difficulty with spiritual dimensions. Looking at this self-perception issue biblically, it becomes clear that this problem is internal, proceeding from within the heart of the person (Mark 7:20-23). Hence, this external behavior has an internal root.

"Being fixated with thoughts about how you appear to other people is not just a contemporary problem," Jill explained. "The apostle Paul, in his first letter to Timothy, instructed the young pastor how to help women in the church to live godly lives (1 Timothy 2:9-10). He drew attention to two characteristics of their apparel: modesty and self-control. *Modesty* is defined as freedom from vanity and boastfulness, which are both biblical terms of pride. *Self-control* is a term that includes the idea of restraint, which for the godly woman would mean to repress the tendency to be absorbed with herself, seeking instead to give attention to the glory due only to God. God opposes the proud (James 4:6) and instead we are called to humility (1 Peter 5:5). A woman who does not give herself over to modesty and self-control, being continually distracted by her appearance, shows herself to be in a great struggle with the sin of pride. Diverting women's attention away from the fixation of their appearance, Scripture exhorts them to be known for good works instead (1 Timothy 2:10)."

Allyssa had been a Christian long enough to know that pride was a vice, not a virtue. Yet she had been blinded to the ways in which pride was manifesting itself in her: first, in her obsession with her appearance, and second, in the attitudes that had resulted. Suddenly, every glance in the mirror made her aware of how she had allowed her thoughts to rest on herself and her appearance, with little thought or care for other people. Every critical thought she entertained—every condescending attitude—opened her eyes further to the selfish way she viewed life. Slowly Allyssa was seeing what she truly looked like—on the inside, where it really matters. And for the first time, she didn't like what she saw.

Jill was compassionate and kind with Allyssa as they studied various passages of the Bible together. They both found that 1 Peter 3 has noteworthy words of wisdom for this problem. Verses 3-4 seemed to speak directly to this issue: "Do not let your adorning be external—the braiding of the hair and the putting on of gold jewelry, or the clothing you wear—but let your adorning be the hidden person of the heart with the imperishable beauty of a gentle and quiet spirit, which in God's sight is very precious." The command in these verses seemed very specific, so in order to understand their meaning, they took time to read the entire book of 1 Peter. Jill pointed out that Christians who desire to know the truth in order to obey it will take the extra time that is necessary to study Bible verses within their larger context.

First, they discovered that Peter was writing to Christians who, due to persecution for their faith in Jesus Christ, had been scattered throughout the cities and villages of the Roman Empire. This, of course, is not the situation most contemporary Christians find themselves in, yet knowing this historical information was helping them to understand the women to whom the letter was written. Men and women who followed Jesus Christ during this time were undergoing severe persecution and various other trials related to their profession of faith. When undergoing trials and especially persecution, one aspect of the Christian's life that is often overlooked is diligence in godly behavior. Peter knew this, and instead of teaching his readers to find ways to end their suffering, he urged them to live godly lives in the midst of their unwelcomed circumstances (1:13-17).

With a careful reading of this letter to persecuted Christians, we notice that Peter taught about submission—a very difficult topic to present to people under persecution. When the early Christians were mistreated because of their faith in Christ, many became justifiably angry at their tormentors. They knew they had done nothing wrong, and that the suffering they were enduring was unjust. So submission to those who were in authority over them—the very people who were either tormenting them or had the power to stop the persecution—was far from their minds. But Peter admonished these suffering Christians and said that submission must govern their lives, even as they experienced affliction at the hands of their superiors (2:13–3:6). Peter then pointed to the wonderful example of Jesus Christ, who had suffered unjustly. Though Jesus had committed no sin and was not deserving of punishment, He yielded His situation to God (2:21-25).

In 1 Peter 2, Peter was pointing out that we do not always do the right thing when difficulties arise. Yes, there are times when we suffer for doing wrong (2:20), and this is not to our credit. But when we are persecuted even as we do what is right, we should not fight back. Jesus Christ never did wrong and still suffered for it—and He did so with a submissive spirit (2:22-24). He is the perfect example we are to follow when suffering for doing good.

Peter further stated the need for godly submission by calling upon wives to submit to their husbands (3:1-6). In this case, he was speaking to wives who had an unbelieving husband or a husband who acted like an unbeliever. Such husbands are described as those who "do not obey the word" (3:1). Thus, the woman's behavior is critical in these circumstances—not only because the temptation to rebel in her marriage is greater, but because such godliness can be an effective tool for winning over a husband acting like an unbeliever (3:1-2).

What we see in verses 3-6 becomes particularly helpful in dealing with the heart of the woman who is fixated on her appearance. Because submission requires *humility* and *self-control*, the way a woman dresses will reveal whether or not her heart is submissive. The woman who puts an excessive amount of attention on her outward appearance demonstrates that she does not yet have a submissive spirit. Humility and self-control, two key components of submission, are nowhere to be found in the woman who is concerned only with the braiding of hair, the putting on of gold jewelry, or the clothing she wears. In contrast, humility and self-control stand out as prominent characteristics of the woman who has let her "adorning be the hidden person of the heart with the imperishable beauty of a gentle and quiet spirit" (3:4). When a woman models this kind of behavior, she will exemplify the godly living of the Old Testament women who went before her (3:5-6).

As their study progressed through 1 Peter, Allyssa was seeing her overt attention to her appearance in a completely new light. She had not realized that submission had anything to do with how much she cared about how she looked. She also began to realize that her attention to her appearance had been characterized by pride, not humility and self-control. The process of cultivating humility was beginning in her, and she was suddenly eager to learn more.

Whatever your situation—married to an unbelieving spouse or not, suffering at the hands of those in authority over you or not—Peter's message to you is the same. If you are a Christian, then you have a citizenship in heaven, not on earth (see Philippians 3:20). So no matter what your situation, you are an exile—a stranger—on this earth, and you are called to godly behavior (1 Peter 2:11). Both in good times and bad, the person you are on the *inside* is what God looks at, which is often reflected in how you dress.

Peter's specific instruction about the heart shows a contrast. First, he said that a woman's primary attention to adornment must not be *outward*—braiding of hair and the putting on of gold (things such as rings, bracelets, necklaces), or the wearing of garments (3:3). It's important to note that adorning and dressing are two different things. To *adorn* means to embellish or enhance one's appearance; to *dress* means to put on clothing. Of course Peter means for women to dress themselves, to put on clothing as a covering, as would be appropriate for a godly woman. But he means that her outward appearance must not be her main focus.

In other words, whatever extra attention you give to adorning (embellishing and enhancing) yourself will tempt you to be prideful and ignore the inner person. The question of contrast is this: Are you going to place emphasis on adorning yourself with external fancies, or are you going to focus your attention on who you are on the inside? For your behavior to manifest a godly attitude, you must demonstrate a clear intent to make your inward character the primary adornment (3:4), and that inward character should include modesty and self-control.

Jill paused in her teaching to give Allyssa a moment to respond to what she was seeing in Scripture. "For a long time I have been repulsed by the idea of modesty, especially as it relates to humility," Allyssa said thoughtfully. "But now I see that it is a very attractive quality for a woman who desires to be godly. I have a lot of changing to do in my thinking, but I am willing to bring my thoughts and actions in line with what the Bible says. I used to think that my appearance was very important. Now I realize that what I *think* about my appearance is so much more important."

Jill nodded in response to Allyssa's observation, then said, "There are some women who, though they may be very attractive in external appearance, are actually unbecoming and even ugly when it comes to their inner attitudes. On the other hand, there are women who are *not* externally attractive—you would never find them on the front cover of a glamour magazine—yet internally they possess a Christlike humility and love for others. Their inner person is lovely and attractive."

In contrast to outward adornment, Peter says that these *internal* attributes are hidden, something that others cannot fully witness (3:4). It is clear that God wants you to pursue the quality of a gentle and quiet heart more than your external appearance. In fact, the internal qualities of your heart have eternal implications. There is nothing eternal about our external appearance. Even the most beautiful celebrities must increase their beauty treatments as they age, and when in the grave, all of us decay and waste away. What makes you look nice today and the attention that you are seeking from others is fleeting. Your body will inevitably wither over the years. Your hair will turn gray (see Ecclesiastes 11:10)[4] and your jewelry will eventually deteriorate (see James 5:1-3). You will not always look the same as you do now. But as Peter stressed, it is vital for you to seek that which is imperishable, undefiled, and unfading—your eternal inheritance, which will last (1 Peter 1:4). The Word of God will last (1:23-25). And according to 1 Peter 3:4, your gentle and quiet spirit that comes from your godly character will also last.[5]

Here's the distinction: When you set the focus of your life on your image before others, you are placing your hope in something that for the moment might bring you joy, but will not remain forever. In fact, the temporary joy of the praise of others is quickly lost in a little-known effect of pride: greed. Once you think you have attained a certain level of approval, in your pride you will lust after more and more approval until your joy is gone—until you can heap up even higher mountains of praise. This becomes a vicious and never-ending cycle, much like a dog chasing its own tail.

In contrast, your inner adornment produces godly character, which has an enduring spiritual quality that is "very precious" in God's sight (3:4). This term "very precious" is also translated "costly" and was used in the everyday life of the New Testament world to refer to the expensive prices of items bought in the market.[6] Peter used this term to communicate what God truly finds valuable. Perhaps you have spent a lot of time and money on your appearance: dresses, diamonds, beauty treatments—they can all be tremendously expensive. But what the Lord calls "more precious than gold that perishes" is the genuineness of your faith (1:7), the sacrificial blood of Christ (1:18-19), and now your gentle and quiet spirit (3:3-4). If these qualities could be monetized, they would far outweigh the price in dollars of any dress or jewelry piece you could adorn yourself with. That's because the beauty of godly character is imperishable. It cannot be destroyed. You will always have it to accompany you throughout eternity.

Peter went on to offer a few more words to Christian women. He stated that when you focus on the inner person of the heart, you are following in the footsteps of the Old Testament women who were known as holy women of God. He wrote, "This is how the holy women who hoped in God used to adorn themselves, by submitting to their own husbands" (3:5). Essentially, the Old Testament women who had a godly reputation were found pleasing to God because they clothed themselves more with the qualities of submission, gentleness, and peace than with external adornments.

Sarah, known for her exceptional beauty (Genesis 12:10-14), was just one example Peter used to illustrate his point. She lived with a believing husband and submitted to him faithfully. But Sarah's godliness was not predicated upon her beauty or her situation—whether she had a believing or unbelieving husband. Rather, her example of cultivating a gentle and quiet spirit—which led her to submit to her husband, even calling him lord—was what gave her the reputation for being a holy woman who hoped in God.

It is this example that Peter is calling upon women today to follow. In other words, when the most important thing about you is that you hope in God, with the result that you develop a gentle and quiet spirit, causing you to manifest the kind of submission and internal obedience that Sarah showed, then you are demonstrating to others that you are in fact part of Abraham's seed of faith through Jesus Christ (see Galatians 3:6-7). No matter what your situation in life, it is incumbent upon you to walk in the character traits that a woman of God is called to represent. Such traits may not be esteemed by this world, but they are indeed rich in the eyes of God.

How do you see yourself after studying through this passage? Do you find that you care more about your external appearance than your internal character? For further study, look at Isaiah 3:16-26, where you will find a description of the hearts of women who were obsessed with their appearance. Notice how they flaunted their beauty, whether overtly or covertly, to garner attention from others (3:16). The result of their sensual arrogance was devastating, as they and their husbands were sent into exile under the ruthless and violent hand of their enemies.

Because of Christ, the believing woman today will not live under condemnation for her sin. However, this example in the Old Testament should inform us as to how God views a woman's heart when she cares more for the praise of men than the gentle and quiet heart which God so greatly values. Think about your own heart; consider what might be ruling it. The seductive nature of pride can cause you to idolize your appearance before others. It is heart motivations such as these that you must assess as you consider what you find truly valuable. Whatever you are living for, that is what you find truly valuable.

Questions for Discussion

1. Read Proverbs 31:30. What does this verse say about beauty and external appearance?

2. What is the opposite quality spoken of in verse 30? Is this

quality material or immaterial? In what ways can you develop this attribute in your life?

3. Read the story of Queen Esther in the Old Testament book of Esther. She was given beauty treatments for many months, and yet her character did not reflect that her attention was on her external adornment. What things was Esther most concerned about? How does her life show that she was a woman who feared the Lord?

4. Read the story of Ruth in the Old Testament book of Ruth. Nothing is said about her external appearance. Rather, we read much about the fact that she was a godly and honorable woman. Name five biblical qualities that Ruth exemplified as a woman who adorned her inner person.

5. Read Luke 1:46-55. If there was any woman who could have claimed a reason for pride it was Mary, for she was chosen by God to be the mother of our Lord Jesus Christ. Based on what you read in the passage, what do you learn about Mary's attitude toward herself, her God, and her circumstances?

4

Bitterness

*Bearing with one another and, if one has a complaint
against another, forgiving each other; as the Lord
has forgiven you, so you also must forgive.*

COLOSSIANS 3:13

Bitter and broken in spirit, Bethany's refusal to forgive had become her weapon of choice. But this had also brought her no peace. An oppressive weight of guilt overwhelmed her as she listened to Pastor Mike preach his Sunday morning message. What a nightmare her life had become! And why did the pastor have to choose Ephesians 4:31-32 as his text? "Let all bitterness and wrath and anger and clamor and slander be put away from you, along with all malice. Be kind to one another, tenderhearted, forgiving one another, as God in Christ forgave you."

Her eyes blurry with tears, Bethany kept her head low. She feared someone would see her moment of weakness and seek an explanation. For the first time in a long time, she was ashamed of the angry person she had become. Then, as usual, thoughts of justification began to flood back into her mind, helping her regain control of her emotions. *He deserves to be punished for what he has done to me and our marriage. He has crushed me so deeply I'll never be the same!*

Bethany's unwillingness to forgive was her deterrent from ever being hurt by Joel again. It helped her remain emotionally detached from her husband. Keeping a distance between them was one way she could ensure he would never be close enough to deliver such a serious wound again. But far more than a mere defense mechanism, her refusal to forgive had become her offensive weapon—Bethany's way of letting him know he would never be free from her accusatory remarks and attitudes. Her anger and lack of willingness to forgive him had turned into a deep-seated bitterness.

On the surface, Bethany and Joel's marriage appeared to be a healthy Christian union that experienced the joys and struggles typically faced by every couple. The people in their church viewed them as a great picture of what a Christian marriage should be. Yet they did not know what went on behind closed doors—the reality was much different than appearances seemed to indicate.

The tension in their home was thick, filled with cutting remarks and short tempers. Joel believed that Bethany was constantly assigning the worst possible motivations to everything he attempted to do. She had made it clear that she could not trust him. Certainly the proverb was true, that "a brother offended is more unyielding than a strong city, and quarreling is like the bars of a castle" (Proverbs 18:19). To Joel, Bethany had become like a walled city hiding behind a tall, dense fortress of emotional protection. She was no longer allowing him to get close to her, physically or emotionally, because even the thought of his mere touch now repulsed her. She used to love his caresses, but that was no longer true.

Everyone who knew Joel believed him to be a caring and likable Christian man. This was the very thing that made the situation so hard for Bethany. The one time she had agreed to go to counseling at their church, Joel and their counselor ended up becoming good friends. She had become enraged over this, for in her way of thinking, the counselor was supposed to fix what was wrong with Joel, not become a friend.

As a result, Bethany lost all interest in seeking counsel and refused to go to future sessions. For her, counseling did not hold much promise, even if the couple were to switch to a different pastor or counselor. Joel would just schmooze the next counselor with his Cheshire-cat smiles, and then she would be accused of making mountains out of molehills. Bethany was not about to be viewed as a discontent, nagging wife! No, Joel was the one with the problem. She had come to despise him and could barely stand being in the same room with him.

As time passed, an agonizing sense of loneliness settled in. They both knew this was not what God had intended for a Christian marriage. And neither of them would even speak of separation or divorce. Bethany knew that her Christian friends would not look favorably upon her leaving or divorcing Joel. Besides, her pride would not allow her to be the one who left. That would hang over her head for the rest of her life. If anyone were going to leave, it had to be Joel so that she would be seen as the one who "had tried to make the relationship work." She wanted to be viewed as the victim of his cruel abandonment, not the other way around. It was simple as that.

There were times, however, when the loneliness became so painful that she secretly wished Joel would have an affair. Then she could respectfully divorce him and move on with her life. Other disturbing thoughts occasionally rushed through her mind. Maybe Joel would have an accident at work or driving home, then she could play the grieving widow for a while and later seek a better husband without criticism from her Christian friends. Bethany knew these reflections were wicked, but they still appealed to her.

From her point of view, Joel was a lying hypocrite. He projected the image of a clean-cut, always-kind Christian man who sacrificed himself for others, but she knew who he really was—a two-faced, shallow people-pleaser. Joel had a secret life, and she had uncovered his secret. That was the fateful day he had mistakenly left his cell phone at home. There it sat, all day long. The temptation to peek into her husband's "online life" eventually overwhelmed Bethany, so she sat down and began to look through some of the entries and pages on his social media sites. Filled with curiosity, she went to the history of his web searches and entries.

Bethany was horrified to discover that his web searches were filled with pornographic websites. There was no mistake: Joel was addicted to porn. A mix of emotions flooded her. First, there was a sense of deep disappointment that her husband would do this. Her second response was a rush of anger that he would do this behind her back. Her heart raced, and her body went numb. Bethany believed this was marital betrayal of the worse kind. To make matters worse, she found web searches for nearby strip clubs. Now her anger was at its peak. Was she not good enough for him? Did he have to go outside of their marriage to find sexual satisfaction like some sick voyeur? The hurt and pain from the deception and rejection burned its way deep inside her heart. How could a man who claimed to be a Christian be associated with such filth?

Sickened by this revelation, Bethany was tempted to leave Joel. *My husband is a pervert, and I don't want to live with a pervert*, she reasoned. Vengeful thoughts pulsed through her mind. She decided she would confront Joel about his secret life of self-indulgence.

As Joel arrived home, Bethany waited in ambush. As soon as he walked through the door, she challenged him. Taken off guard, he immediately went into self-defense mode and denied looking at any pornographic pictures. Bethany knew he was lying and trying to play the "good boy" routine. Then Bethany pulled out his phone and confronted him with the undeniable evidence. "You found my phone?

I thought I had left it at work." Joel had no choice but to admit that he had been on those sites.

The next few days were painful—they were filled with hostility, anger, arguments, more denials, quarrels, and intimidations. Bethany and Joel's marriage was spiraling out of control—until one day, Joel came completely clean. In tears, he admitted to indulging his lust with pornography, which he knew was a sin against God and against his wife. He vowed he had never been with another woman physically, only in his imagination. Then he asked Bethany for forgiveness and promised he would seek out help from a pastor who could counsel him. Joel kept his word and began going to weekly counseling sessions. Bethany, however, could not bring herself to forgive him.

Eighteen months went by and Bethany was still angry, withholding herself physically from Joel in every way. How could anyone know the mental pain she was enduring as she realized that, during all their previous times of intimacy, Joel had been imagining such actions with other women? Even though she knew withholding sex from her husband violated Scripture (1 Corinthians 7:3-5), feelings of justification and self-righteousness took over her emotions when she thought about how Joel had betrayed her.

In the meantime, Joel had truly changed. He was no longer the superficial people-pleaser he had been, and he evidenced genuine care and love for Bethany. He even openly confessed the fact that he was happy Bethany had uncovered his hidden sin, because now he was experiencing freedom from the bondage brought on by his lust-filled indulgence. This angered Bethany all the more, for this meant Joel would never have repented had he not been found out. *What kind of repentance is that?*, she thought. As she questioned Joel's repentance and became more blinded than ever by her growing bitterness, Bethany refused to admit that Joel had really changed. She was loathe to relinquish the role of punisher. Bitterness had taken firm root in her heart.

Bitterness is defined as a perpetual, intense hostility and resentment that leads to harsh treatment and unloving opinions of others. Bitter people are caught in a state of spiritual toxicity, and their poisonous attitudes and actions cause great damage. Worse than cancer, bitterness destroys relationships, corrupts attitudes, breeds hostility, and turns daily life into a living death. It is no wonder, then, that among the sins Christians are to "put off" is bitterness. As Ephesians 4:31 says, "Let all bitterness and wrath and anger and clamor and slander be put away from you, along with all malice."

Bitterness not only wreaks havoc on those around us, it also brings severe misery on the individual who perpetuates it. As Bethany sat listening to Pastor Mike's message on bitterness, the anguish in her soul was so great that she was no longer willing to continue on this way. The emotional agony, combined with the guilt she felt over her sin, was too overwhelming. "The heart knows its own bitterness, and no stranger shares its joy" (Proverbs 14:10). Bethany's unwillingness to forgive—her weapon of bitterness—had brought only misery and heartache.

Serious questions formed in Bethany's mind as she continued to listen that Sunday morning. Pastor Mike pointed out from the Bible that people who choose to hold onto their bitterness have good reason to question whether they are a true Christian. The description of an unrepentant unbeliever was made clear by the apostle Paul: "Their mouth is full of curses and bitterness" (Romans 3:14). One of the chief characteristics of an unbeliever is unrepentance (Psalm 7:12-15; Luke 13:3-5; Hebrews 12:17). Bethany instantly knew this was the present state of her heart. Still very angry at Joel, she could not remember any other time in her life that she was so obstinate in her refusal to repent of obvious sin. Could it be that *she* was not a true Christian? Nursing her own hurt had become her sole focus over the last 18 months, and in the process, she had failed to see that her bitterness was exceedingly sinful in the eyes of God.

The thought that she was acting as an unbeliever frightened Bethany to her core. The words of Ephesians 4:32 haunted her: "Be kind to one another, tenderhearted, forgiving one another, *as God in Christ forgave you.*" She thought, *What if God was withholding His forgiveness from me because of my personal sin against Him?* It would be the worst possible fate. Bethany knew that God had forgiven her a whole lifetime of sin, which was much greater than Joel's sin against her. God had forgiven her instantly and completely when she was saved. Since this was true of her heavenly Master, who was far greater and infinitely more righteous than she was, it should be true of her. Bethany realized that the only thing preventing her from forgiving Joel was her prideful self-righteousness. This realization was a personal revelation of immense proportions. "I must forgive him as I am forgiven in Christ!"

Just a month earlier, Bethany had attended a women's Bible study in which the session was titled "The Evidence of True Saving Faith." The study was centered on the book of 1 John, and her mind immediately went to familiar verses in chapter 4:

> We love because he first loved us. If anyone says, "I love God," and hates his brother, he is a liar; *for he who does not love his brother whom he has seen cannot love God whom he has not seen.* And this commandment we have from him: whoever loves God must also love his brother (verses 19-21).

In her vengeful anger, Bethany had hoped her lack of forgiveness would cause Joel to hurt as much as she hurt. But now her weapon was turning against her, revealing significant sin in her life, her conscience laid raw with conviction. How could she say she loved God and then treat her husband as if he were the most despised man on earth? This was not something a genuine Christian would continue to do. Having been forgiven so much in Christ, how could she not be forgiving to Joel?

There was yet one unanswered question in her mind: Was it possible for someone who had been caught in a sin, and forced to admit the truth, to eventually be genuine in their repentance? Then she remembered the story of King David: his adultery with Bathsheba while arranging the murder of her husband Uriah. After David had married Bathsheba, he refused to acknowledge his sin until Nathan uncovered it through a hypothetical story (2 Samuel 12:1-9). Later, David repented with a broken spirit (Psalm 51). If David could genuinely repent of adultery and murder, it *was* possible for Joel's repentance to be genuine. For the first time in months Bethany began to feel sympathy and compassion for her husband. She began to reflect on all the hateful and mean ways she had treated him, remembering his patient and loving responses. She knew what she needed to do.

As the pastor concluded the service in prayer, Bethany poured her heart out to God asking forgiveness for her bitterness and lack of forgiveness. Her eyes red with many tears, her only thought was to humbly submit to God and repent. The promise of 1 John 1:9 gave her an overwhelming sense of comfort and peace. She felt like a new person—as if a ton of weight had been lifted from her shoulders.

"Are you ok?" Joel inquired.

"Better than I have been in a long time," she responded quietly. "Could we go somewhere, so we can talk?"

Taken aback by her change of tone, Joel replied, "Sure."

Once they were alone, Bethany asked Joel to forgive her for having been so bitter toward him for so long. She told him she knew this was a sin against both him and God (Psalm 51:4, 14). For the first time, Bethany forgave Joel for his sinful involvement with pornography. She acknowledged how she had failed him as a wife and shared her determination to make some radical changes. Joel was quick to forgive her, sharing that he had been praying for her and how he knew he had much more growing to do to be a godly husband to her. That day was the rebirth of their marriage. Even though they had gone through extremely difficult times, God had used all of it to draw them closer to Himself and to each other.

Soon afterward, Bethany and Joel began meeting with Pastor Mike for marriage counseling. Even though they had reconciled and were at peace with one another, they both wanted to learn how to work through the difficulties that would arise when they sinned against one another again. Their most recent experience of extreme conflict and division showed them that they needed to learn how to confess sin to one another and exercise forgiveness much earlier in the reconciliation process—leaving very little room for bitterness to develop.

Pastor Mike was a great help to them. "When the weapon of unforgiveness is unleashed, it leaves broken lives in its wake," he explained. "Bitterness is the inevitable result. It always seeks a target, whether another person in your life or God Himself. You have seen how Christians can become bitter when someone sins against them in an egregious way. Or we can become bitter—usually against God in this case—when we expect Him to change an unpleasant, difficult situation and He does not. But the real answer to this problem is addressing the *unforgiveness* that became the catalyst for bitterness to develop. Understanding what God says about forgiveness is the beginning of addressing your struggle with bitterness."

He then asked Bethany and Joel to open their Bibles to Ephesians 4:31-32, the very passage he had preached from a few weeks back. "'Let all bitterness and wrath and anger and clamor and slander be put away from you, along with all malice. Be kind to one another, tenderhearted, forgiving one another, as God in Christ forgave you.'

It would be easy to just study verse 32 because it speaks directly to the command to forgive one another. However, looking at verse 31 provides the proper context for understanding forgiveness in its fullest sense.

"You see, when no one has sinned in an egregious way against you—perhaps they've been in a very bad mood for a long time—it's easy to read verse 32 and say, 'Hey, I can do that! I can be kind and compassionate to my brother, and of course I will forgive him!' But when we add verse 31 to our reading, we realize that something very bad happened that brought about such reactions as these: bitterness, wrath, anger, clamor, and slander. Suddenly we are so hurt, so offended, that we don't want to forgive, or give the offender freedom from our vengeance and our right to retribution. But no matter what has happened between two Christians, forgiveness is the answer to these difficulties—and specifically we are talking about bitterness today because of what you two have recently experienced in your marriage."

Bethany and Joel listened carefully as Pastor Mike taught them about biblical forgiveness. He shared about two kinds of forgiveness: attitudinal and transactional.

Attitudinal forgiveness is something done in your heart before God—having the attitude of forgiveness and willingness to do so. Attitudinal forgiveness must be completed *before* genuine transactional forgiveness can be granted to an offending party. In Matthew 6:12-15, Mark 11:25, and Luke 11:4, notice how there are only two persons present in each scenario: God and you (the offended person). The offending party is not present, which means attitudinal forgiveness is what is required here. And, in each case, the context is always prayer. Before you can truly say that you forgive someone, you must first forgive him from your heart in prayer to God.

Have you been withholding forgiveness? Then this will involve you confessing and repenting of the sin of unforgiveness (2 Corinthians 7:10; 1 John 1:9-10). Write out your prayer, review it to be sure you have covered everything, and then sincerely humble yourself before God in prayer. Only when this is finished, and your heart is right before God, can you move on to the next step.

Transactional forgiveness is the action of personally granting forgiveness to those who have sinned against you—that is, upon her repentance. If the person seeking your forgiveness is an unbeliever, then it is impossible for her to repent, because she has never repented before God. You should practice *attitudinal* forgiveness with an unbeliever so that your heart will not grow bitter because of her sin against you, but you cannot practice *transactional* forgiveness with an unbeliever until she repents of her sin against God.

In fact, no matter how great you may view a person's sin against you, her sin against God is greater. You must explain this to the unbeliever along with sharing the gospel. You could say, "I know you may believe that you need my forgiveness for the sin you committed against me, but the Bible says you have a greater need, which is to be forgiven by God. Let me share with you how this can be accomplished through faith in Jesus Christ as your Lord and Savior."

If, however, the person who repents of her sin against you is a Christian, then you need to practice Luke 17:3-4. "If your brother sins, rebuke him, and if he repents, forgive him, and if he sins against you seven times in the day, and turns to you seven times, saying, 'I repent,' you must forgive him." This is *transactional* forgiveness.

A word of clarification: The statement about "seven times in the day" means you won't have time to wait to see if that person will manifest the spiritual fruit of repentance. You must offer forgiveness on the basis of her word. This means you must leave it up to

God to deal with that person with regard to determining the genuineness of her repentance. It is not your role to be the Holy Spirit in her life.

Bethany and Joel also learned about the true nature of forgiveness. They had always thought that saying "I'm sorry" would take care of any problems between them. But as they studied the Bible further, they found a much more complete definition and basis for forgiveness. The basis, as we have already seen in Ephesians 4:32, is "as God in Christ forgave you." The definition, however, has to do with remembering, or more specifically, not remembering.

The Old Testament prophet Jeremiah gave great hope to the exiled Israelites as he gave them the Word of the Lord regarding a new covenant—a covenant of forgiveness.

> Behold, the days are coming, declares the LORD, when I will make a new covenant with the house of Israel and the house of Judah, not like the covenant that I made with their fathers on the day when I took them by the hand to bring them out of the land of Egypt, my covenant that they broke, though I was their husband, declares the LORD. For this is the covenant that I will make with the house of Israel after those days, declares the LORD: I will put my law within them, and I will write it on their hearts. And I will be their God, and they shall be my people. And no longer shall each one teach his neighbor and each his brother, saying, "Know the LORD," for they shall all know me, from the least of them to the greatest, declares the LORD. For I will forgive their iniquity, and *I will remember their sin no more* (Jeremiah 31:31-34).

We find this crucial Jeremiah passage cited in the New Testament in Hebrews 10:1-18, because now Christ has come to introduce the new covenant. Previously, under the Old Testament law, the sins of the Jewish people were brought up daily before the Lord in the sacrifices. But under the new covenant, the sacrifices stop. Christ's once-for-all sacrifice on the cross removed any requirement for daily sin sacrifices. Along with Christ's once-for-all sacrifice came *forgiveness*, when God promised to "remember their sins and their lawless deeds no more."

> The Holy Spirit also bears witness to us; for after saying, "This is the covenant that I will make with them after those days, declares the Lord: I will put my laws on their hearts, and write them on their minds," then he adds, "I will remember their sins and their lawless deeds no more." Where there is forgiveness of these, there is no longer any offering for sin (Hebrews 10:15-18).

So what does God mean when He says He will remember their sins no more? God, because of His promise to us in Christ—because of the new covenant—actively chooses not to remember our sins. In other words, He chooses not to hold them against us. He covers them; He conceals them with His forgiveness. It is a promise that He will keep for eternity.

As Bethany thought about this aspect of God's forgiveness, she remembered part of a psalm she had memorized a long time ago.

> The LORD is merciful and gracious, slow to anger and abounding in steadfast love. He will not always chide, nor will he keep his anger forever. He does not deal with us according to our sins, nor repay us according to our iniquities. For as high as the heavens are above the earth, so great is his steadfast love toward those who fear him; as far as the east is from the west, so far does he remove our transgressions from us. As a father shows compassion to his children, so the LORD shows compassion to those

who fear him. For he knows our frame; he remembers
that we are dust (Psalm 103:8-14).

Based on God's promise to not remember our sins against us, Pastor Mike taught Joel and Bethany the threefold promise of forgiveness that must take place between two Christians. "In choosing not to remember the sin against the other, you promise:

- I will not bring this issue up again to *you*, unless it would be for your good.

- I will not bring this issue up again to *others*, unless it would be for your good.

- I will not bring this up to *myself* and become bitter and resentful toward you in the future.

"After the threefold promise of forgiveness is made, the matter becomes a settled issue between the two of you, leaving no opportunity for bitterness. It is your obligation to keep your word concerning the three assurances because it is a promise you are making before God."

Joel and Bethany felt like they were starting out in their married life all over again. And in a sense, they were. They were committing to each other to love and reconcile just like God has done for us: being merciful and gracious, being slow to anger, showing steadfast love and compassion toward one another, and choosing in forgiveness to not remember each other's sins against them.

Questions for Discussion

1. Why do you think Bethany was so resistant to forgiving Joel? How do you think Colossians 3:12-13 would help someone who was using the weapon of unforgiveness?

2. According to Ephesians 4:32 and Colossians 2:13-14, how has God forgiven you in Christ? A person cannot truly forgive anyone until they have been forgiven in Christ and understand the depth of God's forgiveness for their sin. Think carefully about the undeserved riches you enjoy in Christ. What is it that makes God's forgiveness so remarkable? In the same manner, you should practice forgiveness of others (Colossians 3:13; Jeremiah 31:34).

3. Some bitter women will say this when they are faced with the biblical requirement to forgive another: "Well, I'll forgive him [or her] someday, but it will take me a really long time!" What does this reveal about the woman's heart? Can she really say she is forgiving as Christ forgave her? Why or why not?

4. Sometimes Christians will offer forgiveness because they believe doing so will make them feel better. But is that a legitimate reason for showing forgiveness? How would you use the Scripture passages cited above to encourage that Christian to forgive someone based on biblical reasons?

5. Read Acts 8:14-24. What perceived right was Simon bitter about? What needed to be done about his bitterness?

5

Borderline Personality Disorder

In the day of prosperity be joyful, and in the day of adversity
consider: God has made the one as well as the other, so that
man may not find out anything that will be after him.

ECCLESIASTES 7:14

Memories. Bad memories. Sad memories. Haunting memories. Skylar rolled over and looked at the clock. It was 4:13 am. Two hours before she needed to get up for work. As she lay her head on her pillow, tears began to trickle down the side of her face. If only things had been different…

Skylar's growing-up years were marked by two distinct memories: a longing to be loved by her mother, and her mother's enslavement to alcohol. Unfortunately, substance abuse had overpowered her mother, and Skylar was never sure that her mother even noticed her that much. No matter how much Skylar loved her mother, no matter how much she tried to be a good girl, her mother's life continued to spiral out of control and she gave less and less love and attention to the very people who so loved her.

Skylar's father was not a perfect man, but he worked hard to supply for his family. He was visibly grieved over his wife's growing reliance on the bottle. When Skylar was 13 years old, her mother left them and moved all the way across the country. They never saw her alive again because she died of a drug overdose two years later.

Devastated, Skylar had never felt so alone and abandoned. The oldest of three daughters, she had to grow up quickly and take care of her sisters while her father worked long hours to meet their needs. Each new challenge was a reminder of how difficult life had become since her mother had left. Her grief slowly turned to anger against her mother as she realized the hardships and pain this abandonment had caused her and her family. In time, Skylar began to view her mother's abandonment as rejection. She had longed for love and acceptance from the one who gave birth to her, but in the end she felt she had been cast off—like an unwanted old shoe. This produced in her an ache that never seemed to go away.

Three years after her mother's death, when Skylar was 18, her family suffered another terrible loss. Her youngest sister, Bonnie, contracted severe bacterial pneumonia. After battling this deadly infection for three months, she was taken from them. For five years Skylar had been both a sister and a mother to her. Bonnie's death ripped a hole in her already-broken family. At first Skylar was inconsolable, but she learned to be strong for her remaining sister, Adele, and her father.

Once again, grief turned to anger. This time Skylar was angry at God. Unlike her mother, Bonnie had not willingly cast her off. She had fought her illness courageously but had lost—and Skylar was holding God responsible. He could have healed her but had not. Losing her sweet Bonnie was just too much to take.

By this time, the loss of two people so precious to her began to significantly change Skylar. In addition to the grief and anger, a new emotion emerged: fear. What possible loss might be just around the corner? Could she take any more? What started out as fearful questions soon grew into an enormous terror that would grip her heart every time she thought about being left alone or abandoned.

A few years passed, and her sister Adele left for college. The house was feeling empty again—only she and her dad were left. Skylar tried to ignore the growing fear of abandonment again, but what happened next was completely unexpected. Her father began to date a woman, and soon they were married. Even though her new stepmother seemed to be a caring woman, Skylar felt unwanted and in the way. She had felt secure in her relationship with her dad, but his marriage ended up creating an unexpected emotional distance from him. Her father was preoccupied, Bonnie and Adele were gone, and Skylar knew it was time to get a job and move out. No one needed her anymore, and the raw feelings of loneliness settled in like a winter storm. Emotionally weak and unstable, she launched out on her own.

Overwhelmed with loneliness, Skylar sought new friendships and even perhaps a boyfriend, but her inability to maintain a close relationship with anyone soon became evident. The simple possibility of a separation, rejection, or abandonment was too overwhelming for her to handle. She became emotional and clingy, reading "rejection" into every situation. When her friend Denise was sick with a cold for a week, Skylar was sure she was spending more time with other friends and had cast her aside. Skylar became more and more withdrawn and irritable. These responses in her friendships became common and made life difficult for anyone who chose to hang around her.

There was this one friend at work, however, who seemed friendly and caring no matter what. Her name was Grace, and she often found Skylar in the employee cafeteria and asked if she might sit with her for lunch. It was always easy to say yes to Grace's company because after spending a little time with her, Skylar walked away feeling a little better about life. What was it about this girl? They were close in age, but Grace showed a confidence and strength that was hard to explain. Every so often she would mention God's goodness and faithfulness, but Skylar was quick to disregard those comments. If her new friend had been through what she had been through, surely she wouldn't be saying these things about God.

About six months into their friendship, Grace invited Skylar to go to church with her on the following Sunday morning. Even though Skylar still blamed God for Bonnie's death, she found herself accepting the invitation. Desperate for a sincere friendship, she pushed aside her anger with God and met Grace in the parking lot of the Bible church. To her surprise, she actually enjoyed this new experience. She had never met people like these before: gracious, kind, and genuinely interested in getting to know her. Grace kept inviting her back, and she was more than happy to return because it seemed she was forming friendships that appeared to be lasting.

After two months of attending the Bible church, Skylar found herself particularly interested in the pastor's Sunday morning sermon on grace. First he spent some time teaching from Romans 3:10-20, where the apostle Paul declared that no one is righteous—not even one person. Then he spent the rest of the sermon preaching from Ephesians 2:1-10 about God's grace to unworthy sinners. Skylar could readily believe that there were sinful people in this world. Although she didn't like to think of her this way, she would have to say that her mother was sinful. She had sinned badly against her family in drinking her life away and abandoning them.

But now Skylar came to realize that her mother's sin had also been against God. The thought that God was someone whom you should not offend hadn't ever crossed her mind. Further, the Spirit of God began to open her eyes to her own sin, particularly the sin of her anger against God. Conviction over the guilt of her sin came crashing down upon her and, for the first time, Skylar realized that she needed to be redeemed from her own wickedness. She needed a

Savior, and this Savior was the Lord Jesus Christ. That day, she confessed the hopeless state of her sinfulness and her inability to save herself. She repented and surrendered her life to Jesus Christ as her Lord, receiving by grace through faith that redemption and eternal life that was offered to all who believe. This was much more than she had expected from her newly formed friendship with Grace, but it was exactly what she needed.

As the months passed, Skylar's spiritual understanding grew rapidly. She read her Bible, and attended Bible studies and church regularly. She had a joy in her life she had never experienced before, and it was accompanied by a new direction and purpose for living. She was actively witnessing to Adele, her father, and her stepmother, hoping that someday they would come to Christ too. Everyone who knew Skylar could see a real change in her life. But, she still carried into her new Christian life the same fears of abandonment from her childhood. Even though they were not as acute as before, they were still present.

Within a year, the Lord brought a wonderful Christian young man into her life. Darren was the guy of her dreams—kind, loving, and a gentleman who enjoyed being with her. Yet as their love for one another grew, so did her anxious thoughts. What if he walked away and left her? This was a relationship she felt she could not afford to lose. As her fears increased, she became more and more possessive of his time with her, intensely jealous of anything that would take him away. Her abandonment fears were smoldering just under the surface.

One day Darren announced that he would be going away for the weekend to visit a couple of graduate schools. An advanced degree would mean that he could get a better-paying job for the future. Skylar went ballistic! Her worst fears were coming true—she was sure Darren was planning on leaving her. He was surprised and confused by her reaction to the news, thinking that she would be excited about the opportunity. She calmed down and tried to smooth things over by saying that she was really going to miss him and didn't want him to go away for that long.

After work the next day, Darren took Skylar to dinner and happened to discover several cuts and lacerations on her arms. "What happened to you?" he inquired with surprise and disbelief. "Are you a cutter?" Ashamed, Skylar explained that in her anger and fear over his plan to be gone for a full weekend that she had cut herself. Darren had come to genuinely love her, so this greatly disturbed him. Was she so insecure in his love for her that she had to resort to this? He was going to be away for only a few short days, but this seemingly simple problem was a huge difficulty for her. Skylar explained that with both of them working demanding jobs during the week, their time together on the weekends had become a source of emotional stability for her. To Skylar, it seemed he was sacrificing their relationship for an unnecessary trip away. Her anticipated separation anxiety was fueling a suffocating panic deep inside her.

Darren knew that dealing with these deep-seated emotional responses was way beyond his ability to handle. The next words he spoke were, "We need to see a counselor!" He really meant *she* needed to see a counselor. But not wanting to alienate Skylar and realizing she would probably not go without him, he was willing to go with her to get her the help she needed. He explained that if they were going to have a future together, seeing a counselor would be a necessity. Skylar could tell that Darren was very serious, more serious than she had ever seen him. In spite of her disappointment and dismay, she agreed.

Upon the recommendation of a friend, they began to meet weekly with a nearby psychologist who claimed to be a Christian. During the second appointment, the psychologist labeled her with

Borderline Personality Disorder (BPD) and recommended behavioral therapy.

When Darren inquired about the treatments, he was surprised that Scripture was practically ignored and instead behavioral techniques[7] and psychotropic drugs were heavily recommended. Several psychotropic drugs are suggested for BPD (selective serotonin reuptake inhibitors—SSRIs, antidepressants; antipsychotics; mood-stabilizing drugs or opiate receptor antagonists), so they would also need to see a psychiatrist indefinitely to acquire the prescriptions and to have them properly managed over a long period of time. Not only was this going to be costly, but neither one of them believed this would help her.

Although they did not know much about psychological theory, they understood this was *not* what she needed. Both Skylar and Darren had seen how much change for good she had already experienced since her salvation, subsequent worship, and Bible study. They clearly understood one thing: faithful biblical input was life-changing, honoring to God, and what she really needed to deal with her abandonment issues.

One of their friends at church recommended they contact a trained and certified biblical counselor who would take them to Scripture and seek godly answers for her feelings of panic every time she considered the possibility of being alone. They found the website of the Association of Certified Biblical Counselors (ACBC)[8] and were able to contact a woman who lived close by and was highly trained as a biblical counselor. After meeting Mrs. Hunt for an introduction, Skylar was so confident about her care and expertise that she told Darren she was willing to meet with this woman counselor on her own. Mrs. Hunt did not charge for the sessions, which was a great help to them both. This marked the beginning of some huge changes in Skylar's life.

During the counseling sessions, one of the critical areas Mrs. Hunt addressed was Skylar's memories of past situations that had left her feeling alone and abandoned. They carefully discussed the effect of her mother's abandonment, heavy chemical abuse and death, as well as the loss of Bonnie to pneumonia, her father's eventual remarriage, and Adele permanently leaving home for college. Skylar was learning that though her past had a powerful shaping influence upon her, it did not have to define her and dictate her responses. Instead, she could be governed by choices made in the light of two things: past events and the truth of Scripture.

There are two extreme dangers when it comes to the influence a person's past can have on her. First, she can believe that it determines her life, defining who she is; *it is everything*! This is what many psychologists teach their clients, causing them to adopt a "victim mentality" for the rest of their lives. The second extreme view is that the past is not important at all; *it is nothing*! There are many Christians who believe this is true, yet their attitudes and actions betray a significant influence from their past. Skylar's excessive fear of being alone or abandoned demonstrated she was greatly influenced by her past.

Mrs. Hunt turned Skylar's attention to the life of the apostle Paul and how his past had influenced him. Prior to becoming a Christian, Paul was a Pharisee. He was so zealous for the Law of God and Jewish tradition that he persecuted Christians and participated in their murders. He was a "Hebrew of Hebrews" and full of self-righteousness (Philippians 3:5-6). His past had marked and influenced him in deceptively wicked ways. In an attempt to gain favor with God, he was living a life of works-righteousness, much the same way that Skylar was living a life of desperation attempting to gain favor with people.

But because of the transformation Jesus Christ made in Paul's life when he was gloriously saved, he considered that his past accomplishments were nothing compared to "the surpassing worth of knowing Christ Jesus my Lord" (Philippians 3:7-8). The unearned grace of Jesus Christ had changed him. For this reason, Paul was not going to allow his past to determine the person he was. As he said in 2 Corinthians 5:17, "If anyone is in Christ, he is a *new creation*. The old has passed away; behold, the new has come."

Paul was able to say that his thought life—which had formerly been full of self and works-righteousness—was now full of "the righteousness from God that depends on faith" (Philippians 3:9). Skylar learned from Paul's example that as long as she considered herself a victim of abandonment and allowed her mind to dwell on the dread of future abandonment, she too would be consumed with herself and not a knowledge of Christ as Lord.

Mrs. Hunt read these words to Skylar:

> Not that I have already obtained this or am already perfect, but I press on to make it my own, because Christ Jesus has made me his own. Brothers, I do not consider that I have made it my own. But one thing I do: *forgetting what lies behind and straining forward to what lies ahead*, I press on toward the goal for the prize of the upward call of God in Christ Jesus (Philippians 3:12-14).

By God's help, Paul chose to forget his past life of works-righteousness and focus upon the riches of Christ. Skylar knew she too must stop allowing her traumatic past to fill her thoughts with desperation and fear; this would no longer happen when she was fully consumed with Christ as her Lord. She wanted to be like Paul, moving "toward the goal for the prize of the upward call of God in Christ Jesus" (3:14), and letting go of the dominating influence of her past. As with Paul, this was going to require a significant effort of "unselfing" (Luke 9:23).

Skylar was gradually becoming a different young woman. One of the most encouraging truths she learned from Mrs. Hunt was that she did not have a mental disorder or some type of mental illness. Her difficulties in relationships was purely an issue of her heart, and this brought her great hope, for she was convinced that the Bible had the solution to problems of the heart—the inner person. She realized that her abandonment problems came from a fear-driven heart, not from a diseased mind and body.

What was puzzling to Skylar was the profound effect that her past continued to have on her after becoming a Christian. To help her with this, Mrs. Hunt had her begin journaling her thoughts each time she began to feel anxious and fearful. In her journal, she was to answer four questions:

1. What was happening in her life when these thoughts surfaced?
2. Who was she thinking about most at that time?
3. What did she think she wanted so badly that it bothered her and caused her to feel so anxious?
4. What does God say about those anxious thoughts?

Skylar was to try to answer the fourth question as thoroughly as she could. Then she and Mrs. Hunt would discuss her responses in detail during their next counseling session.

After weeks of journaling in this way Skylar began to see patterns in her thinking as well as in her reactions to people with whom she had close relationships. This was still a much bigger problem in her life than she had first realized. She came to realize her relationships had been somewhat artificial as a result of her idolizing the other person and fantasizing as to how closeness to them would be such a benefit and comfort to her. She also noticed that the deep emptiness remaining from her past had motivated her to hold people close in a smothering kind of way.

Skylar could see, from her journaling, that she would begin relationships as a needy and open confider, but then she would become a self-righteous and vicious avenger of mistreatment when friends would not give her the attention she felt she needed. The very people with whom she would form close relationships were the same people upon whom she would vent her emotional anger. The people she would idolize early in a relationship became the same people she would demean and devalue later.

What was causing these dramatic reversals? Evidently her fears would end up overwhelming and controlling her thoughts about others. She believed they did not care enough, or did not give enough, or were not "there for her" enough. And surely that meant that they were going to hurt her—or abandon her, which was her worst nightmare. She now saw that her behavior was extremely alienating toward others because she assumed the worst about their intentions and her goal in relationships was her own self-satisfaction.

Mrs. Hunt explained that relationships do give our lives meaning and purpose. This is true in our relationship with God, and God does use human relationships in this way as well. But Skylar had wanted her friendships to bear the weight of all of her expectations and longing for security. Far beyond enjoying the meaning and purpose that human friends can bring to life, she had demanded of her friends that they be as God to her—that they would never leave or forsake her. But only God can promise that, and only God supplies that kind of meaning and purpose to life. Because of this and the self-serving way in which Skylar viewed her friends, she was never satisfied. Consequently her friends were frustrated by her, because they found it difficult to meet her lofty expectations and handle the abuse she poured out when she was once again disappointed by their humanness.

Biblical counseling helped Skylar to face her fear of abandonment that was alienating so many of her friends, including Darren. She realized that elevating personal relationships to such a high level of importance in her life was robbing her of being the godly woman she could be. Her insistence on chasing after feelings of safety and security in human relationships was taking her confidence off of Christ. This fear became like a god she would bow down to every day and worship; it dominated her life, fueling her controlling and manipulative ways (1 Corinthians 10:6-7, 14). It also caused her to express angry and hateful reactions when she was denied what she really craved.

As Skylar saw these things with eyes now opened, she abhorred what she had become. It disgusted her to think that she had idolized relationships even to the point of slicing and cutting herself in her passionate rage. For the first time in her life, she was able to see herself the way others and God saw her (1 Corinthians 13:12; see also James 1:23-25).

Suddenly Skylar's conscience was plagued with the heavy weight of guilt (John 9:41). In tears, Skylar poured out her new realization to Mrs. Hunt, expressing her sorrowful regret for allowing this idolatrous desire to rule her heart for so long. Mrs. Hunt explained to her how psychology views guilt as an enemy, but the Bible teaches that guilt is a friend. It lets us know that something is wrong and needs to be corrected (Proverbs 14:9).

Guilt functions through a good conscience in the same way a fire alarm does in your home. When a fire alarm goes off, you don't pick up a hammer and smash the alarm! But that is how contemporary psychology deals with guilt. Instead, you rush to find the fire and seek to have it extinguished as quickly as possible. This is what guilt should do in the Christian life. God's fire extinguisher is sincere repentance (Luke 5:32; Romans 2:4), and then through the Lord's forgiveness, the conscience is cleansed from its guilt (Jeremiah 33:8; 1 John 1:8-10).

During that counseling session, Skylar bowed her head, confessed her sin of allowing personal relationships to become her god, and tearfully repented before God. Mrs. Hunt prayed and thanked God for working in Skylar's heart, and then she had Skylar read the following Bible verses:

- "With you there is *forgiveness*, that you may be feared" (Psalm 130:4).

- "In him we have redemption through his blood, the *forgiveness* of our trespasses, according to the riches of his grace" (Ephesians 1:7).

- "If we confess our sins, he is faithful and just to *forgive* us our sins and to *cleanse us* from all unrighteousness" (1 John 1:9).

To Skylar, it was as if there had been an enormous weight removed from her shoulders. She began to experience a refreshing freedom from this idol that had controlled her thoughts and desires for so much of her life. She was now firmly rooted in Jesus Christ and found her confidence in Him, not in maintaining and controlling personal relationships. What she had originally thought was a Borderline Personality Disorder was now clearly seen to be a dominating lust of her heart. This was a damaging lust that found its remedy in the person of Jesus Christ and His forgiveness of sin instead of life-long therapy and psychoactive medication.

Skylar now needed to immerse herself and all of her thinking in Christ. Formerly she was a wicked rebel against God; now she was a forgiven sinner, saved by the rich grace of Jesus Christ. She was also a new creation in Christ who was loved with an everlasting love

(2 Corinthians 5:17; Psalm 100:5). She never had to worry about being abandoned and alone because God would never leave her or forsake her (Deuteronomy 31:6, 8; Joshua 1:5; Hebrews 13:5). Human relationships, while providing joy in this life, are also frail and temporary; her relationship with God the Father through Jesus Christ is eternal (John 12:25). All these truths provided Skylar with a new sense of security and confidence she had never had before in her life. Maybe her relationship with Darren would result in marriage—she hoped this would be true, but she now understood that if it did not, she would still have a solid foundation on which to move forward with her life.

As time passed, Skylar began to realize how dealing with this issue in her heart was the best mood stabilizer on earth. She was no longer subject to extreme swings of emotion or volatile reactions. For too long she had been attributing too much importance to temporary things that pass away with time, instead of anchoring herself in her eternal Lord (2 Corinthians 4:18). Now her life evidenced a much greater stability. Her relationship with Darren was greatly improved as well. Although she enjoyed a measure of meaning and purpose in their relationship, she no longer sought to sinfully control him because her full confidence was now in Christ.

• • • • •

If you have recognized a similar tendency in yourself to allow sinful fear to becoming controlling in your relationships, read through the biblical checklist below. Study through the Bible passages listed there to aid you in your goal in putting the past behind you and living for Christ each day.

Indicators that Sinful Fears Are Contributing to Relationship Idolatry

* Sinful fear is controlling my thoughts when it tempts me to not follow the revealed will of God (Exodus 4:10-14; Matthew 25:14-30).

* Sinful fear is controlling my thoughts when it tempts me to disobey the revealed will of God (Numbers 13:25– 14:5; Mark 4:35-41).

* Sinful fear is controlling my thoughts when it tempts me to act out in selfish and demanding ways (Deuteronomy 7:17-18; Isaiah 51:12-13; Philippians 2:4; 1 John 4:18).

* Sinful fear is controlling my thoughts when it tempts me to think in negative and pessimistic ways, with worst-case scenarios (1 Corinthians 13:4-6; Philippians 4:8).

* Sinful fear is controlling my thoughts when I am tempted to panic and become anxious at the realization of being alone (Matthew 14:23; Luke 10:41; John 16:32; Romans 11:3-5; 1 Corinthians 1:9; Philippians 4:6).

* Sinful fear is controlling my thoughts when I am tempted to fear man or man's absence more than I fear God (Psalm 36:1; Proverbs 29:25; Ecclesiastes 5:7; 12:13; 2 Corinthians 7:1; 1 Peter 2:17).

* Sinful fear is controlling my thoughts when I am tempted to find my joy and meaning in human relation-ships rather than my undeserved union with Christ by grace (Romans 5:8, 11, 17; 8:1-2, 38-39; 12:5; Ephesians 1:3; 2:4-10; Philippians 4:11-13).

Questions for Discussion

1. Many people think that when they become a Christian all their problems will vanish. Read Ephesians 4:17-32. Paul wrote these verses to Christians. How does this passage teach the *opposite* of the misperception that all our problems will vanish?

2. Why would the well-intentioned psychologist's recommendations for behavioral therapy and psychotropic drugs not have benefitted Skylar spiritually?

3. What role does Scripture memorization and meditation have in the life of someone who is attempting to put off sinful fear?

4. Read Psalm 34. What truths in this psalm can provide help to a person who is sinfully fearful? What do you observe about God's character, His promises, and the experience of the psalm writer as he cried out to God?

5. Explain why the gospel of Jesus Christ was the only hope for Skylar in her situation.

6

Chemical Abuse

The time that is past suffices for doing what the Gentiles
want to do, living in sensuality, passions, drunkenness,
orgies, drinking parties, and lawless idolatry.

1 PETER 4:3

There it was in her closet—the shoe box that served as her hiding place. As Sheryl opened the box with great anticipation, her heart sank as soon as she realized the box was empty. What was supposed to be filled with her "happy pills" was now holding only air. *Who took my meds?* She wondered. *Don't they understand how much I need them? Is someone playing a cruel joke? Has someone finally discovered my secret? Could one of the grandchildren have found them?*

As these thoughts swirled through Sheryl's mind, she became nauseously ill. Her hands trembled and her knees grew weak as she wiped cold sweat from her forehead. Feelings of panic began to overwhelm her. Her doctor's office was closed on Friday night. How would she make it through the weekend without her little miracle workers?

It had all started two years ago, after Sheryl had back surgery to fuse two vertebrae that were causing her so much back pain. Her surgeon had prescribed a very powerful post-surgical painkiller to help get her through the healing process. It was the first serious relief she had gotten from those sharp jolts of agony she had experienced for many years. She could not remember feeling so good at any other time in her life. It was all due to her wonderful pain meds, which she fondly thought of as her little angels. For 24 months she had manipulated her doctor and pharmacist so they would provide her with a continual supply.

And now, Sheryl was so used to those painkillers that she could not conceive of life without them. She was hooked on them. Not only that, but this was a secret that she had kept hidden from everyone for the past couple of years, even from the closest members of her family. She had always feared a day like this would someday come.

Thinking she was alone, Sheryl ran in panic to the front room of her house, searching for where she might have misplaced the meds. Upon entering the room, she suddenly stopped. There sat Jack, her husband of 32 years, holding her prescription bottle of meds in his hand. *What was he doing home from work?* she wondered.

"Are you looking for these?" he asked sadly. Sheryl mentally scrambled for an excuse for her panic, "Yes," she replied. "I was afraid the grandchildren had found them." Jack brushed off her response and pressed forward. "Sweetheart, you know I love you! And you know I am saying this in love. These prescription drugs have changed you. You are no longer the gracious woman that I have known for years. You are different—nervous, excitable, scared, and secretive."

In tearful anger Sheryl shot back, "You don't understand the awful pain I deal with. I need those pills to make it through the day!"

Jack looked at Sheryl lovingly with deep disappointment in his eyes.

"I don't have a problem! I have a very painful condition!" she fired at him again in haste. Jack continued to sit quietly, dejected and discouraged.

Sheryl rushed forward and grabbed the medication from her husband, trying to open the prescription bottle as she ran back to their bedroom. In her haste, she bumped against the door frame and the cap prematurely loosened, spilling the precious contents all over the floor.

In an instant Sheryl collapsed to the carpet, trying to grab every pill in sight and return them to the bottle while a new awareness of her desperation startled her. It was as if time was standing still. Kneeling there on the bedroom floor, her eyes filled with tears. Jack was right; she had a serious problem that she was unwilling to admit. She was hooked on these pills and she knew it. A dreadful sense of guilt overwhelmed her. She had lied to herself and her loved ones, excusing her deceptive behavior and attitudes with a charade of excuses. This was not the way a woman who professed to love Christ should be. She had become a lying hypocrite.

Sheryl then looked up to see her husband standing in the doorway of their bedroom. "Will you let me help you?" he said in a soft and loving tone. She was mortified that Jack had found her in this state: desperate and weak. Embarrassed and overwhelmed with guilt, her dignity had suffered a terrible blow. For years she had prided herself on her personal self-discipline, with a healthy and careful diet. But now her lack of self-control revealed a serious weakness that seemed beyond her ability to manage. Her chemical dependency was now causing her to experience the raw feelings of being helplessly out of control.

Recently, in the Bible study she attended, Sheryl and her friends had been studying Proverbs 5. They had memorized verses 22 and 23. It was a passage warning about the habitual nature of sexual sin, but the broader principles of those verses became vividly clear to

Sheryl in her own situation. "The iniquities of the wicked ensnare him, and he is held fast in the cords of his sin. He dies for lack of discipline, and because of his great folly he is led astray."

Sheryl's folly was that she believed the helpless feelings of her body (verse 22) more than she believed the promises of God. She knew that if she continued to go down this path, it would destroy her life and she would cease to be the godly wife, mother, and grandmother that she was called to be.

As Sheryl looked up into her husband's eyes she saw he had tears too. His offer of help gave her a sense of hope—she could tell he was not condemning her. He was being the man she had married: caring and gentle. Unannounced, Jack joined Sheryl in kneeling in the middle of their bedroom floor, his left arm around her shoulders, drawing her close. "Yes," she choked out. "Yes, I need your help!"

Jack immediately began to pray. It was a prayer of a desperate sinner calling upon God to be gracious and merciful to his hurting wife. That Jack was willing to join her in this battle provided a huge amount of encouragement to Sheryl. She too prayed and confessed her sinful behavior and attitudes in allowing her heart to worship the comforting feeling she received from her medication. She confessed that it had become her god—a god she bowed down to every day, a god she paid homage to every time she lied to her doctor and her family in order to acquire another fix. She even prayerfully confessed that she had taken money from their savings without telling Jack in order to purchase reserve supplies of her medication. Then she asked forgiveness from God, and her husband, for all of her deceit and manipulation.

Sheryl felt a sense of relief as her heavy burden of guilt was lifted. She hadn't realized, until now, just how much guilt she'd been hiding. Jack stood up, reached for Sheryl's Bible from the nightstand, and began to read the following verses of encouragement:

> But he gives more grace. Therefore it says, "God opposes
> the proud, but gives grace to the humble." Submit your-
> selves therefore to God. Resist the devil, and he will flee
> from you. Draw near to God, and he will draw near to
> you. Cleanse your hands, you sinners, and purify your
> hearts, you double-minded. Be wretched and mourn and
> weep. Let your laughter be turned to mourning and your
> joy to gloom. Humble yourselves before the Lord, and he
> will exalt you (James 4:6-10).

Jack then told Sheryl that just because she had confessed her sin, that didn't guarantee the road ahead would be easy. But he assured her that he would walk it with her. "Cleanse your hands, you sin-ners," he explained, "is James's way of describing the changes you must make in your outward behavior. The hiding, deceiving, and stealing need to stop, along with the misuse of your medication. Your outward behavior must be open and truthful [Ephesians 4:25]. But, if outward change is all that happens, then you will still be liv-ing a duplicitous life. James also said 'purify your hearts, you double-minded'—which means your heart has to change as well. You can no longer think that this drug is the answer. In fact, your dependency on it will destroy you. Your hope and strength must be found in Jesus Christ alone. Your heart has to be resolved to follow Christ no matter how difficult withdrawal from the drug may be. You must worship Jesus Christ alone; anything less than that is idolatrous. Without deep resolve in your heart, you will experience setbacks instead of lasting change."

Sheryl wanted to change, but she still felt weak and helpless. Looking at Jack with great sincerity, she blurted out, "Why does it have to be so hard? Why doesn't God just instantly take this irresist-ible craving away?" That's the question of every Christian who strug-gles with chemical dependency. Jack thought for a moment, then said, "I can think of two reasons change doesn't necessarily happen quickly. First, it helps to deepen your faith in your Lord."

Jack went on to explain that affliction forces the believer to exercise even greater trust in the Lord and His purposes. In fact, instant relief from the trial tempts us to rejoice only in the temporal things of life—the good feelings associated with release from the pain we're feeling. On the other hand, the hardship of enduring the affliction causes us to look beyond our selfish desire for relief to looking for God Himself. This truth is easily seen in Psalm 119: "Before I was afflicted I went astray, but now I keep your word" (verse 67). "It is good for me that I was afflicted, that I might learn your statutes" (verse 71). In other words, our mind and heart are not captivated by God's Word until we are afflicted.

This difficulty of overcoming dependency would drive Sheryl to the Lord and His Word. Many Christians think that God is being unfaithful when He allows hardship, but that is not what the Bible teaches. Psalm 119:75 says, "I know, O LORD, that your rules are righteous, and that in faithfulness you have afflicted me."

In Sheryl's case, it will be critical that she believe that the Lord is being faithful to her in allowing her to endure the affliction of withdrawal from drug dependency. This will draw her nearer to Him *and* save her from even more consequences of her sin. "If your law had not been my delight, I would have perished in my affliction" (verse 92). Trusting in the Lord through affliction is the only way Sheryl will be able to successfully navigate the tough road of withdrawal.

Jack then shared the second reason he thought change is often not instantaneous. "As you seek the Lord and His Word through your difficulty, you will learn the sufficiency of God's grace so that you can be freed from the illusion of your own self-sufficiency," he said. That is, self-sufficiency had brought Sheryl to the place of physical and spiritual bondage to her medications. Her pride had led to her chemical dependency because she falsely believed she could handle the intense cravings it would bring. She was convinced that she would never succumb to drug dependency as others had done.

Sheryl's cry, "Why does this have to be so hard?" is similar to Paul's struggle with a "thorn in the flesh" that God had allowed in his life. Whatever this thorn was (it is not made clear in Scripture), on three occasions, Paul pleaded with God to remove it. And all three times, God responded, "My grace is sufficient for you, for my power is made perfect in weakness" (2 Corinthians 12:9). Paul was left in his helpless state so that God's power would be evident in his life. Remaining in the difficulty demonstrated to Paul that his own human strength was insufficient; anything he accomplished would be on account of God's enabling grace.

As Sheryl struggled, she too would come to recognize her weakness outside of God's power. Her weakness would be magnified; and God's power would be magnified even more. This would help bring an end to her tendency toward self-sufficiency. Why should God take away this great learning opportunity by dramatically and instantaneously removing her craving? Sheryl was about to experience the power of God's enabling grace in her life.

Remembering what he had learned at a biblical counseling conference at their church, Jack went to his desk and picked up a notebook. In it was a list of symptoms commonly associated with people who were enslaved to chemical dependency, based upon the truths found in Proverbs 23:20-21, 29-35. According to Scripture, drunkenness is a paradigm for any type of chemical dependency. Sheryl and Jack spent the next two hours carefully reviewing and discussing this list so that they could better understand the depth of her dependency.

Seven Symptoms of Chemical Enslavement

1. Willingness to sacrifice hard work, possessions, and all or most of one's wealth in order to secure additional dosages of the chemical (Proverbs 23:20-21)

2. Recurring headaches, feelings of anxiety, insomnia, nausea, or general awful feelings when there has been an extended absence of the chemical, which causes the heart to be strongly attracted to and lust for more (Proverbs 23:29-31)

3. Disregard for adverse personal consequences of the chemical, such as dullness, distortion or denial of reality, loss of judgment, and the entertainment of perverse thoughts (Proverbs 23:32-33; see also 31:4-5)

4. Determined desire for repeated experiences with the chemical regardless of the physical and emotional instability that it engenders (Proverbs 23:34)

5. An insensitivity to the mistreatment of others, frequent arguments and fights with family members or friends (Proverbs 23:35)

6. Occasional and temporary blackouts, forgetfulness, or memory loss that contributes to insecurity and uncertainty (Proverbs 23:35)

7. Ongoing demanding desire to use the chemical of choice in order to relax or sleep, to be happy or content, to resolve personal problems, or to just simply feel "normal" (Proverbs 23:35)

At the conclusion of their discussion, Jack and Sheryl had no doubt that she was dealing with a sinful bondage to her prescription drug. It was time for her to get help from a well-trained counselor.

That afternoon they called their church, and one of their staff pastors gave them the name of a woman in their church who not only had extensive experience in biblical counseling but also understood how to help those dealing with chemical abuse. Before the end of the week, Sheryl had her first appointment with her new counselor, Candace.

During their first session together, Sheryl began to realize why her medication had become such a serious problem in her life. Candace opened God's Word and helped her to see her problem from a theological perspective. All along, Sheryl had thought her problem was primarily a physiological addiction. She learned that although her bondage to this chemical had some very strong physical components, the real source of the problem came from a fundamental desire in her heart that called into question her essential allegiance to the Lord Jesus Christ. In spite of the fact that her back surgery had successfully corrected the problem and removed her pain, Sheryl still held onto the terrifying memories of the overwhelming pain she felt during recovery. Convinced that she was unable to endure such pain ever again, her attachment to pain medication was cemented. She was fearful that if she stopped the medication, the pain would return. And this fear led her to fail to trust God for that possibility. It also led her to lie to the doctors and her loved ones.

Candace further explained the theological nature of Sheryl's addiction by sharing six truths that helped Sheryl to understand why she had become enslaved to her medication.

Six Key Truths About the Nature of Addiction

1. God created man as a creature who is dependent by nature (Matthew 6:25-26).

From the beginning, mankind was created to be dependent upon his environment. He needed food, water, oxygen, atmospheric pressure, gravity, and a moderate temperature in order to survive in the world—even before sin had entered the picture. All these provisions were guaranteed and supplied by God. Man was designed to live as a dependent creature, with God supplying everything he needed in perpetuity.

2. Man was also created to be dependent upon God in order to find life and blessing (Genesis 2:15-17; Deuteronomy 8:3).

Man needed God's direction in order to think and function properly in the world. God provided man with the proper instructions on how to rightly structure his moral universe. He told man he could eat of any tree of the garden, except one. He told man what his role would be in working and maintaining his environment. Man did not naturally know these things, so man was made to be dependent upon God's revealed will from the very beginning of creation. But then man sinned and suffered spiritual and physical death (Genesis 3:1-19). Mankind rebelled against his dependency upon God.

3. Ever since sin came into the world, mankind has continually strived for autonomy and self-sufficiency (Jeremiah 9:23-24; 2 Timothy 3:1-5).

As a fallen, depraved creature, man's natural tendency is to mistrust God. Believing he does not need God, it is the nature of man to elevate his own feelings, ideas, and thoughts above God's. He wants to be free and independent from the God who created him. Human history is a torrid tale of man's ritualistic endeavor to act independent of God. This rebellion will continue all the way till the last days, which will be characterized by man being completely self-consumed.

4. In spite of mankind's feeble efforts at self-autonomy, he remains a dependent creature (Isaiah 31:1-3; Matthew 10:28).

Man fools himself into believing he can function without God. Natural disasters, incurable diseases, and death are constant reminders that God alone is in control and that man is still dependent. When a person comes to a point of desperation due to a chemical dependency, it is a reminder of how dependent and slavishly reliant he is upon God. The answer is that man's will should ultimately surrender to God's will. Yet, the human heart remains stubborn, and man still refuses to turn to God.

5. Instead of turning to God, man turns his heart to idols (Proverbs 25:28; 1 Corinthians 10:6-11; 1 Peter 4:1-6; 1 John 5:21).

Idols are simply *anything* that man worships that is not the God of heaven. An idol can be a person, a possession, a passion, a pleasure, or a place. Anything that is desirable can become an idol. Chemical abusers use legal or illegal substances because they believe the mood-altering experiences they create will enhance their life and give them happiness, when in reality the dependency is robbing them of life and will result in misery. Any type of chemical substance will mock its user, and a person who surrenders to the abuse of such substances is a fool (Proverbs 20:1).

6. Man is captivated and ensnared by the idols he trusts and loves, resulting in a horrible bondage of both body and soul (Proverbs 5:22; 19:3; Ezekiel 14:1-11; Romans 1:24-25).

The mood-changing experiences, the relief from stress, the pain-free feelings of pleasure are the implied promises of this chemical idol. An abuser trusts it and loves the rewarding feelings it provides. But because the human body has mechanisms of adjustment, an abuser soon discovers it requires a greater amount and frequency of use to achieve the same degree of satisfaction. The time between fixes becomes less. The demand for the fixes become greater. The appetite of fully enslaved abusers is never completely satisfied, even though they wrongly believe that all they need is just one more fix. Every indulgence only serves to increase the demand, and satisfying this demanding god magnifies desperation. Instead of bringing joy and happiness, it delivers misery and agony. Scripture proves to be true once again: People become dependent because they are dependent!

Sheryl was beginning to see how the Bible speaks authoritatively about chemical dependency. God's Word had defined the problem, and God's Word had also giving the solutions. To be clear, in many cases of chemical abuse, medical help *is* desirable to assist with the possible adverse effects of withdrawal from a drug. In such situations, a good biblical counselor will encourage the counselee to seek professional assistance from a physician at the same time biblical counsel is being received. But ultimately, chemical dependency is a heart issue, and the counselee's behavior will not change unless there is a change of heart. While medical attention will help take care of the physical damage or effects of withdrawal, it cannot change the ways of the heart. Only biblical counsel can do that.

Candace pointed out to Sheryl that the world calls chemical dependency a *disease* or an *addiction*, but that is not the terminology Scripture uses. Both contemporary terms imply that the solution is primarily medical and beyond our personal responsibility. They are terms of helpless dependency and hopeless determinism. Studies have demonstrated that many people have quit their chemical dependencies entirely on their own.[9] People don't quit a disease. If that were true, there would be no more cancer or even the common cold. Chemical dependency is primarily spiritual in nature. And the terminology the Bible uses to speak of it is *idolatry*—that is, the replacement of the true and living God with a substance.

Substance abuse is reliance upon one's own self-judgment and self-sufficiency in determining what is best for their life, and a turning away from God's will and purposes. Because the critical sin of the substance abuser's heart is the worship of the experience that is provided through a chemical substance, the remedy is repentance from worshipping the wrong god. Jesus Christ did not come to provide atonement for a disease; He came to provide atonement for the willful sin of the heart (Hebrews 2:17; 1 John 4:10—"propitiation" means an atoning sacrifice). True biblical repentance, which is the beginning of permanent change, must involve a total acknowledgement and ownership of one's personal sin of seeking self-gratification over the Savior's glory (Ezekiel 14:6; Luke 13:5; Acts 8:22).

In addition, Candace pointed out that this repentance has another important dimension: reconciliation. Anyone whom Sheryl had sinned against while abusing this drug should be sought out for reconciliation. She needed to go to each person, acknowledge her sin, seek their forgiveness, and make restitution. Then she needed to pray that the offended party will be gracious and will forgive her (Luke 17:3-5). God is honored when a sweet reconciliation is restored among His people.

For example, to hide her habit, there had been times when Sheryl had lied or misrepresented the truth. And to support her habit, she had deceitfully used money that had been set aside for other uses. She needed to confess her wrongdoing to those whom had been affected by her behavior. Sheryl knew doing this would be difficult and humbling, but she recognized the importance of mortally wounding her pride. This severe act of "unselfing" would make the temptation to sin much less appealing in the future. She made immediate plans to reconcile with her husband and her doctor, with a willingness to pay back all she had deceitfully taken (Exodus 22:10-15; Luke 19:8-9). Restitution proves repentance to be genuine.

The Word of God held such great hope for Sheryl. She had heard people coming out of 12-step programs dutifully reciting this mantra as though it were fact: "Once an addict, always an addict." This is not what the Bible teaches concerning the Christian, Candace explained. There is no such thing as a "recovering Christian abuser" who spends the remainder of her life attending group therapy sessions because she will never fully recover from her chemical dependency. People who are in an endless state of recovery should question whether they are truly Christians because our Lord promises full and complete recovery through the transforming work of justification. Look at how Paul describes this transformation:

> Do you not know that the unrighteous will not inherit the kingdom of God? Do not be deceived: neither the sexually immoral, nor idolaters, nor adulterers, nor men who practice homosexuality, nor thieves, nor the greedy, nor *drunkards*, nor revilers, nor swindlers will inherit the kingdom of God (1 Corinthians 6:9-10).

The immoral conduct and practices listed in that passage describes unbelievers. They are the ones who continually practice these things, including the continual abuse of alcohol, a very common form of chemical abuse. People who continually identify themselves as abusers cannot identify themselves as Christians. They "will not inherit the kingdom of God"! The Christian understands the transforming power of Jesus Christ. In fact, the next verse in this text affirms that complete transformation really is possible: "And such were some of you. But you were washed, you were sanctified, you were justified in the name of the Lord Jesus Christ and by the Spirit of our God" (1 Corinthians 6:11).

Paul was saying that those who at one time were marked by immoral conduct and practices were now transformed. Their identity was no longer that of being a "recovering abuser." Rather, their identity was found in Christ.

Now, such transformation does not mean we will no longer endure the weaknesses of the flesh. Though we are Christians, we are still indwelling a sinful body. Yet the fact we now identify as being in Christ will directly affect how we function.

Candace provided Sheryl with an illustration: Imagine you are a very poor migrant worker who has spent most of your life laboring for very low wages. Then you discover that you are an heir of a king's fortune. However, you will not receive your inheritance for several years. Do you think that would change the way you think about yourself and how you conduct your life, even though you still have several years left in your poverty? It certainly would! Likewise, if Sheryl continues to think of herself as a "recovering chemical abuser," she will act like one. But if she considers herself a child of the King, she will act like royalty. In fact, her spiritual position in Christ is infinitely better than the material inheritance of an earthly king.

As Sheryl progressed in counseling, she found the discipline of self-denial to be quite difficult. Some days she felt so weak that she was seriously tempted to return to her chemical god. Candace helped Sheryl to work through a plan to facilitate righteous decisions and actions, but there were times when doing this was exceedingly hard. To resist the temptations that came her way, Sheryl found it helpful to remind herself that she is an undeserving child of the King.

In addition, Candace encouraged Sheryl to memorize the words of Jesus Christ in Luke 9:23: "If anyone would come after me, let him deny himself and take up his cross daily and follow me." Sheryl learned what it meant to take up a cross—that she would need to treat *self* like a wicked criminal and nail *self* to the cross every day. Gradually Sheryl found that the more she practiced righteous living, the more a great sense of satisfaction in knowing she had obeyed her Lord encouraged her. Guilt-free living was a refreshing way to experience her new life without a drug-induced euphoria.

Another verse that came to mean a lot to Sheryl came from the pen of King David. It was part of a psalm written about how the Lord had given David relief during times of distress. The Hebrew text of Psalm 4:1 literally says, "In tightness you have made space." When circumstances of life were closing in on David, God gave him space. God loosened the tightness of his circumstances. In verse 7 David wrote, "You have put more joy in my heart than they have when their grain and wine abound." As Sheryl made daily decisions to be faithful to the Lord, denying her self-sufficiency and trusting the Lord's sovereign purposes, God was gracious to her by loosening the tightness of her circumstances. And as family members recognized the changes in Sheryl's life, she was always careful to give the praise and glory to God.

Questions for Discussion

1. Read James 4:6-10, the passage Jack had read to Sheryl. Explain how "God opposes the proud, but gives grace to the humble" (verse 6) can help someone who has become enslaved to drugs. As you consider your answer, keep in mind the roles that pride and humility have in the thinking of the person who deceives herself and others with regard to her problem.

2. What can a woman who is abusing drugs or alcohol do to "cleanse her hands"—that is, stop abusing the chemical? What can she do to "purify her heart"? What do you think James meant when he used the term "double-minded"? (See James 1:5-8.)

3. Describe the difference between self-sufficiency and working hard to be obedient to Christ.

4. In Sheryl's experience, what was the relationship of her fears to her enslavement to her medication?

5. Explain, in your own words, why chemical dependency is not a disease or an addiction. How is it helpful to use the term "enslavement"?

7

Depression

Why are you cast down, O my soul, and why are
you in turmoil within me? Hope in God; for I shall
again praise him, my salvation and my God.

PSALM 42:5-6

With a long sigh escaping her lips, Donna lay in bed, trying to find
the energy and motivation to start the day. Today would be the same
as every day: shower, dress, eat breakfast, commute, work, commute,
dinner, weariness, sighing...

Donna was tired. Tired of sighing. Tired of unending fatigue.
Tired of the joyless routine of her life. When would this dark and
heavy cloud of depression lift so that she could find happiness once
again?

With her training as a registered nurse, Donna recognized the
signs of chronic long-term depression. Throughout her life she had
experienced bouts of depression, but this most recent episode was
much more persistent. Long days stretched into weeks, and then
months, and then years. It was difficult for her to remember the last
time she could say she had had a good day. Everything appeared dark
and foreboding. Just getting out of bed in the morning was a hercu-
lean task. It took all of her strength and fortitude to sit up, move her

body to the edge of the bed, and place her feet on the floor. All she felt like doing was curling up in a fetal position, pulling the covers over her head, and staying in bed all day.

Donna's thoughts were increasingly full of hopelessness and despondency. She found herself dwelling on the most negative aspects of her life, even though she actually had many things to be thankful for. On the rare occasion that the idea of thankfulness crossed her mind, she cringed as she realized that she gave very little thought to God and His Word. Ten years ago, Donna had responded in repentance and faith to the good news that Jesus Christ receives sinners like her. Filled with new joy and gratitude, she read the Bible and reveled in the love and grace of God toward her. Her attendance at a Bible church had helped her in her newfound faith, and her bouts with depression had become fewer.

Then her husband had an affair. Donna's world came crashing down around her, and new waves of depression swept over her. Three years ago, the divorce was finalized. All that time, she remained in dark depression. "God, why are You so far from me?" she asked. "How could You have let this happen to me? When will You rescue me from this darkness?"

As Donna continued to lay in bed, the words of the great British preacher Martin Lloyd-Jones came to her mind: "A depressed Christian is a contradiction in terms and is a very poor recommendation for the gospel." What did he mean? Can a genuine Christian be so depressed? Maybe a depressed Christian is an oxymoron? These thoughts penetrated deep into her soul, contributing to an even greater feeling of hopelessness. Donna knew it was time to get some help.

During her recent annual physical, Donna had mentioned her ongoing depression to her physician. After a thorough exam and several tests there appeared to be no abnormalities, but her doctor still wanted her to begin seeing a psychiatrist so that she could start taking antidepressant medication. Donna was uneasy about this recommendation. She had close acquaintances who had become physically and emotionally dependent on their medications, and that had ended up causing a whole different set of problems.

In addition, her experience in the medical field had informed her concerning the biological mechanisms involved in taking psychotropic drugs. She remembered reading about a well-researched double-blind study of the effectiveness of selective serotonin reuptake inhibitors (SSRIs, or antidepressants). The article in the *Journal of the American Medical Association* (JAMA) concluded, "An increasing number of studies have failed to show a difference between active anti-depressants and placebo."[10] This study was able to establish the fact that St. John's Wort (an herbal supplement), Zoloft (a commonly used antidepressant), and a placebo (a pill with inert ingredients) were equally effective in improving patients who were identified with severe depression according to the Hamilton Depression Scale. If there were no identifiable organic difficulties or a discernible pathophysiological imbalance, Donna was not interested in psycho-medication or a psychiatrist. She told her doctor she would seek a counselor who would work with her.

After researching the classic symptoms of depression, Donna was even more convinced that she needed to get some help:

- Feelings of moodiness and depression throughout most of the day

- Persistent depression occurring most days for a period of six months

- A continual experience of unexplained sadness

- The absence of interest or pleasure in normal daily responsibilities or activities

- An increased desire for caloric intake, raising the blood glucose level in order to provide a momentary feeling of euphoria and often resulting in weight gain, or an almost complete disinterest in food, resulting in serious weight loss

- Difficulty in sleeping or falling into a deep sleep (insomnia) or excessive sleeping lasting more than nine or ten hours a night (hypersomnia)

- Going to bed tired and, after a good night's sleep, waking up tired

- Agitated or repetitive behavior such as pacing, rocking back and forth, wringing of the hands (psychomotor agitation) or reduction and withdrawal from most or all behavior, a general behavioral slowdown (psychomotor retardation)

- The experience of constant fatigue or a lack of energy to complete tasks

- A general sense of worthlessness with no clear purpose in life

- A persistent feeling of guilt plaguing the conscience

- Difficulty in thinking, reading, and concentrating; an inability to focus on the task at hand

- Repeated or involuntary thoughts of death or suicide

Mustering up all the motivation and energy she could, Donna called her church for a counseling recommendation. A woman named Rebecca returned her call and, before she knew it, she had her first appointment with a biblical counselor. A glimmer of hope appeared on the horizon of Donna's life.

At the beginning of their first session, Rebecca revealed that in the past, she had also struggled greatly with depression. She was happy to show Donna that God and His Word could help her remove the dark cloud of depression and get her back to the joy she had previously known.

Rebecca began by carefully exploring the possibility of this depression being medically induced—either from an illness or perhaps a side-effect of regular medication. The human body and soul, while a person is alive, have a true symbiotic relationship—the soul affecting the body, and the body the soul. Research has shown that distressing news or prolonged discouragement can repress the body's immune system. Consequently, depressed people tend to experience more aches, pain, and illness than those who are not depressed. Inversely, a person who has been chronically ill for an extended time can experience a deep depression of the soul. It is because of this interconnectedness of soul and body that a biblical counselor will be careful to examine a person's depression from more than one angle.

Finding that all the possible medical issues had been eliminated as the cause, Rebecca then explained that Donna should look at the spiritual dimension of her depression. It should be viewed as a soul-problem and not as a somatic-problem. From a biblical standpoint, "feeling down" is not depression. Many people experience moodiness or low feelings because God created us in His image as emotional creatures. Part of the communicable attributes of God is the human ability to experience emotions of the soul. Our God has emotions of love, sadness, anger, and grief (Exodus 34:6-7; Mark 3:5; Ephesians 4:30). In fact, He "feels indignation every day" (Psalm 7:11). Because God the Father, who is spirit without a body (John 4:24), experiences emotions, it follows that the source of overwhelming emotions should not be reduced to mere physiological responses of the body.

What is a good definition of depression from a theological perspective? Depression is a persistent debilitating mood, feeling, or sense of hopelessness that becomes a person's reason for not handling the most important issues of life. This is a spiritual depression of the soul that has not come from any organic/chemical disorder of the body, or from the side-effects of medication or illegal drugs.

When severely depressed, a person stops functioning completely—refusing to get out of bed. Lesser degrees of persistent depression, such as what Donna was experiencing, can be quite agonizing, but somehow the person manages to keep up with the basics of life: getting up, going to work, keeping oneself clean and fed. Yet life is viewed as hard and joyless—not worth living. Thinking becomes cloudy and concentrating on something can become difficult. One depressed counselee remarked, "When I was depressed, the mere act of thinking required an enormous amount of energy. It was like trying to walk through waist-deep mud. Every step forward was excruciating and exhausting." Donna understood the feeling—it had been her experience for a long time. Understanding how the body and soul interact with one another was very helpful to Donna. She could directly relate to everything her counselor was describing.

During this first session, Rebecca asked a lot of questions so she could become familiar with Donna's background and struggle with this stubborn darkness. She wanted to know if Donna had truly placed her full trust in Jesus as Lord. Finding that to be true, Rebecca reminded her of the reasons why she as a Christian could be hopeful in her battle with depression. The true believer serves a resurrected Lord who is familiar with her sufferings because He came to earth in flesh and blood and suffered as a human so that He might be a "merciful and faithful high priest...to help those who are being tempted" (Hebrews 2:17-18; 4:15). Jesus Christ defeated death and the grave so that "he might destroy the one who has the power of death, that is, the devil, and deliver all those who through fear of death were subject to lifelong slavery" (2:14-15).

Now, we can rightly conclude that if God has the keys to conquer death, then He also has the keys to conquer depression. The hope that Donna needs is found in faithfully following His Word (Romans 15:4, 13).

However, because Donna's depression had so overwhelmed her, she described her own experience as uniquely miserable, essentially implying that no one had ever experienced the degree of depression that she was experiencing. Rebecca understood the feelings Donna was trying to express, but wanted her to understand that she was not the first person to struggle with such intense depression. Even though Donna felt very alone in this dreadful torment, others like her had found answers in God's Word and left depression behind for good. In fact, Scripture clearly teaches, "No temptation has overtaken you that is not common to man. God is faithful, and he will not let you be tempted beyond your ability, but with the temptation he will also provide the way of escape, that you may be able to endure it" (1 Corinthians 10:13). Another bright ray of hope pierced through Donna's dark soul.

At the end of their first session together, Rebecca gave Donna a few assignments to complete. This proved to be an insightful plan of action. Depressed persons who finally come to counseling have felt down and hopeless for so long that they have fallen into a kind of slump where they don't do much of anything besides the bare necessities of living: eating, sleeping, going to work. Because of their inactivity, they tend to view counseling sessions as "the magic hour of the week" during which they expect all their problems will be resolved and their feelings will return to normal.

That's why it was crucial that Donna become actively involved in the process of moving herself out of depression. As she would come to see, most of her depression was not so much something that "happened" to her; it was largely a result of wrong thinking and choices that she had made when she faced difficulties, or her hopes and dreams were dashed, or the realities of daily life had failed to meet her expectations. The homework given to Donna was designed to help her correct her thinking and choices, leading her to work her way out of the depression through the help of God's Spirit in His Word.

Donna's first homework assignment involved two simple things. First, she was to look up all the references in Scripture they had discussed on hope and write down how each text provided hope in Donna's situation. Second, she was required to keep a thought journal, writing down her thoughts when her feelings of depression were most intense. She was to answer four simple questions:

1. What was happening at that time you began to experience depression?

2. Who was present or absent?

3. What were you thinking, and what did you want?

4. What does God say you should think or want?

Donna agreed to make the effort to complete the homework even though she knew it was going to be difficult to even be moderately motivated to do so.

A week later, Donna and Rebecca met again. In spite of the fact that it was one of the most difficult weeks Donna had experienced in a while, she kept her word and completed her homework. She told Rebecca that the verses of hope had been especially helpful and encouraging to her during this tough week, and she even had committed Romans 15:4 to memory. Rebecca was very pleased that Donna had completed her homework and even gone beyond the assignment. But what was most revealing were the entries in

Donna's thought journal. It demonstrated why she was struggling with such severe depression. Here is a shortened summary of what she wrote:

> **Entry #1:** *It's Saturday and I'm drinking my morning coffee. I'm in so much emotional pain today. It's like my depression is my own private hell. It is exhausting me to the point of giving up on life. My apartment is empty as usual. There is no one to see. Nothing to do. Nothing to look forward to. Just the same emptiness as every other day. I hate my life.*

> **Entry #2:** *It's Sunday and I know I should be at church. But I just can't get myself going today. It feels like God has forgotten and forsaken me. It's difficult to pray, and I'm not sure God even hears me anymore. I say I believe in Him, but some days I'm not so sure He exists.*

> **Entry #3:** *Today at work I saw a 7-year-old girl with a severe case of bacterial pneumonia lying still in her bed, barely breathing. The sight of her suffering just overcame me and I ran into a nearby supply closet and burst into tears. I could barely hold my emotions together the rest of my shift. And so tonight I am questioning God: Are You really good when bad things happen to innocent children? Are You really powerful enough to heal? Why don't You make everything better, including this awful depression I live with? What's wrong with You, God?*

> **Entry #4:** *Oh God, I hurt so badly. I've heard of people dying of a broken heart, but this is worse. I am living with a broken heart. I am so alone. Please God, please let me die. I am not anything that I've thought I was. I thought I was a good wife, but my husband didn't think so. When I was*

*so sure of our marriage and our extremely good relation-
ship, it was like I was a nobody. And now I'm convinced
that I am just a plain, boring person. How could I have
thought so highly of myself? The most confusing part to me
is that I only thought I was trying to be a submissive wife,
as commanded by the Bible. I was submissive like You told
me to be, and instead of being an asset, it was a liability. I
don't think I'll ever love again. I can't because I'm so afraid.
Please help me.*[11]

Tears filled Rebecca's eyes as Donna read the reflections written
in the journal. They exposed Donna's unfulfilled hopes and expectations, and provided insights into why she was experiencing such
strong and unrelenting bouts with depression. It was time to unleash
the life-changing Word of God. This would provide the best possible help for her depression.

What does the Bible say about depression? First, Donna needed
to understand that depression is possible only in a fallen world.
When Adam and Eve chose to do things their own way, rejecting
God's rule and authority over them, their sin resulted in alienation
from God. This brought all kinds of problems and pain into the
world—losses, setbacks, discouragement, depression, and ultimately,
death (Genesis 3:1-19; Romans 5:12-21).

These were the consequences of man and woman attempting to
live free from God's Word ("Did God actually *say*?..." Genesis 3:1).
The effects of man's rebellion is chronicled throughout Scripture, but
can be clearly seen shortly after the fall. Cain, the oldest son of Adam
and Eve, became angry over God's rejection of his sacrifice of "the
fruit of the ground." God had accepted his brother Abel's blood sacrifice, but not Cain's agricultural sacrifice. "So Cain was very angry,
and his face fell" (4:5).

God proceeded to confront Cain: "Why are you angry, and why

has your face fallen?" (4:6). Cain was angry and depressed because his brother's sacrifice was accepted and his was rejected. When life fails to meet expectations, there is a sinful human tendency to become angry and depressed. "The LORD said to Cain...'If you do well, will you not be accepted? And if you do not do well, sin is crouching at the door. Its desire is for you, but you must rule over it'" (verses 6-7). The phrase "will you not be accepted?" means "will not your countenance be lifted up?" God was saying that if Cain did the right thing, his countenance would be lifted up, meaning that Cain would no longer be angry and depressed. His emotions would change for the better if he did the right thing. This biblical principle is still true today. God has ordained there is always eventual joy in obedience. Discouragement and depression will be a part of this sin-cursed world, but obedience to the Lord will bring joy.

There was a second important truth for Donna to understand. Depression is the only logical, rationally consistent conclusion of living *without God* (Romans 15:13; Ephesians 2:11-12; 1 Timothy 1:2). Even depressed Christians can display attitudes and actions that betray a "practical atheism"—thinking and responding to life's difficulties as though God does not exist.

Donna's thought journal revealed serious doubts about God's goodness, power, promises to help, and even His very existence. The foundation of her world crumbled when her husband cheated on her. Although she had come to believe in Christ, her doubts about God demonstrated that her hopes and expectations had been planted in this world and not in heaven, where things do not change (Philippians 3:19; James 1:17). Hope that rests upon temporal things will take the emotions on a roller-coaster ride: overwhelming joy when things are pleasant, crushing disappointment and depression when hopes and dreams are smashed.

Donna realized that she had lost sight of God and what He can do. Where man will fail her, God will always be faithful (Romans 3:3; 1 Corinthians 10:13). Where human relationships will always change, God will never change. He is our immutable (unchanging) God (Numbers 23:19). Donna could identify where she had begun to abandon the idea of God's faithfulness in her past and how this abandonment of good theology had resulted in her despair and hopelessness.

The third biblical truth that Rebecca taught Donna had to do with where deliverance from depression would come. Psychological theories of counseling grasp at weak and temporary solutions, which are really not solutions at all. For example, rarely will a doctor treat depression without some form of pharmaceutical drug, which only helps the patient to feel a little better without eliminating the cause of the depression. Other forms of treatment have to do with talk therapy, increasing exercise, changing your diet. While these things may help you feel better, they do not bring permanent change in the soul, which is where all nonmedical-related depression is from.

True and lasting deliverance from depression, which we have seen is one of the effects of mankind's fall into sin, is made possible through the redeeming work of Jesus Christ and the subsequent work of the Holy Spirit (Hebrews 10:10-14, 19-23). Because of the atoning sacrifice of Jesus Christ, unworthy sinners are now fully justified before God in heaven. Jesus died to save Donna from God's judgment. Without Christ's atoning sacrifice, God's wrath would be poured out upon her because of her sin—her determination to live for herself and not for His glory. But now that she has been redeemed by Christ's blood, she is numbered among His beloved children. Such unmerited grace is a cause for daily rejoicing and thanksgiving (Romans 5:2, 11).

Depression comes upon us when we are focused on our deficiencies: what we want but don't have, or what we think we deserve yet can't seem to attain. Redemption in Christ focuses us on the gospel: what we don't deserve—forgiveness and eternal life—yet possess by faith. Just like every redeemed sinner, Donna does not deserve eternal life, fellowship with Christ, the inheritance of heaven, and a guilt-free conscience. But she possesses all that, and more. It is time for Donna to stop dwelling on earth's losses and begin dwelling on heaven's gains. The unmerited grace of Jesus Christ should become her chief cause for joy.

There is yet another truth which will help Donna look at her battle with depression biblically. Practical and experiential deliverance from depression, and other effects of the fall, is not the automatic result of becoming a Christian (2 Corinthians 4:16-18; Galatians 5:22-23; Philippians 2:12-13; Hebrews 12:1-2; James 1:2-5). Even though the final answer and deliverance from depression is secured because of the atoning work of Jesus Christ, it does not guarantee that it will be instantaneous and automatic in the Christian life. Often the Christian, like Donna, will have to daily battle against her feelings to appropriate these truths into her life.

Why is there this ongoing spiritual battle with depression? There are two theological dimensions to our battle with sin. First, the penalty for the sin has been paid by the death of Jesus Christ, and the Christian stands no longer condemned. Sin is no longer her master (Romans 6), and she has been declared to be fully righteous in Christ (2 Corinthians 5:17). This is called *positional sanctification*.

Second, there are remaining habits of sinful thinking and doing that the Christian must work hard to change. This is called *practical sanctification*, which is the process of the Christian putting to death fleshly desires and actions, and living in new obedience to Jesus Christ (Colossians 3:5-17). There is a tension in the life of the believer between the "already" (I've been declared righteous) and the "not yet" (I'm still struggling with sin but learning to obey).

Christians are already declared legally righteous in the court of God's law, but they await full practical sanctification (holiness), which is yet to come. Understanding these two key aspects in the defeat of sin is essential for Donna as she looks for God's help with her depression. Christ has brought victory over her sinful responses to her circumstances, but she must now work hard to deny herself and follow Christ, being obedient to Him in all things (Luke 9:23).

Donna found great hope and encouragement in her efforts to work her way out of the darkness of depression. A troubling question in her struggle with depression had been answered: Can a true Christian struggle with depression? The clear answer was yes, that is very possible. She was discovering that someone like her, a Christian who fell into the blackness of depression, could face her darkest days with God's unchanging truth: Christ had redeemed her, and He would help her defeat the enemy of sin.

This realization led her to confess that her heart had not been right with God for a long time. At the core of her depression was anger over the many unmet expectations she had experienced. Like so many Christians, Donna was not aware of how her heart had latched onto her hopes and dreams—how she had found such security in the hope of the fulfillment of these ambitions.

God had used the affliction of her husband's sin against her to open her eyes to where she had placed her hope. Donna should have seen that as a reminder that all of her hope for today and the future was to be firmly placed in God and His will for her life. Instead, her anger and subsequent depression revealed that her hope had been placed in seeing her earthly desire satisfied: "I must have a husband who loves and cares for me." It had become like a god to her to have the warmth of her husband's love, and when that was ripped away, her world was shattered. From that point onward, she felt less and less like doing anything worthwhile. Everything in her life went into a tight downward spiral. It became so serious that there were days when she would lie in bed just wanting to die.

The pain of marital rejection is severe; there is no mistaking that reality. Though a Christian woman will suffer greatly through this agonizing crisis, the one who chooses to live by faith and put her complete trust in God will turn away from the inevitable anger that results when she is treated unjustly. She will resist the temptation to become bitter toward her husband and especially toward God for allowing this severe trial. What she had once wanted more than anything, to have a perfect Christian home, she will now see had become a desire more important than taking what God had permitted her to experience—the affliction and sorrow of a broken marriage.

Donna's repentance was the beginning of real change in her life. She confessed idolizing her marriage, the sin of not loving God first, and sought the Lord's forgiveness (1 John 1:9-10). She was still tempted with depression, and gave into that temptation every now and then. But now she was motivated to be faithful to her Lord and began to change with the strength that God supplied.

Another truth that brought Donna great joy was the fact that believers will eventually experience complete and continuous, uninterrupted deliverance from depression and all other effects of the fall (Revelation 21–22; Psalm 16). There is no depression in heaven, and there will be no depression in the new heavens and the new earth! Once Donna receives her full inheritance, her battle with depression will be a part of her past. The only person who has this kind of hope in this world is the Christian. During counseling sessions, Donna and Rebecca spent a good deal of time discussing the glories of heaven, where they would know freedom from the difficulties and suffering of this world. But they also acknowledged that as long as God gave them life, they were responsible to faithfully trust and serve Him in this world.

Early in the counseling process, Donna memorized a passage that became very significant as she and Rebecca did several biblical character studies as they discussed conquering depression. The passasge was Romans 15:4: "Whatever was written in former days was written for our instruction, that through endurance and through the encouragement of the Scriptures we might have hope."

Together, Donna and Rebecca studied the lives of Cain (Genesis 4:1-19), Elijah (1 Kings 19:1-18), the psalmist (Psalm 42–43), Jonah (Jonah 1–4), David (Psalm 32:38), and the apostle Paul (2 Corinthians 4:1-18). Being immersed so persistently in biblical truth helped to slowly lift Donna from her despair and darkness. It was the grace of the Lord Jesus Christ that showed her that God's plan for her life was infinitely better than her own plan.

More and more, Donna came to trust God and His plan for her life. The dark shadow of depression slowly went away, and she found new reasons to rejoice in the hope God had given her. Her thinking, desires, expectations, and goals were different now. It was apparent to everyone who knew her: Donna was a changed woman with a renewed love for Jesus Christ.

Questions for Discussion

1. Read Psalm 32:3-4. How do the soul and the body affect each other in the problem of depression?

2. What is the difference between discouragement and depression?

3. If depression like that which Donna experienced is brought on by discouraging circumstances, then why is repentance part of the solution?

4. How is depression an expression of "practical atheism"—thinking and responding to life's difficulties as though God does not exist?

5. Read Jonah 4:1-11. What was the source of Jonah's depression that led him to say, "It is better for me to die than to live"? How can anger against God often become a stimulus for depression?

8

Eating Disorder: Anorexia

Be not overly righteous, and do not make yourself too wise.
Why should you destroy yourself?

Ecclesiastes 7:16

Lisa's cell phone sounded again—another text message from Erica. *Why won't that girl leave me alone?* she thought. For weeks she had been bugging her about her weight loss, and Lisa was sick of the constant pressure and nagging. Lisa grumbled to herself: *Erica doesn't understand. She's always been beautiful—thin and athletic. All the girls at school admire her. What seems to come so naturally for her I have to work hard at achieving. It just isn't fair.*

It was lunchtime, and once again Lisa was face-to-face with food. Sitting alone in the high school cafeteria, she used her fork to slowly maneuver the vegetable salad around her plate. Her stomach no longer felt empty. The appetite suppressant she had taken an hour ago had its intended effect, and Lisa reveled in the thought that—for this meal at least—she didn't have to dread gaining weight. She could continue to pursue that perfectly thin body she longed for.

A deep sense of pride filled Lisa as she cut her lettuce into small squares. She is not like her undisciplined friends, gorging themselves on plates full of high-calorie foods. Standing up to carry her lunch tray to the conveyor belt, Lisa wobbled a little, finding herself unsteady. But she was okay; she was getting used to feeling lightheaded at times. It was a small price to pay for the self-control she was so proud of.

"Self-control: that long-lost virtue in the struggle to tame the appetite in a world of specialty restaurants and appetizing advertisements. Overweight people seem to be everywhere, unable to effectively manage their caloric intake in a world full of delectable delicacies—from pizza to pot roast, from Snickers pie to Krispy Kreme donuts. How can anyone resist? The bounty of food in America is overwhelming—and therein lies part of the problem. Thinness is valued only in the context of abundance; and while there are many malnourished, starving people in impoverished countries, you'll not find true anorexics there." Ah yes! That paper she had written for her sociology class. She remembered that paragraph with glee. It sounded so poetic and yet was full of truth. Lisa smiled with satisfaction at the high grade her teacher had given her. Yes, she knew something about self-control in a world that had gone nuts over food. *Erica had better keep her distance because she doesn't really know what she's talking about,* Lisa thought smugly.

But Erica had good reason to be concerned. Lisa had become so accustomed to her daily rituals of weight control that she didn't realize how steeped she had become in a dangerous eating pattern. So carefully had she counted calories, fat grams, and carb grams that she had begun to view food as an enemy. Eating had become a disgusting exercise, so much so that she positioned her food on her fork so that it wouldn't touch her lips as she ate. Once in her mouth, the morsel was quickly swallowed. What once was an enjoyable part of daily life had now been reduced to a necessary evil.

In addition to her restricted eating, Lisa committed herself to a rigorous daily exercise plan designed to burn off whatever calories she had eaten. Every 100 calories meant another mile she needed to run that day. When she thought no one was looking, she pulled out a small food scale, carefully weighing everything she ate and recording the weight of her food in a dietary app on her smart phone. If she could manage it, she also weighed her bowel movements; Lisa wanted to make sure that whatever amount of food she consumed was equivalent to the waste being eliminated from her body. If the food outweighed the feces, she would punish herself with extra-strenuous exercise.

This extreme form of self-torture had gone on for a long time. By now Lisa had lost between 20-25 percent of her body weight. Everyone who knew and loved her could see she was wasting away; it was clearly evident in her gaunt face and very thin arms. If they had been able to see her sides, they would have noticed her protruding ribs. Yet Lisa made every effort to keep her body hidden under heavy clothes and coats. Even during the heat of summer she constantly complained of being cold.

Lisa's parents were beside themselves. It had been apparent to them for months that their daughter was suffering from a self-induced condition called anorexia nervosa. They had been powerless to help her because she wouldn't admit she had a problem. She refused to go to the doctor, and she went into a full rage if they even tried to bring up the subject of her weight loss. They had done some research on reputable medical websites, and what they had read frightened them, to say the least, because it matched with the evidences of the condition that they observed in Lisa.

Restricting calories for an extended period of time will result in a reduction of blood volume in the body. The blood helps to maintain normal body temperature, especially in the extremities of the feet and hands. With less blood volume, the anorexic will feel cold constantly. Even on warm days Lisa dressed in heavy sweaters and gloves. Furthermore, she had developed a condition called *amenor-rhea,* or the loss of her monthly menstrual cycle due to energy imbalance and severe weight loss. Her pulse rate was extremely slow due to the reduced amount of blood in her body, which caused her heart to work extra hard to pump this reduced blood volume throughout her body. Many women with extreme anorexic nervosa die from heart failure because they overwork their heart. Lisa was getting dangerously close to this tragic result, and her parents were becoming increasingly worried.

Loved ones who had known Lisa since she was a young child were noticing a dramatic change in her temperament as well. She had become more impulsive, distracted, irritable, and aggressive with close friends and family. She seemed to be suspicious of the people around her, as if they were judging her. Helpful suggestions intended to restore her to health and strength had brought out a new scornful side of Lisa. *No one seems to appreciate my sacrifice and self-discipline,* she thought to herself. *I am not fat and undisciplined like many of my family and friends. They should look in their own mirrors before becoming critical of the way I look!*

As Lisa distanced herself from people, she found herself struggling with loneliness and depression. Her attention span had shortened, and she had difficulty concentrating. Her love of reading had diminished as a result. Constantly moving and fidgeting, it was now difficult for her to even sit still—so unlike her formerly content and joyful self.

Lisa's health continued to decline as weeks turned into months. There was hardly a day during which she felt good or normal. For several weeks she had not attended church or her favorite Bible study because she had a cold, the flu, or generally felt lousy.

In spite of all this, she continued to maintain her highly disciplined regimen of exercise. She wanted her body to be a fat-burning machine. Her thoughts were consumed by her difficulties, even though she did not realize how seriously her health was in decline. "I hate my life and I hate my body. All I want is to be thin," she confided in her journal. Full of internal conflict, she had to admit that she still experienced hunger and at times enjoyed the taste and satisfaction of food, even though she had come to think of food as a toxic necessity. *I like food,* she would admit to herself, *but I don't want it.*

Brokenhearted at what was happening to their daughter, Lisa's parents called the pastor of their church for some advice and counsel. Together they talked through Lisa's behavior and the resulting physical and spiritual problems. Pastor Tom explained, "The issue is much deeper in Lisa's life than the simple concept of thinness. Being thin is merely an external measurement of success to her, regardless of how harmful it is to her body. Many believe that thinness is all that matters to an anorexic. This is not the case for Lisa, and is not the exclusive issue for most anorexics. But getting Lisa to see that she has a serious, life-threatening problem will be difficult. Let us first pray together for her and ask God to also provide a way for us to help reverse this deadly pattern in her life."

The answer to their prayers was not long in coming. As Lisa was playing volleyball in her P.E. class the following week, she passed out and fell to the floor, hitting her head as she landed. She sustained a laceration that required stitches and was taken to the local hospital's emergency room for treatment. There, her vital signs were taken. Her low blood pressure and pulse was alarming to the medical staff, and so Lisa underwent a full physical examination.

This was the first time Lisa had been subjected to such an intrusion into her private life, but because she was so weak, she gave little resistance. *After all,* she thought, *there's nothing wrong with me. There's nothing to fear. They will just have me drink a little juice and send me home.*

But to her dismay, she was not sent home immediately. After several hours of tests, Lisa was diagnosed with anorexia nervosa and strongly urged to see both her family doctor and a psychiatrist. She was released to her concerned parents and advised to get some food into her body as soon as possible.

As soon as Lisa heard the doctor's report, she was filled with panic. *They can't do this to me. They can't force me to eat. I'll gain weight and blow up like a balloon. I'll give up my self-control and that will be bad for me. No, I can't and I won't do what they say. Somehow I have to remain in control of my life.* But even as she said these things in her own mind, Lisa knew that she had begun to lose the battle. She could see that her worried parents were determined to follow the doctors' orders. And to be honest, she had also begun to feel the weariness that comes with being continually vigilant about not eating, weighing food and excrement, and the endless exercise required to keep her from gaining weight. Suddenly she was so tired that all she wanted to do was sleep. Upon arriving home, her parents were able to get Lisa to down half a cup of chicken broth before she fell into bed exhausted, sleeping for the next three hours.

While she slept, Lisa's parents prayed together again, thanking God for providing an opportunity to speak to their daughter about her condition. Then they called Pastor Tom and explained what had happened. He agreed to stop by their house that evening to try to talk with Lisa about her situation.

As Lisa sat calmly in the living room, her parents and Pastor Tom were surprised to hear her express a willingness to listen to their concerns. They detected a look of defeat on her face, yet they proceeded with caution so that they might gently show their love for her and their hope that God would help her to overcome her problems.

After sharing with her their reasons for concern—the medical data and statistics regarding those who have stopped nourishing themselves for various reasons—they asked her if she would be willing to be helped by their family doctor and a woman counselor from their church. The doctor would provide weekly monitoring of her vital signs, weight, and other physical manifestations of the anorexia. The biblical counselor would help her to make changes that would bring joy back into her life and share with her the Bible's teaching on self-control.

Lisa thought carefully about all they were saying. Having been a Christian for the past five years, she found herself drawn to the idea of getting God's help. While she still did not like the idea of eating food on a regular basis, she agreed to their proposed twofold plan, knowing the loving support she would receive from her mom and dad. Desiring to show them her sincere intention of following through, she was able to eat another half cup of broth along with half a slice of toast. Already feeling a release from the pressure that her self-imposed rituals had placed upon her, she went to bed again, sleeping better through the night than she had in a long time.

The following week, Lisa began meeting with her biblical counselor from church. Anne had taken several classes teaching her how to provide counsel from the Bible, and one of the classes was specifically directed at helping young women with eating disorders. Although this was one of the more difficult problems to help with, Anne was eager to direct Lisa to God's Word to enable her to regain both her health and her trust in God her Savior.

A good biblical counselor will listen carefully to what her counselee has to say about her problem. Anne asked a lot of questions about Lisa's thinking and behavior, but mostly about her hopes and dreams for her life. She wanted to hear Lisa express what goals were the most important to her; what desires were the strongest within her. This gathering of data would be very helpful in directing Lisa to see herself and God's Word accurately. At the conclusion of their first session, Anne said, "With everything I've heard you say today about yourself and your goals for your life, I can assure you that God's Word has the answers for the difficulties that you've gotten yourself into. Together we will help you reverse the avoidance of food, but we will also see the hope that is laid out for you in Scripture. Let's read 2 Peter 1:3-4 together:

> His divine power has granted to us all things that pertain to life and godliness, through the knowledge of him who called us to his own glory and excellence, by which he has granted to us his precious and very great promises, so that through them you may become partakers of the divine nature, having escaped from the corruption that is in the world because of sinful desire.

"Because you are a Christian," Anne continued, "you belong to Jesus Christ, and there are some great benefits to that relationship with Him. One is the divine power that the apostle Peter spoke of—the power that helps us overcome the temptation to live for self, to please only ourselves. As you increase in your knowledge of God and His Word, He will help you to change and to grow in godliness."

In subsequent sessions, Anne went on to clarify the diagnosis of anorexia nervosa. The term *anorexia* is an unfortunate and misleading psychological label. It is a Latin term borrowed from the Greek language with an alpha-negative as a prefix. Literally, it means to not desire or want. It mislabels the condition itself because it suggests a loss of appetite. But this is not an accurate assessment of the problem. An anorexic generally still has a tremendous interest in food, will experience hunger, and wants to eat. This is not about loss of appetite; rather, this is a matter of self-denial for the purpose of getting what she wants. And what does the anorexic want?

Cultural norms have framed the female's thinking about the

shape and size of her body. Add to that her desire to be admired, respected, and in control of her own body, and you have the perfect setup for anorexia. Fear of not measuring up in the eyes of others drives women to do almost anything to change their appearance. For Lisa, what began as a simple desire to find acceptance among peers, or even just to please herself, had turned into a nightmare with food—which was now viewed as the enemy.

After carefully thinking through these things, Anne helped Lisa to realize that what she really wanted was to be in control. Why was control so important to her? She believed that taking control of this area of her life—practicing extreme self-denial—made her a strong person and gave her a focused and uncomplicated life. To many women, simple living is pure and perfect living. The concepts of purity and perfection appeal to an essential fundamental in Christian thinking as well. Because Lisa could strictly adhere to this level of self-sacrifice in her diet, she felt more righteous and noble in comparison to so many Christians who appeared lazy and undisciplined. In her way of thinking, she far surpassed any justified criticism from her friends. They simply did not have the moral authority to make any judgment on her life unless they practiced the same level of self-control as she.

The downside is that anorexia nervosa can cause irreversible damage to the body that will require substantial medical treatment. It is imperative for a person who has had a sustained practice of serious malnutrition to seek professional medical help immediately with the goal of restoring the anorexic back to a functionally healthy lifestyle and a proper and realistic body weight. Without careful medical treatment, the mortality rate can be as high as 3.9%.[12] In many cases death is a result of cardiac failure, critical organ failure, malnutrition, or suicide. Anne warned Lisa that if she continues her anorexic behavior, she will soon need to be hospitalized and fed through an intravenous tube.

With a growing concern about her physical condition, Lisa listened carefully as Anne shared even more information. There are certain biological factors that can contribute to anorexic weight loss. Some of them may include the activity of the hypothalamic centers of the brain or how the body utilizes blood glucose. Sometimes factors like hormonal regulation with insulin and cholecystokinin (a peptide hormone which belongs to the gastrointestinal system responsible for stimulating the digestion of fat and protein) can be concerns. Or, the basal metabolic rate (BMR), which is the amount of energy expended while the body is at rest, can be a contributor. The right types of medical tests should be able to identify if these are causes for concern.

Sometimes environmental factors contribute to anorexic practices. This includes the way that a person has acquired their food preferences or their exposure and sensitivity to food-related cues. How the person has developed eating habits—like tendencies to snack, eat at night, or eat while watching TV—can bring understanding as to how these practices got started and developed. This would include the relationship that their moods and ability to deal with stress has with their eating habits.

"Properly addressing the needs of anorexia requires much more than a physiological change of behavior and medical treatment," Anne explained to Lisa. "That only deals with the symptomology and consequences of the problem, not the heart of the problem. While it is vitally important to provide you with proper medical attention so that you can preserve your health and your life, the spiritual dimensions of your behavior must be brought to light to bring about permanent change. Merely focusing on the physical manifestations of anorexia without attending to the heart that motivates the behavior is utterly useless. Catastrophic failure is still imminent."

To further clarify the spiritual dimension, Anne observed that

Lisa practiced her anorexia because of the way she viewed her life. She had adopted a sinful outlook on her life that drove her behavior, feeding both her attitudes and actions. It not only determined how she ate and how much she exercised, it also motivated her alienating behavior toward her friends and family, and even effected the way she thought about God's relationship to her and her problems. She doubted God's care and love for her, believing she must to do all she could to earn His love. Therefore, she had assumed the self-denying life reminiscent of an aesthetic monk. She had erroneously assumed, "When God sees all of my self-denial, He will love me and accept me."

Lisa's self-denial was fundamentally flawed because it was rooted in a deep sense of self-righteousness. She believed that through her rigorous self-neglect, self-denial, and even self-inflicted pain, she could control her own life for her own good. The apostle Paul confronted a similar problem in the church at Colossae in the first century, where a rigid form of self-denial that was detrimental to Christianity and the doctrine of Christ was threatening sincere Christians. Carefully note how Paul admonished the believers in Colossae:

> If with Christ you died to the elemental spirits of the world, why, as if you were still alive in the world, do you submit to regulations—"Do not handle, Do not taste, Do not touch" (referring to things that all perish as they are used)—according to human precepts and teachings? These have indeed an appearance of wisdom in promoting self-made religion and asceticism and severity to the body, but they are of no value in stopping the indulgence of the flesh (Colossians 2:20-23).

Such practices are moral time bombs because even though they may *subdue* physical desires, they fail to *stop* sinful desires. Christians who indulge in such practices appear to be religiously self-disciplined, but inwardly their passions are out of control and are of no eternal value. Anorexics like Lisa are focused on worldly values—such as loving the praise of people and seeking to show themselves as superior—and are not focused on Christ and His redemption.

If Lisa is a genuine Christian, then she has died to such things and now lives for Christ. Lately, she has been self-deceived, thinking that she was living for Christ. She wrongly believed that through her good works of self-denial and self-control she could reach a simple life of purity and perfection. She was also attempting to prove herself more righteous than others around her, taking great pride and comfort in her extreme self-discipline. But no matter what effort she exerts, she cannot be pure and perfect apart from Christ. When she humbly admits her imperfection and confesses her sin of self-righteousness, she will realize that—better than any control she might accomplish—Christ has given her His perfect and eternal righteousness through her faith in Him. God will accept no other righteousness than that of His Son.

Lisa learned that the single greatest issue that determines anorexic behavior is the heart: What does the heart worship? Or you could say, What does the heart desire more than God? Common heart desires for anorexics are:

"I must be thin so I can have significance."

"I am unhappy with my life, and I want to eat whatever I want without gaining weight."

"I deserve pleasure, but I don't want to pay the consequences."

"I have to be perfect!"

"I deserve the attention!"

But for many like Lisa, their heart demands, "I want everyone to see me for the perfect person that I am, and by refusing to be controlled by food, everyone will know that I do not give in to sinful overindulgences in the same ways my friends do. For this they will respect me!"

Lisa had been attempting to control her friends' and family's estimation of her, and when their opinion differed from what she expected and craved, she became irritable and angry. And anytime such desires for perfection and respect reign in the heart, then God is not worshipped. It is critical to recognize that the cravings of the heart can become so demanding that they become a person's functional gods. These gods promise happiness and contentment, but they deliver pain and misery. The Christian has the responsibility to worship the God of heaven alone; anything less is a destructive lie (Exodus 34:14; Psalm 81:9; Matthew 4:10).

"Complete and lasting change for the anorexic begins with confession and repentance," Anne gently admonished. "I know it doesn't seem that way, because your motivations were driven by a desire for purity and perfection. Because the Bible calls Christians to be pure and perfect—as in Matthew 5:48 and Philippians 1:9-11—you may have thought you were right in what you were doing. But our righteousness is found in Jesus Christ alone. He gave His righteousness to us because we had none of our own. Thus any attempt to purify and perfect ourselves so that others will glorify us only robs God of His glory. Do you see, Lisa, how this has gotten twisted in your thinking?"

With her head bowed reverently, Lisa confessed her pride-driven goals of purity and perfection, recognizing how she had dishonored Christ in the process. She readily confessed and repented of desiring glory due only to God Himself. She felt more ready and energized than ever to make the necessary changes in her eating and exercise so that her life would once again bring glory to God.

• • • • •

Whatever you or someone you are counseling might identify as their heart desire, *confessing* these idolatrous desires before God and *repenting* of them as sin are the necessary steps to total change (1 John 1:8-10). First, confession identifies these cravings of the heart as sinful. When a person truly confesses her sin, she refuses to make excuses for allowing her cravings to rule over her and become more important than living for God's glory. Second, repentance is that declaration before God that her mind has conclusively changed. True repentance is a change of mind that is so complete that it leads to a permanent change of behavior. When you give counsel that removes only the biological and environmental factors (the body's struggle with food), you deal solely with the external contributors to the problem. There must be a fundamental change on a much deeper level—that is, in the heart—for the anorexic to be restored to a healthy, God-honoring life.

After a heartfelt repentance has taken place, then comes a biblical re-education concerning the anorexic's view of food. This is a critical step to take for the change process to be irreversible. Careful study should be given to the following principles, along with the Scripture references listed while writing out a *personal response and plan* to make each of these truths a reality in daily thinking. It may even be helpful to write them out on display cards and place them in close proximity to the locations where meals are consumed.

- God has graciously provided food, and because everything that God provides is good, this food is good (Genesis 1:29-30; 2:9; Acts 10:10-16; 1 Timothy 4:3-5; James 1:17).

- God intends mankind to find enjoyment in food, therefore eating should be an enjoyable activity (Psalm

104:14-15; Ecclesiastes 2:24-25; 8:15; 9:7; 1 Timothy 6:17).

- Eating is done for strength to honor and serve God, and not for self-centered denial or indulgence (Ecclesiastes 10:16-17; 1 Corinthians 10:31; Colossians 3:17; 1 Peter 4:11).

- Instead of eating being subservient to sinful desires, eating should be subservient to faithful service to God and His Word (Job 23:12; John 4:34; 1 Peter 4:1-5).

- Love for God and others should be evident in eating, instead of loving the sinful desires that rule the heart (Matthew 22:37-40; Luke 10:27; Romans 14:21; 1 Corinthians 8:13; 11:20-22).

- Obedience to God, motivated by a redeemed heart, must overrule all eating habits, rather than the desire for personal control (Proverbs 23:1-3, 6-8; Romans 14:17; Hebrews 12:16).

- Being controlled by Jesus Christ is of greater importance than the idolatry of personal control (Proverbs 13:25; 16:18; Mark 7:15,20-23; Romans 16:17-18; Philippians 3:18-19).

• • • • •

Lisa was so grateful for God's work through Anne in leading her to repentance. It was clear to her now that her anorexia was simply a symptom of an even more serious problem in her heart. She was broken over her sinfulness and lack of trust in God. Her behavior had been destroying the healthy body God had given her, and she acknowledged that she had been a very poor steward of her life, her health, and her time. The realization of how selfish she had become overwhelmed her. She could see the ugliness of her pride and self-righteousness, and it grieved her. It was time for her to draw near to God (James 4:8-10).

Humility was the fruit of Lisa's repentance, which meant she was teachable and eager for biblical instruction on how her newly strengthened walk with Christ should affect her view of herself and her eating habits. She excitedly poured herself into studying the principles shared by Anne, writing out her personal response to each and making a detailed plan on how she was going to implement changes in her new lifestyle and eating.

Knowing how difficult it would be for Lisa to implement these changes, Anne helped even further by enlisting a couple of mature Christian women in the church to help keep Lisa accountable. They began meeting regularly, praying together, eating together, and reviewing the scriptural principles for life change. One of the women even brought a weight scale to their meetings in order to ensure that Lisa was sticking to her plan.

Lisa's mother joined the group after a few weeks, eager to see how she could be of help to her daughter at home. Lisa gained back the weight she needed to be healthy, and even learned to enjoy eating moderate amounts of food again. She was careful to let her friends know that it was the conviction of the Holy Spirit and the truth of God's Word that brought about the lasting changes in her life. Lisa was a changed young woman, inside and out, and Jesus Christ was at the core of her change.

Questions for Discussion

1. What effects do current societal expectations have on young women today? What do these expectations reveal about the philosophy of the world in which we live?

2. How was Lisa influenced by her incorrect theological understanding of purity and perfection? Describe the strong temptations Christian young women face today when they are confronted with ungodly societal expectations and, at the same time, fail to understand the source of purity and perfection for the believer.

3. After a Christian young woman rightly understands that purity and perfection are given to her by Christ, how would you teach her to live a life of holiness? What should be her motivation to holy living? (See Matthew 22:37-40, Philippians 2:3-11, 1 Peter 1:13-25.)

4. Why are confession and repentance vital so that Lisa and other anorexics like her can experience true change?

5. Scripture memory is a key component of change in the Christian's life. What passage of Scripture would you have Lisa memorize so that she might have the Word of God ready when she is tempted to fall back into a self-righteous controlling lifestyle?

9

Grief

Be gracious to me, O LORD, for I am in distress;
my eye is wasted from grief; my soul and my body also.

PSALM 31:9

Kate walked through the front door of her house, laying her keys on the entry table. The house was quiet—too quiet. She tried to wrap her mind around the reality that just two months ago she had buried the love of her life, Kevin, her husband of 37 years. It still seemed like he was away on an extended business trip. The agony she felt was so deep and continuous, she was incapable of explaining it even to her closest friends. The darkness of her sorrow was her constant companion now. She felt as though no one could fully understand the awful ache and lasting loss she was experiencing. It was her grief to bear and hers alone.

As the days went by, nothing seemed to improve Kate's spirits, not even the things that formerly brought her great joy. Food did not seem to interest her, not even her favorite dishes. She had lost 20 pounds in the weeks since Kevin's passing. Eating reminded her of him and the many times they enjoyed eating together, often going to their favorite restaurants. When Kate sat down to a meal, she found herself lost in a seemingly irrecoverable nostalgic state, recalling the vibrant conversations she and Kevin experienced over dinner. Dinnertime had become their special time together, finding out how each other's day had gone and just relaxing at the end of the day.

All that was changed. The house unnaturally quiet in the evening, Kate now ate her solitary meal for strength; food was a necessity, not a pleasurable experience. In fact, she had an additional reason not to eat too much. She was experiencing consistent digestive problems after eating even small amounts. Kate had never had digestive issues before now. As time progressed, these problems were complicated by fatigue, headaches, occasional chest pains, and sore muscles. In every way, she felt miserable: physically, emotionally, and spiritually.

Kate's friends meant well when they tried to help; they were always very careful, loving, and gentle. But their spiritual clichés and quoting of Scripture only served to irritate her. She could feel herself becoming less patient and more short-tempered with them, even though she tried to disguise it under a veneer of attentiveness and respect. All of their verses and offers to pray with her only served to magnify her bitterness. *They do not have a clue as to what I am going through,* her angry thoughts accused them. *They still have their husbands! You would not see them acting so optimistically if God had suddenly taken them away.* As Kate's unhappiness grew, she withdrew from her friends.

Widow. There was that word she had hoped would never be said of her. And yet here she was. There was no place to hide from the truth of it. She was a widow, and that was that. It was especially difficult to go to church as a new widow. Seeing the people she and Kevin had known together just renewed her pain. She knew they missed him too. These friends often avoided making eye contact with her, and when they did look, their eyes were full of pity. Kate could see that her relationships with them had dramatically changed. She could see in her friends' awkward reactions and responses that they were always used to seeing her with Kevin.

Kevin had been the outgoing one, and she had secretly enjoyed being a spectator to his lively banter when among their friends. Personally, because she was the quieter one, it was difficult for her to maintain a conversation alone. She could see how hard it was for their friends to interact with her when she was so quiet. It seemed like she had not only been cut off from her husband, but from her friends as well. Occasionally one of them would bravely step forward to offer condolences—"I cannot imagine what you are going through, Kate. It must be truly difficult!" And Kate would privately think, *You have no idea how difficult this is! You do not realize the excruciating agony of forever losing someone you so dearly loved.* The faces and comments of her friends were empty and meaningless to her now. She was numb, except to the despair of her own private little hell.

Kate and Kevin had been committed Christians actively serving in their home church for many years. Kevin had served on the board of the church, and Kate had been active in teaching Sunday school classes and helping with the women's ministry. She especially loved serving behind the scenes. However, Kevin had served as their main personal link to their church and all its ministries. Now that link was permanently severed. Her connection to her friends and her church had suffered a fatal blow with his passing.

Their pastor had been amazingly helpful during the time of the funeral and the weeks immediately afterward, but he had returned to his usual duties and Kate was soon left to herself. She could not sing in church, nor did she enjoy the worship music any longer. She used to love to sing the rich and vibrant hymns of faith, but there was no song in her groaning heart. She recalled the words of King Solomon in Proverbs: "Whoever sings songs to a heavy heart is like one who takes off a garment on a cold day, and like vinegar on soda" (25:20). Singing and making music was not a pleasant experience for her any longer. Church attendance became increasingly infrequent. She continued to withdrawal into deeper darkness and insolation.

An unfamiliar loneliness settled in. Kate remembered enjoying Bible study and lengthy spiritual discussions with Kevin in their home. They would have wonderful times of prayer together, but that was no longer possible. Kate's Bible sat unopened on her bedroom dresser, gathering dust. Occasionally she would attempt to pray, but the attitude and content of her prayers had dramatically changed. Full of complaints and accusations, she sent up indicting questions for God. "What have You done? Why did You allow this to happen to me? What good can ever come of taking Kevin away from me? Do You even love me? Can't You see the excruciating pain I am suffering? Do You even care? Can You even sympathize with my loneliness, or have You abandoned me too?" These prayers only served to stoke her fiery anger. They did not provide answers or any solace for her grief.

Six more months passed, and eventually Kate's fatigue, chest pains, and weight loss motivated her to see her physician. After reviewing her symptoms and doing a brief examination, he concluded she was healthy, but suffering from mild depression. He recommended that she see the resident psychiatrist in their practice as soon as possible.

Later that same day, Kate was able to schedule an appointment that had become available with the psychiatrist. Her name was Dr. Garcia. After carefully reviewing her circumstances, Dr. Garcia diagnosed Kate as suffering from a psychological condition known as Prolonged Grief Disorder (PGD). It is a syndrome characterized by a distinct set of symptoms that normally is sustained after the death of a close loved one. It is different than normal grief because the symptoms extend indefinitely and involve painful, disabling, and life-altering mental and physical effects.

Dr. Garcia wanted Kate to know that her grief was a part of the natural processes of life and the effects were predictable. Kate had become fixated on one or more of the five stages of grief: (1) denial and isolation, (2) anger, (3) bargaining, (4) depression, and (5) acceptance.[13] According to Dr. Garcia, Kate had not yet moved on to stage five. She was stuck in various degrees of stages one through four. Dr. Garcia recommended she begin a treatment similar to psychotherapeutic techniques used for post-traumatic stress disorder (PTSD)—which included a class of psychotherapy drugs known as selective serotonin reuptake inhibitors (SSRIs) or antidepressants—until she was able to move on to stage five.

Kate was given a prescription and she left the psychiatrist's office feeling somewhat overwhelmed and confused. Originally she had gone to her primary care doctor for help with her loss of appetite and chest pains, but now she was being treated for a psychological disorder with drugs. She was unclear about how to proceed. *If only Kevin were here,* she thought to herself, *he would know what to do!* Starting on psychotropic drugs was a huge decision for her; she decided to wait before filling the prescription.

That night Kate got very little sleep. All the events of the previous day swirled like a windstorm in her brain. Before dawn, she finally decided to go and see her pastor. He had been so helpful after the funeral, maybe he could help her now. She needed clarity and a new perspective, since her thinking had become so muddled and unreliable. Lately, trying to concentrate on even the simplest thought had become an impossible task. Before 9:00 in the morning, she had called the church office, and her pastor and his wife agreed to meet with her the next day.

Pastor Tim and his wife, Becca, had always been the most gracious and caring couple. Kate believed she could share her most troubling thoughts with them, and that they would lovingly listen without being judgmental. In addition, both he and his wife had taken special steps to secure biblical counseling training, and they had completed their full certification two years ago.[14] This gave Kate confidence that she was doing the right thing. She knew she needed help from a Christian viewpoint, and she believed Kevin would be happy she was seeking out competent help from them. Kevin had always trusted Pastor Tim's wisdom and had often gone to him for spiritual advice.

• • • • •

Pastor Tim and Becca were warm and welcoming when Kate arrived for her appointment. They perceived that Kate did not look well. She appeared tired and thin. Grief had etched deep furrows in her face. It was obvious that Kate's smile was politely manufactured. They began the appointment by praying together with her, asking God to minister deeply to Kate's heart through the work of the Holy Spirit and the truth of Scripture.

After prayer, they told her they loved her and were happy she had sought them out for help. They had been praying frequently for her since the day they found out about Kevin's death. They also encouraged her by affirming their confidence that the Word of God was sufficient to address the heartache and grief she was experiencing (2 Peter 1:3). Nothing was going to change the fact that the Lord had chosen to take Kevin home to be with Him (Ecclesiastes 3:14; Hebrews 9:27). And, as her counselors, they wanted to show her how the Lord would provide comfort and hope to her despairing soul (John 14:1). They wanted to help her understand how she could produce righteous fruit in the midst of her storm (Psalm 1:1-6).

Tim and Becca had worked with a number of people in their church after the loss of a loved one. They understood how grief could slowly rob a widow of her focus and purpose in living. They had seen the agonizing pain that death delivers when it suddenly tears a person away from the one they love, leaving them empty and wounded inside. An unwanted darkness invades the soul without warning, suppressing any glimmer of light or hope. This was Kate's life—her new reality. Her mental dexterity was traumatized by death's blow; her thoughts were plagued with hopeless despair. As a Christian she knew that suicide was not an option, but her will to go on living was almost nonexistent. Tim and Becca could see what Kate was experiencing, and they knew that tenderness, patience, and genuine Christian love was what she needed now along with a huge dose of hope.

Understanding Kate's despair, Tim and Becca encouraged her to look at her circumstances through God's eyes. They turned to the book of Philippians and drew her attention to chapter 1, verses 21-23:

> For to me to live is Christ, and to die is gain. If I am to live in the flesh, that means fruitful labor for me. Yet which I shall choose I cannot tell. I am hard pressed between the two. My desire is to depart and be with Christ, for that is far better.

Here the apostle Paul was writing while in captivity as a prisoner in Rome. It was his first Roman imprisonment (ca. AD 60–62). From a human perspective, the apostle was at his lowest state and longing for heaven. These words written to his friends at Philippi indicate that heaven was considered gain to him because he would be released from the misery of life and ushered into the presence of the Lord Jesus Christ. To him, that was much more preferable to the conditions he was in. He clearly stated his "desire is to depart and be with Christ, for that is far better." Kate nodded, affirming the same feelings. She fully could relate to Paul's desire. She had had similar thoughts. She felt there was no reason to continue on in her present misery. If she could escape this life, she could join Kevin and Jesus in heaven. Like Paul, her will to remain on earth was dwindling.

However, if Paul had given up the will to live and died as a prisoner after writing those words, he would have never written 1 and 2 Timothy or Titus. He would have never finished his missionary work or been such a tremendous testimony for Christ in the palace of the Emperor Nero during his second Roman imprisonment (ca. AD 66).

As Paul continued his letter to the Philippian Christians, he expressed his determination to live.

> To remain in the flesh is more necessary on your account. Convinced of this, I know that I will remain and continue with you all, for your progress and joy in the faith, so that in me you may have ample cause to glory in Christ Jesus, because of my coming to you again (Philippians 1:24-26).

Paul's will to live was directly related to the furtherance of the gospel through him in the lives of the Philippians believers. He saw this as his God-given motivation to press forward.

Kate pondered this thought and began to examine her real motivation for living. Becca reminded Kate of the many years of experience she had as a Sunday school teacher and in the women's ministry at the church. Women who knew Kate considered her to be a great encouragement to them with the gospel. So many children in their church had grown up loving her as a teacher. Some of them had come to Christ because of her careful teaching of the Word of God. There was still a lot of work yet to be done in those ministries, and there were few women as experienced as Kate. God was not finished with her yet!

This gave Kate a lot to think about, but it did not remove the awful agony of daily existence without Kevin. The deep pain of her loss was very difficult to bear. Where there has been great love, there is always the potential for great grief.

Perceiving the intensity of her struggle, Tim gently said, "Too often we use the term *hope* carelessly because it is used to express uncertainty. 'I *hope* my children grow up healthy and happy.' 'I *hope* I have enough money to make it until the end of the month.' There is a serious lack of certainty or reality in such expressions. However, when your concept of hope is anchored in biblical promises, all ambiguity and doubt is removed. Biblical hope is backed up by the very character and faithfulness of God. Unlike 'I hope so' hope, it is absolute and full of confident assurance.

"Remember what 1 Corinthians 10:13 says? 'No temptation has overtaken you that is not common to man. God is faithful, and he will not let you be tempted beyond your ability, but with the temptation he will also provide the way of escape, that you may be able to endure it.' This verse provides confident assurance that there is nothing that God allows to come into our lives whereby it will be too much to bear. He understands our limits better than we do. Losing Kevin was a tragic and devastating loss, but God is still faithful. He will enable and strengthen you personally in this trial."

Tim paused for a moment, then went on. "When the verse says 'no temptation has overtaken you that is not common to man,' it means that other Christians have faced crushing losses as well, and they have been able to face them successfully. He has not given you more than you can handle, even though this is the hardest thing you have ever experienced. So even though you are tempted to give up the will to live, tempted to surrender yourself to dark despair, tempted to get angry with God, you must remember that God, in His faithfulness, has provided a righteous way of escape. He will give you the grace to endure such loss and still bring Him glory."

The Encouragement of Scripture

Practically, how is this possible? How is it possible for a person like Kate, barely surviving each day with such enormous grief, to live a meaningful life to the glory of God? Kate knew Kevin was with his Lord (2 Corinthians 5:6-8). She was not concerned about him or his welfare because she knew him to be a man who fully trusted the atoning work of Jesus Christ on the cross to pay for his sins (Romans 8:38-39). And she herself had trusted the same saving work of Jesus Christ (Ephesians 2:8-10). Someday she would see the fulfillment of her joy in heaven. But the question now was this: How was she to live until then? How could she endure through such suffering until then? Kate knew something was not right in the way she was handling her grief. She just did not know what was wrong.

What Kate hadn't realized yet was her need to take a close look at the desires of her heart. She needed to be honest with herself concerning what she really wanted for her life. Times of hardship and suffering are opportunities to examine the allegiances of the heart.

Kate had dearly loved Kevin. Over the years, their love for one another had grown. It was deep and satisfying. She had depended upon Kevin and completely trusted him. Her reliance upon him had developed with time until almost everything in her life was dependent upon him. And now he was gone! It felt like the foundation of her whole life had suddenly been kicked out from underneath her. Now she felt like she was in a freefall, spiraling downward into a dark abyss. She knew this is not the way a Christian should be, but her emotional state made it difficult to identify what was wrong.

"What has happened to me?" she wondered out loud to her counselors. "I know this is not the way a Christian handles grief. But I can't help myself!"

While Kate's love for her husband was good and honoring to Christ, even a legitimate love over the years can become a controlling love when its intensity overcomes one's love for the Lord. Slowly and imperceptibly, Kate had permitted her fierce love for her husband to be elevated to an ungodly level in her heart. In reality, Kevin had become her functional god, even though she still professed Jesus Christ as her Savior and Lord. Once Kevin was removed from her life, her whole world caved in. Without realizing it, she had grown to love him more than her Savior.

Familial love is a wonderful gift from God; but it should never replace our love for the Lord (Matthew 10:34-40; Mark 10:28-31; Luke 14:25-27). Ashamedly, Kate's mind went to a place that she was not yet willing to reveal to her counselors. Every time she would open her bedroom closet, tears would flow as she saw Kevin's clothes. She would drop to her knees, burying her face in his shirts—the sweet aroma of his cologne still lingering there. She would not let friends or family touch any of the items in his wardrobe. Her closet had become a shrine, a memorial to his memory. It was a place where she daily worshipped his remembrance with Kevin's scent bringing back so many fond memories of their life together. Her idolized view of the past with him was her escape from the misery of the present. More and more, she was living in the past, and her nostalgic memories were beginning to command all of her thoughts.

Tim and Becca could see that Kate was lost in thought. They let her have a few moments, and then gently asked about what she was thinking. With tears spilling down her cheeks, Kate confessed her idolatry. Sparing no details, she told them everything about her daily ritual in the closet. With great compassion, her counselors reminded her that "living in the past" was not what God wanted. "Say not, 'Why were the former days better than these?' For it is not from wisdom that you ask this" (Ecclesiastes 7:10).

To dwell in the past demonstrates a serious and sinful discontentment with what God has provided in the present. It rejects the goodness of God for today (Psalm 23:6). Kate realized that her love for Kevin was not wrong, but the fact that she had allowed it to become greater than her love for Jesus Christ made it a ruling sin. She had become more passionate about Kevin than about his Lord. And she knew that if Kevin were still living, he would not want that. Kevin would never have wanted to be Kate's god.

Through this painful loss, Kate could learn how to live a better life for Christ. In fact, death is a great teacher about life. This is one of the lessons of the book of Ecclesiastes. Through the first six chapters, the writer, King Solomon, describes the failure of finding the true meaning of life through materialistic pursuit. Kate, Tim, and Becca began to study this insightful Old Testament book together. Solomon sought wine, women, and wealth and all the materialistic pursuits he thought would bring him happiness, but then he observed, "Vanity of vanities...All is vanity" (1:2).

"The Hebrew word translated *vanity*," Tim explained, "means 'vapor' or 'breath.' That is true of everything in this world. Everything is mere vapor or smoke. It is here for a short time, then it is gone." He went on to illustrate: "Soap bubbles, soap bubbles, everything and everybody in this world is temporary and quickly passing away. Like a soap bubble that looks so pretty for a moment, it is gone and disappears forever. That is the destiny of everything we see and touch, including people."

Tim went on: "The real meaning and substance of life cannot be found in the world that is passing away; it is death that teaches us that lesson. Later in Ecclesiastes Solomon wrote, 'It is better to go to the house of mourning than to go to the house of feasting, for this is the end of all mankind, and the living will lay it to heart'" (7:2).

"Why is it better?" Becca asked Kate rhetorically. "Because it helps us to see how frail and unreliable our lives are, so that our hope and trust will rest in God alone. In verse 4, Solomon went on to say, 'The heart of the wise is in the house of mourning, but the heart of fools is in the house of mirth.'

"When was the last time you went to a party and afterwards thought, *I am a better person after being there?*" Becca asked. "That doesn't really happen. But after you stand by the casket of someone you dearly love, it forces you to reevaluate everything in your life. It helps you to see what really is important."

Becca then pointed Kate to Ecclesiastes 12:13: "Fear God and keep his commandments, for this is the whole duty of man." She wanted Kate to realize what was of primary importance. Solomon had learned that it was not the tangible things of the world that ultimately mattered; rather, it was the intangible reality of a God-centered life that did.

How could Kate learn and grow from her grief? Tim and Becca's goal was to help her see how God intended to use Kevin's death for her good. Up to this time, Kate had struggled with anger toward God for taking Kevin from her. But now she began to recognize how she had made her desire for Kevin's presence an idol in her life. She saw her anger as the fruit of that idol. Repenting of her idol and her anger against God (James 1:20), she asked the Lord to forgive her. She wanted to love the Lord her God with all her heart and use the remainder of her life to please Him.

For the next several weeks, Tim, Becca, and Kate studied through the book of Romans to see how the apostle Paul had dealt with adversity in his life. How did he handle trials and suffering? Tim highlighted Paul's perspective on suffering in Romans 5:3-5:

> Not only that, but we rejoice in our sufferings, knowing that suffering produces endurance, and endurance produces character, and character produces hope, and hope does not put us to shame, because God's love has been

poured into our hearts through the Holy Spirit who has been given to us.

Kate could immediately see how her view of suffering differed from Paul's. In the course of her grieving, she could see no good coming from Kevin's death. All she could think about, from her perspective, was the injustice of it. She had allowed her grief to make her bitter and angry. By contrast, Paul had rejoiced in his sufferings because he could see that a good and righteous God stood behind the difficulties, which God had intended for his good.

Kate was awakened to the way the Lord works in people's lives to bring about greater righteousness through suffering. With the help of the Holy Spirit, she would not lose faith. Instead, her faith would endure and deepen through the suffering. As she persevered, God would strengthen her character, especially through changes in her thinking, feeling, and behavior. And as her character became more Christlike, it would develop a firm resolve. Then as her character grew, so would her hope. This is the type of hope that is full of absolute assurance (Hebrews 10:23). Because God would walk with her through this most difficult trial, she could be absolutely certain that He would take her through any other difficulties the future might hold.

In the counseling sessions, Kate learned how the Christian has a hope that the non-Christian does not understand. Becca pointed out that it is the Christian's hope that changes the grief process of the believer (Lamentations 3:21-24). When a believer trusts the promises of God, she does not have to go through the five stages of grief mentioned by Kate's psychiatrist. In fact, the grief of the Christian is substantially different than that of the non-Christian. Writing to the Thessalonian Christians in his first epistle to them, Paul said, "We do not want you to be uninformed, brothers, about those who are asleep [are dead], that you may not grieve as others do who have no hope" (1 Thessalonians 4:13). Christians understand that those who have died in Christ are present with the Lord and will return with Him at the second coming (1 Thessalonians 4:14-18). This knowledge changes the Christian's grief from a worldly desperation to a wonderful expectation.

In light of this truth, Tim and Becca encouraged Kate to study hope throughout the New Testament (for example, 1 Corinthians 15:51-52) and especially in the book of Romans. Romans 15 was particularly helpful in providing Kate with what she needed to do in order to build her hope in Christ. This study proved to be a better help than taking any drug to stabilize her moods. It enabled her to see the bigger picture, through God's eyes, and this calmed her spirit.

When Kate began to look at things God's way, the ache of her heart started to slowly diminish. Joy returned to her life. Tim and Becca encouraged her with these words from Romans 15:4: "Whatever was written in former days was written for our instruction, that through endurance and through the encouragement of the Scriptures we might have hope." As Kate maintained her trust in Christ through her grief, with the enabling work of the Holy Spirit, her endurance grew (Jeremiah 17:7; John 14:1). As she studied how Jesus Christ and the saints throughout the Old and New Testaments faced death, her hope grew stronger. She still mourned the loss of her husband, but her grief was no longer hopeless. It was no longer covered with a dark cloud. The light of God's Word had filled her life again with a renewed faith in the Lord.

In all this, Romans 15:13 was becoming more and more a reality in Kate's life: "May the God of hope fill you with all joy and peace in believing, so that by the power of the Holy Spirit you may abound in hope."

The Comfort of Christ and the Cross

After Kevin's death, there was a time Kate seriously questioned whether God even cared for her. She doubted if God even understood what she was experiencing. The ache within was unbearable, and she felt abandoned and alone in her grief. Kate felt like the prophet Jeremiah as he watched the destruction, death, and mayhem of Jerusalem in 586 BC. He kept repeating, "She has no one to comfort her...She has no comforter...for a comforter is far from me, one to revive my spirit...but there is none to comfort her...there is no one to comfort me" (1:2, 9, 16, 17, 21). Kate could identify with this overwhelming sense of isolation and aloneness. It had gotten to the point where she had come perilously close to abandoning her faith in Christ because she had been tempted to believe God had abandoned her.

But nothing could be further from the truth. The Lord not only knew her plight, He was also ready to comfort her. Even Jeremiah, in the midst of his horrendous loss, came to his senses, remembering the faithfulness and lovingkindness of the Lord as stated in Lamentations 3:21-26:

> But this I call to mind, and therefore I have hope: The steadfast love of the LORD never ceases; his mercies never come to an end; they are new every morning; great is your faithfulness. "The LORD is my portion," says my soul, "therefore I will hope in him." The LORD is good to those who wait for him, to the soul who seeks him. It is good that one should wait quietly for the salvation of the LORD.

Kate's repentance brought her back to her senses. Jeremiah's observation was profound and eternally true: In spite of her severe loss, the Lord's lovingkindness and mercy had continued to shine on her. Tim and Becca encouraged Kate to write a list of 20 things that she could be truly grateful for, beginning with the fact that she would see Kevin again one day and rejoice with him in glory. This brought a smile to her face.

The Lord's lovingkindness is fully realized in the death, burial, and resurrection of Jesus Christ. No other human news could provide a Christian more comfort than the news that death has been conquered. As Hebrews 2:14-18 says:

> Since therefore the children share in flesh and blood, he himself likewise partook of the same things, that through death he might destroy the one who has the power of death, that is, the devil, and deliver all those who through fear of death were subject to lifelong slavery. For surely it is not angels that he helps, but he helps the offspring of Abraham. Therefore he had to be made like his brothers in every respect, so that he might become a merciful and faithful high priest in the service of God, to make propitiation for the sins of the people. For because he himself has suffered when tempted, he is able to help those who are being tempted.

On the cross, Christ conquered sin and death, destroying the power of the devil. He did not do this for the angels, but only for those who would have faith in Him, "the offspring of Abraham." He provided propitiation or atonement for the sins of His people. This is the greatest comfort a believer can receive, especially in the face of death.

The Lord walked among those who experienced grief (John 11:33-35). He suffered when being tempted. Because of this He was moved with compassion and sympathy for them (Hebrews 4:15). Even more amazing is that He not only feels our sorrow, but as Hebrews 12:18 says, "He is able to help those who are being tempted."

Kate was now beginning to understand the importance of the cross and to experience the comfort Christ provides as He "sympathize[s] with our weaknesses."

Kate no longer grieved as a woman without hope. There were still many times when she would recall a precious memory of Kevin, and that would bring her to tears. Often she longed to have Kevin by her side. But the dark cloud of faithlessness was gone from her heart. She was able to remove Kevin's clothes from the bedroom closet and give them away to other men who could wear them. She "destroyed" the closet shrine where she had been worshipping and returned to worshipping the God of heaven. She also returned to church with a new song in her heart, enjoying the corporate worship and hymns. And she even returned to teaching her Sunday school class and her role in the women's ministry.

As Kate poured her life into the people she was ministering to, a radiant joy returned to her face. She no longer looked pale and gaunt. Her appetite and energy returned, and her chest pains vanished. She was very grateful for Pastor Tim and Becca's patient love in counseling her. And she was careful to give the Lord the credit for delivering her from the darkest hours of her life.

Questions for Discussion

1. In counseling Kate, Pastor Tim and Becca did not walk her through the five stages of grief. Why do you think that is so? What did they do instead?

2. When we lose a loved one, we are tempted to hold onto that person in one way or another. Kate's weakness was Kevin's clothing. What are some other ways in which widows can end up holding onto the past in an obsessive way, leading them to further difficulties?

3. What are some different types of thoughtless responses we might show to someone in grief? Describe what you believe would be a comforting and encouraging way to come alongside of a widow who has suffered a great loss.

4. If you are married, take some time to examine your attachment to your husband, knowing that your love for Christ must always supersede your love for your spouse. What changes do you think you need to make now to be a wife who glorifies God in her marriage?

5. What Scripture given in the chapter was most helpful to you as you thought through Kate's grief? Take some time to memorize it so that it is a help to you both today and in the future as you ponder the reality of God's comfort and help in time of extreme grief.

10

Guilt

I am not aware of anything against myself,
but I am not thereby acquitted.
It is the Lord who judges me.

1 Corinthians 4:4

Jennifer made herself comfortable, sinking into a beautiful Italian leather chair in her therapist's office. She could not help but notice the exquisite furnishings, thick maroon carpet, and picturesque paintings. It made her feel at ease and relaxed. This was her second session with the psychologist, and even though the first session did not seem to help much, she felt fairly free to talk with her. Her therapist was a woman, the nearest one to her home who was on the list of psychologists approved by her medical insurance company.

Even though each session cost more than $200 an hour, Jennifer was desperate and willing to try anything to deal with the overwhelming problem disturbing her. Yet she was a little anxious about where this next therapy session might go. Jennifer had not yet shared her most troubling secret; she was still testing the waters to see if the woman was trustworthy and non-condemning. Condemnation from this person who she didn't really know, and who she was sure was not a Christian, would be devastating.

In the previous session, Jennifer brought up her struggle with depression, fear, and anxiety. Her psychologist had said very little. Occasionally she would ask a question concerning her childhood or whether she had thoughts of suicide. Jennifer described a rather normal childhood with loving Christian parents and siblings. She grew up happy as the youngest of five children. She then reluctantly revealed that in the past three years she had entertained thoughts of suicide on a few occasions, especially when she was battling with another bout of serious depression.

"What happened three years ago that is so significant?" her therapist probed. This was the question Jennifer dreaded. As a Christian, she knew she needed to tell the truth to someone. But was this the right time? Was this the right person? An awful sense of humiliation swept over her. Confessing it openly would bring an unbearable feeling of shame. Noticing her turmoil, her therapist commented, "Sometimes unwanted shame blocks your willingness to be honest with yourself and others. Your psychic defenses cause you to deny, repress, and eventually suppress being truthful." There was an element of truth in her therapist's words, but Jennifer was sure her unbelieving therapist did not understand how immeasurably shameful her secret was.

"I am not sure I want to talk about it," she had fired back at her therapist. Jennifer began to realize that her continuing struggle with depression, fear, and anxiety were only symptoms of this much deeper issue. "The shame that comes from guilty feelings is not healthy," her therapist had said. "Shame is 'the radioactive waste of your psyche.' It will not take long for it to leech through your efforts to repress it and mess up your entire life."

Jennifer knew about feeling messed-up. The guilt she experienced from repressing her secret had already taken a huge toll on the quality of her life. "In William Shakespeare's *Macbeth*, guilt is described as 'life's fitful fever,'" her therapist had said. "It will make your life uncomfortable and miserable until it is cured."

The therapist's words had played over and over again in Jennifer's mind since that first visit. As a result, Jennifer decided it was time to expose her most carefully hidden problem.

Three years earlier, while she was a university student and actively involved in a campus ministry, she had met a handsome young man. They began dating. He said he too was a Christian. All her girlfriends told her that he was a real catch, and she could not deny her attraction for him.

They had been dating for only two months when heavy petting unexpectedly turned into sexual intimacy. The next morning, she felt terrible. She knew this was not the way Christians were to act prior to marriage. The intense weight of her guilt caused her to withdraw into a shell. She earnestly prayed for God's forgiveness and broke off the relationship with her boyfriend. She told him they had gone too far, and she accepted her part of the responsibility for this sin.

He had pleaded with her to continue the relationship, rationalizing that they were no different than the other university students. "We can work this out together," he had said. But his justification was his big mistake; it helped her to realize he was not the type of a guy she would want to pursue and marry. She felt better as she walked away from him that day, but she still grieved over her lack of self-control.

After Jennifer shared all this, her therapist leaned back in her chair with a dismissive grin. "Honey, you are merely describing the life of the average female university student. Don't you see that your guilt is merely the toxic residue of your strict moral upbringing? If you get rid of your guilt, you will no longer feel so miserable."

The therapist continued, "This is how you deal with guilty feelings. You need to have multiple sexual relationships until you no longer feel guilty about it. If you continue to nurture this unhealthy guilt and hold onto these inflexible moral values, they will destroy you."

Jennifer was troubled by her therapist's dismissive attitude, but she was not all that surprised at the advice she was receiving. In her psychology class, she had learned that B.F. Skinner advocated a behaviorist model that stressed that continuing to act against the conscience was like taking allergy shots: Eventually there would no longer be an adverse reaction.

It suddenly became clear to Jennifer that she was paying a lot of money to have her therapist tell her that her moral code was obsolete and that the solution to her depression and anxiety was to practice fornication until she felt no more guilt. Jennifer had to agree with the part about feeling guilty. She knew enough about the Bible to know that if she continued to sin against her conscience she would no longer feel guilty (Ephesians 4:19; 1 Timothy 4:2; Titus 1:15). Her conscience would be silenced due to her repeated sin. But would that really solve her problem?

In spite of her misgivings, Jennifer then told her therapist that her problem had an even more serious dimension. Two months after having sex with her boyfriend, she learned she was pregnant. This was devastating news. She thought she had privately put this situation behind her. But eventually everyone would know, including her parents and her Christian friends. They would all be deeply disappointed in her and she could not bear the thought of informing them. Her parents had an unrealistic and idealistic view of their daughter she did not wish to spoil. They believed her to be a wonderful, sexually pure, committed Christian young lady, and Jennifer knew pregnancy outside of wedlock would permanently shatter how they viewed her.

In desperation, Jennifer had secretly gone to the university health clinic and collected information on abortifacient procedures and clinics. The shame and guilt she felt as she read the materials was overwhelming. But she was panicked and believed she had no other option. This was the quickest and quietest way to take care of her problem while saving face.

Without consulting the father of the baby, Jennifer proceeded with the abortion. Throughout the procedure she tried to silence her conscience by repeating, "This is not a baby; it is a mass of tissue." But her guilt would not be quieted. Afterward, Jennifer knew a fleeting sense of relief. She had taken care of the problem without anyone knowing. But God knew! And her Christian conscience would not leave her in peace.

It hadn't taken long for a deep sadness to settle within her. She had killed her baby for the sake of convenience and to preserve a superficial image. These thoughts would not let her go. As weeks turned into months and months turned into years, her depression had deepened and she had withdrawn from social interaction. It had become extremely difficult for her to go to church and act normal. Much more than feeling that she was a disgrace, her conscience convicted her every time she sat under biblical preaching. She had murdered her baby. Was it possible that she had committed the unpardonable sin?

Jennifer's parents knew something was very wrong, but they did not know what. Her last couple of years at the university evidenced declining grades and a complete change of personality. She was no longer the outgoing and energetic daughter that grew up in their home. They thought perhaps the secular instruction she was receiving had served to adversely affect her faith and trust in God. But they could not get her to open up to them. Whenever she visited home, she would reluctantly agree to go to church.

Jennifer's therapist decided she had heard enough. Leaning

forward in her chair, she looked Jennifer in the eye and informed her that *guilt* was her problem—her only problem. In fact, guilt was her enemy. As long as she allowed guilt to plague her thoughts, she would never be able to live with full authenticity as a person. She would never be whole. Her self-esteem had been badly damaged by this notion of guilt and it was imperative that she do everything she could to begin to put guilt behind her and feel better about herself. She had to learn to defy guilt, which the therapist described as a self-mutilating exercise that wastes time and energy.

The therapist then said Jennifer needed to think of herself as good. She may be naïve, weak, and emotional, but she was nevertheless good. One of the worst things she could do was to pollute her mind with thoughts of worthlessness and self-hatred.

And finally, the therapist urged Jennifer to see herself as a victim of a false set of religious and social values. "These values restrict women and keep them oppressed," said the therapist. "You need to be free to make your own decisions about your body without being made to feel guilty. That is the toxicity of false guilt. You need to move on and get a new start in life."

Jennifer sat in silence, unable to respond. According to the therapist, every moral value she had learned from her family and church was to be repressed, denied, and rejected. There was no doubt she needed help, but was this the type of help she needed? Was guilt really her enemy? She left the therapist's office that day more confused than ever before.

It had been months since she had been to church, but Jennifer made sure she was there the following Sunday. She saw many old friends she had not seen for a long time, and it was refreshing to see them again. Their kind reception was encouraging, but she knew they did not know her big secret. She was fearful as she entered the main auditorium, yet the hymns being sung brought back many warm memories of her growing-up years. Providentially, the pastor's message that Sunday was on Psalm 51, in which King David admits his guilt after committing adultery with Bathsheba and then subsequently plotting the murder of Uriah, her husband (2 Samuel 12:9).

Jennifer was riveted on every word. She placed herself into David's emotional sandals and could directly relate to his guilt and grief. He too had believed that his sin was a secret that no one would know, except God. The pastor explained the meaning of what David had written in Psalm 51:4: "Against you, you only, have I sinned and done what is evil in your sight, so that you may be justified in your words and blameless in your judgment."

In that verse, the Hebrew preposition "against" can also be legitimately translated "before." It is very possible David was highlighting the secretiveness of his sin, "*Before* you, you only, have I sinned and done what is evil in your sight." Evidently David believed his sin was a private matter (2 Samuel 12:12)—that is, before Nathan the prophet made it public. Yes, David had sinned against God. But he had also sinned against Uriah—as evident by his admission of "bloodguiltiness" in Psalm 51:14. As Jennifer listened, she realized that David was not treating guilt as his enemy. Rather, it had become the source of his conviction, which, in turn, led to his repentance.

The turning point of Psalm 51 was David's cry for deliverance from his bloodguiltiness. David realized that his sin was so grievous that it could not be atoned for by any animal sacrifice (Numbers 15:30-31).[15] Such offenses called for capital punishment for each one of David's sins, adultery (Leviticus 20:10) and murder (Numbers 35:30). David knew he deserved death for what he had done. That's the reason David's prayer for deliverance is so poignant. "You will not delight in sacrifice, or I would give it; you will not be pleased with a burnt offering. The sacrifices of God are a broken spirit; a broken and contrite heart, O God, you will not despise" (Psalm 51:16-17).

Jennifer's misconceptions about guilt began to change. David did not deny his guilt. He did not attempt to reject his self-hatred and worthless feelings about himself. And he did not act like a victim of his circumstances. Instead, he totally owned his sins. As appalling as they were—adultery and murder—he confessed them before both God and man by writing this psalm. David was broken over his sin, and it was his guilt that had brought him to seek God's forgiveness. In verse 10 David wrote, "Create in me a clean heart, O God, and renew a right spirit within me."

Jennifer understood this was precisely what she needed. She had heard this psalm taught many times before, but it had never meant as much to her as it did on this day. Her sins were just like David's. She had committed a sexual sin, and she had murdered her baby.

After the church service concluded, Jennifer made it a point to see the pastor and ask for biblical counseling. He explained that his wife would be more than willing to meet with her and that she was a trained biblical counselor. Jennifer asked, "How much will this cost? I don't know if I can afford this because church counselors aren't covered by my medical insurance plan."

The pastor reassured Jennifer that the counseling was a free ministry of the church. He explained, "I don't charge for the public ministry of the Word when I preach. Similarly, we do not charge for the private ministry of the Word when we counsel." Jennifer was relieved and eagerly agreed to meet with the pastor's wife. This was the first time in more than three years that she had begun to sense any kind of hope for dealing with the immense guilt that plagued her.

During the first visit with Mrs. Edwards, Jennifer quickly revealed all the reasons behind her guilt and the counsel she had received from her psychologist. Mrs. Edwards listened carefully, then proceeded to explain that psychology treats guilt as an enemy, whereas Scripture treats it as a friend. Guilt is a lot like a smoke detector—when the detector goes off, you don't smash it with a hammer. Instead, you check to see what's wrong so that your house doesn't burn down. Many people treat guilt as if it *itself* were the problem—as if it were a pollutant that needed to be eliminated from your life. But for a Christian, guilt is an asset. It alerts you that something is wrong in your life.

Mrs. Edwards explained that psychology views guilt primarily as an awful *feeling* or an unnecessary nuisance, while Scripture views guilt as an important *fact* that needs attention. Biblically speaking, guilt is defined as "a legal liability or culpability to punishment." In Scripture, the theological idea of guilt stresses the fact of culpability before God and not the dreadful feelings that will often accompany it. Bad or negative feelings are often the *result* of guilt, but they are not the *same* as guilt. Therefore it is possible to be guilty (the fact of guilt) in God's eyes and yet not *feel* guilty.

It is like slowing down from 50 miles per hour to 35 miles per hour while driving through a 20-miles-per-hour school zone. You will feel good that you've slowed down, but you are still exceeding the 20-miles-per-hour speed limit. A police officer will still give you a ticket for going 15 miles per hour over the speed limit, even though you slowed down some. The problem is you just didn't slow down enough.

"Let me get this straight," said Jennifer. "*Feeling* guilty is not the same as *being* guilty. Does that mean that when a Christian feels guilty that she is experiencing false guilt?"

"When people speak of experiencing false guilt," said Mrs. Edwards, "they are often referring to deep regret or remorse, not guilt. Guilt is always a fact. Either you broke God's law or you did not. *False guilt* is an oxymoron, like *deafening silence*. That's because you cannot truly have a *false fact*. When your psychologist accuses you of having false guilt, it is her way of rejecting biblical standards and replacing them with worldly values. Either you are guilty by biblical standards, or you are not."

"Well, what if I feel guilty about something and yet I am not guilty according to Scripture?" Jennifer asked.

"That is not false guilt because you are guilty of nothing," said Mrs. Edwards. "Rather, it shows your conscience has been trained to respond to an unbiblical standard. Your conscience feels bad about the wrong things because it is informed by a human standard and not God's standard. You are guilty about having a false standard, but that is not what you feel guilty about. The key is to have your conscience trained by Scripture."

Jennifer pondered her counselor's insight, but still struggled with one thought. She asked, "If I feel guilty about something that is not biblically wrong, and still act against my feelings, am I being a hypocrite?"

"No," said Mrs. Edwards. "In fact, there are many things you do against your feelings. For example—getting up early in the morning to go to work or school when you would rather stay in your nice, warm bed. Getting up when you want to stay in bed doesn't make you a hypocrite. A hypocrite is someone who claims to believe something is right or wrong but behaves in a way that denies those beliefs.

"Now, if you firmly believe that an activity or pattern of thought is wrong, even though Scripture does not define it as wrong, and you still proceed to violate it against your conscience, then it is a sin for you to practice it, because you are not doing this in faith, as stated in Romans 14:23. Our Lord would have us protect our conscience instead of continually repeating perceived sins and hardening the conscience. And we should never underestimate the effects of guilt on the conscience by continuing on with unconfessed sin" (see Psalm 32:1-5; 38:1-8).

• • • • •

God has given us the gift of a sensitive conscience to help us identify when we have violated His truth. The New Testament word for
"conscience" (Greek, συνείδησις) literally means "a knowing with."
Some theologians have defined it as "the soul reflecting on itself." It
is an awareness of and culpability for transgressing God's commandments. It is similar to metacognition as the mind is aware of its own
learning and thinking, but with the added understanding of personal accountability to God's standard, a standard beyond you that
is your final authority. Your inner person uses the information or
knowledge it has to evaluate its own thinking and actions in a similar way that diagnostic software runs on a computer. When an error
is found, a warning is issued through your emotions.

It is important to see that your conscience is what you know or
believe—not what you feel. You can believe something is right but
feel hesitant or even hostile toward practicing it. For example, suppose a friend comes to you and begins to gossip about someone else,
slandering her behind her back. You know that gossip is wrong. You
may feel awful about confronting your friend about her gossip, even
though you know it is the right thing to do.

Conversely, you can feel good about what you know is wrong.
For example, Jennifer remembered her initial feelings after aborting
her child. She knew it was wrong, but she felt good for a short time
about getting rid of the social stigma of an unwed pregnancy. So
feelings are not the same thing as the conscience. They are, however,
often the result of the functional effect of the conscience.

The Bible teaches that it is important for the believer to have a
clean conscience. This means that any unconfessed sin in your life
needs to be taken care of before God. In his defense before Ananias,
the high priest of Jews, the apostle Paul spoke of the care he took in
maintaining his own conscience: "So I always take pains to have a
clear conscience toward both God and man" (Acts 24:16). Paul also

wrote, "I thank God whom I serve, as did my ancestors, with a clear conscience, as I remember you constantly in my prayers night and day" (2 Timothy 1:3).

When a Christian fails to keep the conscience clear, it is possible for the conscience to become desensitized to sin. Scripture refers to those who continually live with a defiled conscience as having a "seared conscience" (1 Timothy 4:2; see also Ephesians 4:19; Titus 1:15). A seared conscience usually belongs to unbelievers, because they are apathetic concerning their sin before God. But for a time, a Christian can act and behave as an unbeliever, refusing to confess and repent of her sin, with the growing danger that her conscience might also be seared.

$$\bullet \ \bullet \ \bullet \ \bullet \ \bullet$$

Thankfully Jennifer's conscience had not stopped working in that way.

For the first time, Jennifer realized why she was still struggling with depression and anxiety. She had never sought out the Lord and genuinely confessed and repented of her sin (1 John 1:9-10). Her counselor helped her to see that the reason she had committed these sins was because of her "fear of man"—which is a fear of what others think and a longing for their approval (Proverbs 29:25; John 12:43; Galatians 1:10). This had become an idol in her heart—fearing others more than she feared the Lord.

With tears rolling down her cheeks, Jennifer prayed and asked the Lord to forgive her of committing sexual sin and then killing her baby through abortion as a means to cover her fornication. She confessed that the idol of her heart had been pleasing people rather than pleasing God. In God's kindness and mercy, she was forgiven (Exodus 34:6-7), and the weight of this guilt she had carried for three years was finally removed.

Mrs. Edwards then showed Jennifer Romans 8:1, and asked her to read the verse out loud: "There is therefore now no condemnation for those who are in Christ Jesus." She then told Jennifer, "All your sins are covered under the blood of Jesus Christ. And in case you're wondering whether God would really forgive you, consider that the apostle Paul, who wrote those words, participated in the murder of Christians before he was saved. That's what he confessed in Philippians 3:6-7. And yet God forgave him—he no longer faced any condemnation. If Paul's grievous sins could be forgiven, then yours can be forgiven too."

Jennifer was guilty of lying to her parents, and especially of keeping her pregnancy and abortion a secret from the father of her child. She knew she needed to confess her sins to those whom she had deceived. After all, the baby was not just her baby, it also belonged to her former boyfriend too. She had taken something that was his as well and destroyed it, in addition to putting on a façade before her parents.

After repenting before God, Jennifer realized that her sin had affected others, and that she needed to do whatever she could to turn her relationships with her former boyfriend and her parents into truthful and edifying friendships (Matthew 5:24; Romans 12:18). She and Mrs. Edwards worked through likely scenarios of how Jennifer's former boyfriend and her parents might react when she confessed her deceitfulness to them and sought their forgiveness. Jennifer understood that their reactions would be part of the consequences of her sin, and she was willing to face whatever might happen because she wanted to have a clear conscience.

Jennifer contacted her former boyfriend and confessed what had happened to their baby. Then she asked for his forgiveness. It was a very difficult conversation, but it ended well. He then sought her forgiveness for having sex with her and accepted the responsibility of having put her in this difficult situation. He was grateful that she had contacted him, and they both believed that this brought a Christ-honoring closure to their relationship.

Telling her parents was more difficult. Many tears were shed over her sin. She was so relieved to find out that her parents had long suspected something was wrong, so they were not totally surprised. They were actually hoping Jennifer would let them know what had been bothering her for the past few years. As Christians, they readily forgave her and they were happy to hear that she was receiving the help of a biblical counselor.

Several months after confessing her sins, Jennifer still found herself becoming very sorrowful when she thought about what she had done. Her counselor had warned her this would happen if she was truly repentant.

Jennifer no longer felt the weight of the guilt that had plagued her. She no longer experienced severe depression, fear, or anxiety. But she was sorrowful over her sin, and she grieved over the fact that the idol of pleasing people had become so powerful in her life that she had gone so far as to kill her baby. This was a godly sorrow that she accepted as a reminder of the weaknesses of her own flesh (2 Corinthians 7:10-11; James 4:8-10). She saw this sorrow as something that would keep her clinging to Jesus daily.

Questions for Discussion

1. God defines guilt in relation to sins committed (Psalms 32:5; 78:38; 85:2). Describe how this definition is viewed by secular culture. Many evangelical churches are slowly moving away from this definition. What effect will this have on sincere Christians who are seeking cleansing for their sin?

2. Why did Jennifer still feel sorrowful even though she was completely forgiven and cleansed from the guilt of her sins? Some would say that she still felt "guilty." Describe the biblical teaching on guilt as a fact, and how Jennifer should respond to her lingering sorrow over her sin.

3. The heavy feelings brought about by our conscience after we sin often bring thoughts of worthlessness and self-hatred. Many Christian psychologists urge their counselees in this situation to learn to value and love themselves more. Based on the Scripture's teaching in Matthew 22:35-40, how many commands did Jesus give in regard to love? Also study Jesus' Sermon on the Mount in Matthew 5–7. How is "loving yourself more" actually in opposition to Jesus' teaching?

4. Proverbs 29:25 says, "The fear of man lays a snare, but whoever trusts in the LORD is safe." What are some ways in which you have sinned because you longed for the approval of man more than God's approval? What are some ways you can make yourself more mindful of living for God's approval in all that you do?

5. What part did pride play in Jennifer's rationalization of her abortion? Read Proverbs 8:13, 11:2, 16:18, 29:23. What warnings are we given about pride and its effects?

11

Marital Unfaithfulness: Adultery

Let each one of you love his wife as himself,
and let the wife see that she respects her husband.

EPHESIANS 5:33

Staring in disbelief at the paper in her hand, Veronica could feel a knot forming in her stomach. Smelling of perfume and embellished with a lipstick kiss, the handwritten love note sent a sharp pain through her heart. *Who was this "Charity" person? Where did Jordan meet her? How long had this affair been going on? How did I not see the signs?* Agonizing, unanswered questions swirled through her mind, almost to the point of making her feel dizzy.

Veronica could not imagine any emotional pain greater than what she was feeling in this moment. The knowledge that her beloved husband had been deceiving her was devastating: lying every time he kissed her, lying every time he told her she was the only one for him. One of her friends who had gone through the same ordeal described her experience as the most dramatic turning point of her life: "I was sick for weeks. I had a deep emotional ache inside that robbed my life of all joys, both great and small. It was not long before an intense anger grew up in my heart. How could he do this to our children? How could he do this to me? Once there was a time I longed to be near him, but now I am nauseated at the sight of him!" Veronica now knew just how her friend had felt.

Jordan and Veronica were faithful churchgoers. They had both submitted to the claims of the gospel on their lives, part of which is understanding their own sinfulness as well as the sinfulness of their spouse. Christians are sinful—true—but they are forgiven sinners. On this point both husband and wife agreed. But this revelation about Jordan was changing everything for Veronica. Whereas once she casually acknowledged Jordan's sinfulness as a matter of fact, she now saw his depravity everywhere she turned. What clothes did he wear when he was with *her*? What credit card of *ours* had he been using to wine and dine this unwanted intruder? What other deceit had he perpetrated that was yet to be revealed? She shuddered at these imaginations, dreading the next moment of the day, fearful of what more might come to light.

Marriage is the most intimate of all human relationships by God's design. When a spouse commits adultery, the protective barrier of the marital vows has been breached and a serious trust has been violated. Where there has been a great capacity for love there is an equally great capacity for hate. History has repeatedly demonstrated that sweet love can instantaneously turn to a sick loathing. Overnight, it seems, your lovebird has become your albatross.

When Jordan came home from work that night, Veronica stared coldly at him as she placed the love note in his hand. Then she turned and walked from the room. Going to their guest room, she lay down on the bed and wept. How would she ever get through this? As her sobs subsided, her thoughts went to a recent sermon series their pastor had preached on the family. He had discussed adultery and other sexual sins at length, and Veronica found herself carefully thinking about biblical truths regarding her situation.

Adultery. Even saying the word out loud sounded sinful to her.

She could think of a lot of other equally condemning words: cheating, betrayal, and wickedness. The Bible has a lot to say about adultery. Adultery is sexual intercourse by a married person with another married or unmarried person who is not his or her spouse (Exodus 20:14; Leviticus 20:10; Mark 10:19). For the married man, when he has physically copulated with someone other than his spouse, he has committed adultery (Proverbs 5:20; 6:29, 32). But for the unmarried man participating in sexual immorality, he has not committed adultery; though he has committed an egregious act of fornication in its own right and has become a willful perpetrator in the adultery committed by his married sexual partner (Acts 21:25; 1 Thessalonians 4:3).

What about "mental" adultery? That is, using the mind to imagine lustful acts with someone who is not your spouse? Does the Bible teach that this kind of adultery is also sin? Jesus Himself condemned the Pharisees and Jewish leaders because they arrogantly maintained that they had never committed physical adultery. In their minds, this proved that they were more righteous than other Jews, and therefore worthy of being held in highest esteem as role models.

But Jesus unmasked their self-righteousness by revealing that God's kingdom begins in the heart. His words were indicting: "You have heard that it was said, 'You shall not commit adultery.' But I say to you that everyone who looks at a woman with lustful intent has already committed adultery with her in his heart" (Matthew 5:27-28). In other words, the heart of a man who lusts after a woman is the same as the heart of a man who commits physical adultery.

Deeply embedded sexual cravings, even though there has been no sexual involvement with someone other than your spouse, are just as grievous of a sin in God's eyes. This teaching opened Veronica's eyes to the fact that even she could be guilty of adultery—adultery of the heart, that is. But in spite of the Bible truths she had been

192 The Biblical Counseling Guide for Women

learning, her anger continued to rage within. She found herself wondering about how many other ways Jordan might have sinned against her.

What about pornography? *What man* hasn't *looked at pornography?* she asked herself. *Isn't a porn addict the same as an adulterer?* Thinking back to her pastor's sermons, she remembered again the Bible's teaching. Being the wife of a man who has been caught in some type of sexual voyeurism can be extremely repulsive and painful. Sexual cravings are often privately satisfied by pictures, television programs, movies, books, and the Internet. While the husband who views pornography has not committed physical adultery, he has broken his promise in marriage to seek his sexual fulfillment only with his wife, not with some imaginary person (Proverbs 5:15-19; Hebrews 13:4).

Continual pornographic indulgence trains a man's mind and body to desire someone other than his spouse, which can eventually lead to actual physical adultery. Many a man will claim that pornography improves the intimacy he experiences with his wife, but this is a thinly veiled lie. Such a man, when he is having relations with his wife, is mentally entertaining relations with the image of another woman.

Secular psychologists and counselors do not often talk about adultery, much less mental adultery, because to them, the term contains religious connotations that do not comport well with naturalistic counsel and practices. At best, some will only go as far as to call actual adultery "an affair," but the colloquial term has blunted the impact and shame that this is a grievously serious sin before God. The Bible simply calls it adultery. Furthermore, for the secular mind, pornographic scenes are merely the indulgence of the animalistic nature of man. For the Christian mind, however, pornographic scenes are manifestations of a covetous and demanding heart that seeks fulfillment (Exodus 20:17; Ephesians 5:3-5).

Knowing she would find no help in psychological counseling, Veronica admitted to herself that she did still need help—the kind of help that would teach her the ways of the Lord. Before she could change her mind, she quickly called Mrs. Wilson, a biblical counselor in her church who had a solid knowledge of God's Word.

Mrs. Wilson listened carefully as Veronica shared about her recent discovery. It seemed that so far, Jordan was not repentant—he was not willing to give up Charity. If so, Mrs. Wilson knew that, at least for now, she would need to teach Veronica how to handle the struggle within her heart. One of the first battles she would face was over her own self-righteousness.

As Veronica continued to talk, she became more and more angry. "How could he do that to me? I would *never* do that to him!" Forgiveness had been far from her mind as she entertained indignation, anger, and hostility toward Jordan. She imagined herself unloading a barrage of bitter and hateful verbal attacks upon him. She wanted very much to hurt him as much as he had hurt her.

But at the same time, Veronica wanted to appear godly in the eyes of others—she wanted others to perceive her as being in the right, and not stooping to Jordan's level. She decided it would be better to feign a tough exterior and silently withdraw from all affection and communication. She felt justified in taking this approach—as if she were saying, "See how good of a Christian I am? I would never have an affair, and I certainly will not explode in anger! How sad that he has sinned so greatly against me, a godly wife."

Veronica was blind to the self-righteousness she was nursing in her heart. She had somehow forgotten all the grievous ways she had sinned against God and others over the years. That her own heart had an equal capacity to be drawn away into unfaithfulness with an illicit lover was completely lost on her in this moment. Instead, her thoughts were like those of the Pharisee who had prayed, "God, I thank you that I am not like other people: swindlers, unjust, adulterers…" (Luke 18:11-12 NASB).

Mrs. Wilson was quick to show from the Bible how history demonstrates that the natural inclination of the sinful human nature is to violate commitments if it brings momentary pleasure (2 Samuel 11:2-4). "When you break even one promise to Jordan, you know how quick you are to rationalize your action. This is the reason Jesus discouraged us from making oaths—because we falsely presume upon our ability to keep them [Matthew 5:33-37]. Jordan's violation of your marriage covenant is not uncommon; it is just that you believed your marriage would be the exception. If you will look honestly at your own heart, you will realize that it could just as easily have been you who violated the sacred covenant of marriage."

God's Word gives us a real-life illustration of how a loving spouse should treat and live with an adulterer. The Old Testament prophet Hosea married a woman named Gomer upon the instructions of the Lord God, a woman who violated her vows and repeatedly committed adultery. Imagine how Hosea felt when the Lord told him that he was to love her and her children of harlotry as a godly husband and father should (Hosea 1:2). His marriage became a mosaic of God's love for His adulterous people, Israel, though they had committed adultery by worshipping the gods of Baal (2:13). It is hard to imagine that Hosea had any affection for Gomer, yet he did as he was commanded. "And the LORD said to me, 'Go again, love a woman who is loved by another man and is an adulteress, even as the LORD loves the children of Israel, though they turn to other gods and love cakes of raisins'" (Hosea 3:1).

Is it possible that your marriage could become a mosaic of God's love for His people? Absolutely! This will depend upon how you intentionally choose to love even as you have been loved in Christ. He loved you in spite of your unworthiness. There was nothing in you that merited the love and supreme sacrifice of Jesus Christ and yet He became the all-sufficient atonement for your sin.

After sharing about Hosea's example, Mrs. Wilson said, "Veronica, your love for your unfaithful husband can mirror Christ's love for you."

"Jesus is God!" Veronica objected. "I can't love the way He loves."

"Hosea could have said the same thing, but he didn't," explained Mrs. Wilson. "Why? Because he knew that God is not unreasonable in His expectations. He knew God would never command him to do something that was impossible. And God does not expect of you something you cannot do. Scripture tells us that if you cannot love your husband in a romantic way at this time, then you can learn to love him as a friend or neighbor [Leviticus 19:18; Matthew 19:19]. And if you have a difficulty loving him as a friend or neighbor, then Scripture says you can learn to love him as your enemy [Matthew 5:44-48]. You may have to start at the lowest rung on the ladder, but that's the first step toward rebuilding your marriage."

• • • • •

Kinds of Forgiveness

Such unworthy love is first evidenced as a wife learns what it means to forgive her adulterous husband. Whether he is repentant or not, she must settle this issue with God. This is where it is important to understand the theological difference between *attitudinal forgiveness* and *transactional forgiveness*. Transactional forgiveness can take place when a husband confesses his sin and repents, seeking God's forgiveness and his wife's. The transaction is completed when his wife then forgives him.

Attitudinal forgiveness is a wife's biblical obligation if her husband refuses to repent. According to the intentionality of her heart, it grows out of her relationship to God in Christ. Because of God's forgiveness of her in Christ, she now stands in the place of one who is ready to forgive (Ephesians 4:32). Jesus taught about this "heart forgiveness" in Mark 11:25: "Whenever you stand praying, forgive, if you have anything against anyone, so that your Father also who is in heaven may forgive you your trespasses."

In that passage, Jesus was speaking of the offended person going to the temple to pray where only he and God were present; the offender was not present. So the issue of the offense, no matter how minor or serious it may be, must be forgiven in the person's heart before God in prayer.

Other Bible passages speak to this same attitude of forgiveness (Luke 23:34; see also Matthew 6:12-15; Luke 17:3). If a wife fails to forgive her unrepentant husband in her heart, she will continue to struggle with sinful responses that will sabotage all efforts to rebuild her marriage. In fact, transactional forgiveness (in which the husband has repented and sought his wife's forgiveness) cannot take place until attitudinal forgiveness is settled. Otherwise, the wife would be agreeing to forgive her husband verbally, but not really intending to forgive him actually.

Repentance Linked to Forgiveness

Notice how the issue of repentance is linked to forgiveness. Jesus said in Luke 17:3, "Pay attention to yourselves! If your brother sins, rebuke him, and if he repents, forgive him." In the original language of the New Testament, the term for "rebuke" means to reprove or warn your brother, but to do so in a non-indicting way. This means being willing to fairly hear his side of the story. There are occasions when well-meaning wives have falsely accused their husbands and have not been willing to hear the husband's side of the story. But, if the husband hears his wife's rebuke and agrees he has violated the covenant of marriage he made with her, and he repents, she must forgive him. If she decides to not forgive him, then Jesus is clear that it is she who is sinning.

* * * * *

Having been so devastated by the pain of marital unfaithfulness, Veronica wondered if she should wait for obvious signs of repentance before forgiving Jordan. Jesus answered this question in Luke 17:4 when He said, "If he sins against you seven times in the day, and turns to you seven times, saying, 'I repent,' you must forgive him." Obviously, seven offenses and requests for forgiveness in one day's time does not give the needed opportunity to see fruit of the repentance. The disciples, to whom Jesus was speaking, realized the difficulty of practicing this type of repeated forgiveness in such a short period of time, because they immediately remarked, "Increase our faith!" (verse 5).

Jesus continued to patiently instruct them, pointing out that one's ability to forgive like this was not dependent upon the amount of their faith, but whether they saw themselves as "unworthy servants" (verse 10). Remember, a self-righteous attitude will fuel a person's inability to forgive; but the one who concludes that she is an "unworthy servant"—as Jesus illustrates—will have a heart that's willing to forgive.

Veronica realized that her unwillingness to forgive showed that she had forgotten the enormous debt of sin that Christ had forgiven on her behalf. Mrs. Wilson encouraged Veronica to ask herself, "Have I so quickly forgotten the undeserved transformation that Jesus Christ has worked in me?"

> You were dead in the trespasses and sins in which you once walked, following the course of this world, following the prince of the power of the air, the spirit that is now

> at work in the sons of disobedience—among whom we all once lived in the passions of our flesh, carrying out the desires of the body and the mind, and were by nature children of wrath, like the rest of mankind. But God, being rich in mercy, because of the great love with which he loved us, even when we were dead in our trespasses, made us alive together with Christ—by grace you have been saved (Ephesians 2:1-5).

The Christian has been consumed and covered by grace—and all of this in spite of her previous rebellious attitudes and actions. Only when Veronica understood the enormity of her sin, and the magnitude of her forgiveness in Christ, would she understand how to forgive like Christ. Grace had saved her, and grace provides the necessary forgiving attitudes and actions that she is called upon to give to others. A woman who realizes she has been forgiven much will herself forgive much.

The primary meaning of forgiveness in the New Testament is "to send away" or "to release." With regard to a sin like adultery, it means "to pardon." When it comes to forgiving sin, God has publicly promised that His forgiveness is lasting (Isaiah 43:25; Jeremiah 31:34). For a wife to forgive in a similar manner, she too must make a public promise to pardon her husband. This involves three elements—publicly (or verbally), she promises...

- she will not bring up his sin to him (in continual accusations)
- she will not bring up his sin to others (in gossip)
- she will not bring up his sin to herself (in bitterness of spirit)

In other words, she promises she will not use this information against him in the future. An exception would be if she needs to revisit the offense with him in the future if it is intended for his benefit, but not for the purpose of holding it against him.

Mrs. Wilson helped Veronica think through what God would have her do if Jordan failed to repent. Because he was a member of the church, the church leaders would need to carefully and lovingly walk him through the proper steps of church discipline as outlined in Matthew 18:15-18, with the goal of lovingly restoring him back into good fellowship upon the basis of his repentance. Church discipline shows that there is a distinct difference in the way that Christians and non-Christians respond to sin. Genuine Christians do not continue to sin and refuse to repent (1 John 1:8-10). Only unbelievers act this way. So if Jordan were to repent, then Veronica and the church should forgive him. Then Veronica and Jordan could begin the process of rebuilding their marriage, making it better than it was before.

If Jordan were to refuse to repent, then he would be acting as an unbeliever, and should be treated as an unbeliever. As far as Veronica was concerned, whether he repented or not, the attitudinal forgiveness in her heart would keep her from becoming bitter and resentful. Even if Jordan refused to repent, she would still be kind and gracious, but she wouldn't be able to offer him transactional forgiveness. That way, she would indicate she was taking his ongoing sin seriously. And she would then commit to praying for his rebellious soul.

Mrs. Wilson's guidance about repentance and forgiveness raised a question in Veronica's mind. "Is it permissible for a wife to divorce her adulterous husband who is unrepentant?" she asked.

"It is permissible in Scripture," said Mrs. Wilson, "but it is not commanded. The scriptural texts that permit a divorce in the case of physical adultery are Matthew 5:32 and 19:9. The mental adultery that we addressed earlier is a cause for personal and marital counseling, and not for divorce. If mental adultery were a sufficient reason for divorce, then every married woman and man could potentially have biblical cause for divorce. Only unrepentant physical adultery is a justifiable reason for divorce, and in such a case, the Christian woman is free to remarry another Christian man if our Lord sovereignly provides such a godly spouse."

Veronica had not only learned much about what God says about adultery, she had also come to realize her need to humbly repent of her wrath and self-righteous attitude toward Jordan. She needed to be willing to forgive him, and let God teach her how to love her unfaithful husband so that this love would showcase the great love that the Most High God has for His people. Although Veronica was still tempted with anger and bitterness, she prayed for God's help to live through this trial in a way that would honor Him.

Veronica continued to meet with Mrs. Wilson weekly to learn more from God's Word about how to respect Jordan and submit to him as her husband (Ephesians 5:22-33), even though he had not yet repented. She learned how to humbly pray for his soul, recognizing that if he never repented of his adultery, God's judgment was upon him (1 Corinthians 6:9-10). And finally, she began to study Scripture to find out how to love Jordan as a friend and a brother in Christ, even though he was as yet unwilling to repent and give up his lover. This was perhaps the most difficult thing Veronica had ever attempted to do, and she was not sure exactly how to go about it.

Following Mrs. Wilson's direction, Veronica began to study Romans 12:9-21. There she found the apostle Paul's teaching on how to love another person with a godly genuineness and without hypocrisy. In these verses she found several instances where Paul described what it looks like to love another person who is difficult to love. Phrases like "be patient in tribulation" and "bless those who persecute you" and "repay no one evil for evil" seemed to leap off the page at her. This was what she really needed: teaching and encouragement to love in a godly way while enduring a truly difficult trial. Veronica proceeded to commit this entire section of Scripture to memory, knowing she would need to meditate on these truths daily.

> Let love be genuine. Abhor what is evil; hold fast to what is good. Love one another with brotherly affection. Outdo one another in showing honor. Do not be slothful in zeal, be fervent in spirit, serve the Lord. Rejoice in hope, be patient in tribulation, be constant in prayer. Contribute to the needs of the saints and seek to show hospitality.
>
> Bless those who persecute you; bless and do not curse them. Rejoice with those who rejoice, weep with those who weep. Live in harmony with one another. Do not be haughty, but associate with the lowly. Never be wise in your own sight. Repay no one evil for evil, but give thought to do what is honorable in the sight of all. If possible, so far as it depends on you, live peaceably with all. Beloved, never avenge yourselves, but leave it to the wrath of God, for it is written, "Vengeance is mine, I will repay, says the Lord." To the contrary, "if your enemy is hungry, feed him; if he is thirsty, give him something to drink; for by so doing you will heap burning coals on his head." Do not be overcome by evil, but overcome evil with good (Romans 12:9-21).

After memorizing this passage, Veronica then began to plan how to actively show love to her husband. For example, prior to repenting of her self-righteous anger against Jordan, she had stopped making his breakfast and lunch each day. If he showed up for the evening meal, she coldly told him he could heat up leftovers from the refrigerator. Now directed by Romans 12, she began to obey verse 20: "If your enemy is hungry, feed him." She quietly and humbly returned to making Jordan's breakfast at home and preparing a lunch for him to take to work. Each evening, she had a delicious hot meal ready for him whether he came home or not. This was just one of the practical ways that she began to love her husband, who was difficult to love.

Veronica found great joy in committing herself to obeying God's Word, and this, in turn, produced a peace in her heart. Her thoughts of anger and retaliation slowly dissipated as she found more and more ways to love, honor, and respect Jordan. God was at work through His Word, changing Veronica from a bitter, self-righteous wife to a humble, loving wife. Regardless of whether or not Jordan repented of and ended his adultery, Veronica's hope was in God and His Word to strengthen her in this most difficult time.

• • • • •

Not all adultery is perpetrated by the husband. Many women have betrayed their husbands as well.

Perhaps you yourself have been the adulterer; or you may be at this very time tempted to be unfaithful to your husband. Does the guilt of this offense, or potential offense, weigh heavy in your conscience? You may be wondering if there is help and hope for you.

While it is clear that God takes adultery very seriously, He is compassionate toward men and women who have committed the sin of adultery. The good news is that you can be forgiven. One of the most poignant passages concerning adultery is found in 1 Corinthians, where Paul described how the Corinthian believers had formerly lived as adulterers, and in many other sinful ways as well:

> Do you not know that the unrighteous will not inherit the kingdom of God? Do not be deceived: neither the sexually immoral...nor adulterers...will inherit the kingdom of God. And such *were* some of you. But you were washed, you were sanctified, you were justified in the name of the Lord Jesus Christ and by the Spirit of our God (1 Corinthians 6:9-11).

The tense of the verb in verse 11, "such were some of you," indicates that this was not a one-time act committed by these believers prior to their conversion; it was a continuous practice of adultery that characterized their lives. In the case of these new Christians, Paul extended hope to them: "and such *were* some of you." It is astounding and humbling that God would take any sinner from any kind of background and make him or her an heir of His kingdom. But that is the wonderful grace of God! There is forgiveness in Christ for those who repent and forsake their life of sin.

However, it is sobering to read that those who continue to pursue adultery and remain unrepentant will not inherit the kingdom of God. How is this so? Are the consequences of continual sexual sin this devastating? Indeed. Earlier in 1 Corinthians, Paul had directed his readers' attention to an egregious situation in the church at Corinth, where a man was living in a sexual relationship with his stepmother (5:1). Then in chapter 6, Paul pointed out the dire consequences of sexual immorality and adultery. Hoping his readers would see why ongoing sexual immorality is so scandalous that it would bar one from the kingdom of God, he then illustrated the nature of this sin. Using food and the stomach as an example, he said, "'Food is meant for the stomach and the stomach is for food'—and God will destroy both one and the other" (6:13).

In other words, the purpose of food is that it is for the stomach, and conversely, the stomach was made for food to go into it. Both are inextricably linked to each other. In the same way, the purpose of the human body is for the Lord, and the Lord for the body. Thus the body of the believer is not to be dedicated to sexual immorality, but to the Lord.

To put it another way, when a person comes to know the Lord, he is grafted into the body of Christ Himself. They are inextricably linked to each other. The body of the believer is for the Lord, and the

Lord is for the body. Therefore, if you alter or change the status of your body in any way (that is, if you join yourself sexually to a man who is not your husband), it has a direct effect on the Lord. Because your body will be raised physically by God's power (6:14), your body is eternally important. It matters what you give your body over to. Paul explained in verse 12 that he did not let himself become mastered by anything that would keep him from being committed to the Lord. It is this same attitude and goal that a godly woman must have for her body, for it belongs to God.

That is why Paul said that our bodies are individual members of Jesus Christ Himself (6:15). Our bodies act as a representation of our Lord. Because our bodies are linked to Christ, should we then link them immorally to another person who is not our spouse? Of course not, said Paul.

Genesis 2:24 teaches of the marriage relationship that the husband and wife "shall become one flesh." When a woman chooses to sexually unite with a man, she is fulfilling this principle in marriage (1 Corinthians 6:16). She and her partner become one flesh.

And when we as believers are joined to the Lord, we are in a superior way united with Him and corporately linked together by the Holy Spirit Himself (6:17, 19). This oneness with the Spirit of God supersedes all other unions, putting under His authority any union with other humans. That superior union with Christ brings with it weighty qualifications and consequences. That is why Paul says that when we sin any other kind of sin that is not sexual immorality or adultery, we are sinning "outside of the body." That is, our sin is being directed against someone outside of ourselves, whether it be God or another person. But when we sin in an adulterous way, our sin is directed toward our own body, and because the Holy Spirit is residing in us, He is directly affected when a foreign and immoral partner becomes one flesh with us (6:18). And even more so, those in the body of Christ are impacted as well because they are linked with us to the Holy Spirit.

Ultimately, if you are a true believer in Christ, it is clear that God will not allow this sin to go unseen. It will become evident to the church and affect the people in it. Furthermore, when we ally ourselves with someone else in such an egregious way, we grieve the Holy Spirit by whom we were sealed for the day of redemption (Ephesians 4:30). That word redemption in Ephesians 4 is the same root as the word "bought" in 1 Corinthians 6:20. It is like Paul is saying, "You were bought with a price! So glorify God with your corporate body. But the flip side is that you will grieve Him when you immorally cleave to another person, and the whole body of Christ will suffer as a result of it."

But even for the adulterer, still there is great hope. A godly man in Israel's history not only committed adultery, but murdered the husband of the woman with whom he committed the adultery. King David was the man, and he expressed his sorrow in the words of Psalm 51. You will find there the heart of repentance in full bloom. Take encouragement that this man was completely forgiven by God for what he had done.

And as for us, if we are in Christ, we share that same privilege and joy. This does not mean that all consequences will be taken away because we've turned to the Lord in repentance. But it does mean that God will not hold this sin over our head. He will forgive us and restore us to His corporate body when we uncover our sin before Him.

What we attempt to cover, God will uncover. But what we uncover, God will compassionately cover (see Psalm 32:1, 5). If you have engaged in adultery, now is the time to run to Christ for forgiveness and recommit yourself to your marriage vows.

Questions for Discussion

1. Read Luke 18:9-14. Write out the similarities you see between the Pharisee in Jesus' parable and the "old" Veronica—before she repented. Then write out the similarities you see between the attitude of the tax collector in Jesus' parable with the "new" Veronica.

2. Read through Romans 12:9-21. List five practical ways that Veronica can show love to Jordan.

3. Thinking about the Bible's teaching on forgiveness as taught in this chapter, list three excuses a Christian woman would likely give for not forgiving her husband. Then read Ephesians 4:32 and Colossians 3:12-14. How do the truths in these two passages help a Christian woman realize her need to forgive her husband?

4. In your own words, explain why the sin of unrepentant adultery results in the person being prohibited from entrance into the kingdom of God (1 Corinthians 6:9-20; see also Matthew 5:17-20; James 2:10).

5. Read Psalm 32. In your own words, describe the benefits and blessings of being forgiven by God.

12

Obsessive Compulsive Disorder

Whatever gain I had, I counted as loss for the sake of Christ.

Philippians 3:7

Carla's early childhood memories were pleasant enough. There hadn't been much to worry about then. She enjoyed being the only child…for a time…until fourth grade. That year her teacher began to send home not just a quarterly report card, but weekly progress reports. Was her homework done on time? Were there any errors in her assignments? How many math problems did she get wrong on the weekly quiz? Mom and Dad were teachers themselves, tenured professors at the local university. Mom had a doctorate in English literature. Dad's was in agricultural science. Of course they stressed excellence and top achievements in every subject. Nothing but the best grades in Carla's class were tolerated. Her parents were kindhearted people in their own way, but nothing would deter them from making sure their little girl was the best and had every opportunity for her future career.

Carla's response was to internalize any stress she experienced from these huge expectations because she loved to please her parents. As a child, she never considered that her parents were unrealistic. Not until she was a teenager did she realize the parents of her friends were not as exacting in their expectations as her own parents were with her. Still, she attributed this to the fact that they were simply high-achievers and exceptional in their own right. Education was important to them, and she shrugged off the extra effort and hard-earned praise. The last thing she wanted to do was to disappoint Mom and Dad.

Through grade school, middle school, and high school, Carla remained at the top of her classes. Studying constantly with very little social life, she was able to pull off straight As in every subject. Her devotion to excellence even included sports. She loved her fitness classes and sought to remain thin and trim through her teenage years. Carla knew that her parents wanted her to maintain a disciplined image in public; this was important to their social standing in the academic community. It was no surprise that near the end of high school, Carla was offered several full-ride scholarships to prestigious universities. She chose a university, and then proceeded to excel through college and graduate school just as she had in all her previous studies.

Carla's family was a churchgoing family. Her parents went to a Protestant church where many of their university colleagues attended. While she was still living at home, Carla began to see that her parents went to this church because it helped them with their social standing in the academic community. Seldom was the Bible taken seriously during the Sunday services. Most sermons were full of politics or pop psychology. When the Bible was mentioned, it was often dismissed as generally good advice but full of unenlightened errors. However, there was an older woman in that church—her Sunday school teacher—whom Carla really respected. She first heard the gospel message from this teacher, and she had noticed how reverently this teacher spoke of the Bible and the person of Jesus Christ.

While at the university, Carla's roommate invited her to attend a campus ministry meeting. There, she heard the gospel for the second time. Carla was surprised to see so many of her peers taking the Bible seriously—fellow students who were intelligent and very academically oriented. With more than just a little curiosity, Carla began to read a Bible that had been given to her, and as she read God's Word, she began to feel conviction of sin for the first time.

One evening, Carla's college roommate explained the gospel to her. Realizing her need for salvation, Carla repented of her sins and entrusted her life to Jesus Christ as Lord and Savior. This was a major turning point in her life—up till now, she had lived to please her parents. But she was learning from Scripture that she was to live to please Jesus Christ.

When Carla informed her parents about her newfound faith in Jesus Christ, they immediately showed disdain toward her—the first time that had ever happened. They let her know they were not happy with her news and expressed the unwelcome opinion that they believed she had taken up with some type of religious fanaticism on her campus. They begged her to get out of that group as quickly as possible and focus on her schooling. Although her parents' displeasure was extremely distressing to her, Carla was firm in her faith in Christ.

With help from her Christian friends, Carla found a Bible-teaching church and began attending every Sunday. The anxiety she experienced because of her parents' demands was somewhat eased by the growing relationships she enjoyed with her new Christian friends. Busy with her studies in the university, Carla tried not to think about her parents' displeasure and the alienation that had resulted.

Yet a growing unsettledness lingered. Carla's drive to regain their approval grew ever stronger as she approached graduation and it began to manifest itself in a kind of perfectionism. From girlhood, Carla had always been careful and precise about her daily habits—every hair in place, clothing clean and pressed, bed made each morning, and tidying up the bathroom sink after each use. Things like these were a part of who she was. But now, in her uncertainty brought on by the disapproval of her parents, she began to second-guess herself and pay far more attention to the daily details of life than she had previously—continually assessing and reassessing everything she did.

Following graduate school, Carla secured a high-paying job at a local law firm, and she remained active in her church. But as she adjusted into her new job, both Carla and her close friends could see certain behaviors becoming increasingly repetitive in her life. One day while Carla was having lunch with Marcia, one of her Christian friends, they both talked about obsessive compulsive behavior. Marcia had noticed Carla checking and rechecking certain things in an obsessive way.

For example, when Carla was asked to help clean up after refreshments were served to their Bible study group, she would go back and forth several times to make sure the coffee dispenser was turned off. On another occasion, after they had collected money to help a missionary family, Marcia observed Carla remaining after the meeting in a side room counting and recounting the money. What should have been a 15-minute task ended up taking Carla two hours to do.

On still another occasion, during a silent prayer time in their group, Marcia heard Carla whispering the same words over and over again: "Thank You, Jesus! Forgive me, Jesus! Thank You, Jesus! Forgive me, Jesus!" This went on for 20 minutes. Concerned for her friend, Marcia gently asked the obvious question: "If this is the way you are acting when you're around your friends, what are you doing at home and work?"

Carla's eyes filled with tears, and she looked away to regain her composure. Then she confessed to her friend that she was on probation at work. Her failures at work involved a similar problem of irresistible urges to check and recheck her work. Lately, she had been staying at the office longer, after everyone had gone home, just to be sure her work was done with excellence.

But even with all of this overtime, Carla was falling farther and farther behind. Her boss was emphatic that though he greatly appreciated her thoroughness, she was slowing down the entire office's productivity—so much so that if she did not improve the speed of her duties, she would be let go. This was new territory for Carla, never having failed at anything, but it appeared that she was headed toward losing her job. She was crushed at this prospect, but even more disturbing was the knowledge that her parents would likely blame her failure on her recent profession of faith in Christ. She did not want to bring reproach on Jesus Christ in her parents' eyes because she wanted them to surrender their lives to Him as well.

Marcia was not surprised by this news. This was a serious problem, and she was wanted to help her good friend. "I've done a little research about your behavior and I want you to read a short synopsis of it. Then tell me if this describes you. Whatever happens, I want you to know that I am committed to praying with you and for you about this." Carla was grateful for Marcia's offer of help and read the material her friend provided:

> The research in the area of Obsessive-Compulsive Disorder (OCD) is extensive and can be found in its own chapter in the DSM-5 under "Obsessive-Compulsive and Related Disorders."[16] OCD is classified as its own disorder, but is also related to disorders like "body dysmorphic disorder [consistent dissatisfaction with appearance or constant mirror checking], hoarding disorder, trichotillomania (hair-pulling disorder), excoriation (skin-picking) disorder," etc.[17]

Psychologists neatly define the difference between obsessions and compulsions. Obsessions are involuntary and undesirable. They are the unwanted, yet recurring, thoughts, desires, cravings, feelings, or images that a person experiences. Compulsions, on the other hand, are willful and voluntary. They are the repetitive behaviors that the individual feels driven by and has learned as a means to cope with life or a particular recurring situation.[18]

Compulsions are like inexorable rules that must be followed. It is admitted that many OCD conditions may overlap with some anxiety disorders. Hence, psychiatrists take special care to define what is taking place in the life of each patient. Where OCD differs from developmentally immature habits is in the recurrence of behavior far beyond the typical age of maturity in which the behavior generally stops.[19]

Specifically with OCD, those diagnosed with it generally have both obsessions and compulsions. In fact, it is often the case that a compulsion grows out of an undesirable obsession. "The aim is to reduce the distress triggered by obsessions or to prevent a feared event (e.g., becoming ill). However, these compulsions either are not connected in a realistic way to the feared event (e.g., arranging items symmetrically to prevent harm to a loved one) or are clearly excessive (e.g., showing for hours each day)."[20] Though a person may experience a reprieve from an unwanted obsession due to the implementation of his compulsive behavior, it is rarely true that a person derives pleasure from it.

There is a wide range of severity when it comes to compulsive behavior. Some have only a mild case (e.g., spending a few hours a day obsessing over a situation), while others live lives of relentless, moment-by-moment obsession and compulsion.[21] The most classic forms of OCD are as follows: "those of cleaning (contamination obsessions and cleaning compulsions); symmetry (symmetry obsessions and repeating, and counting compulsions); forbidden or taboo thoughts (e.g., aggressive, sexual, and religious obsessions and related compulsions); and harm (e.g., fears of harm to oneself or others and related checking compulsions)."[22]

Finally, OCD often appears with other disorders, including panic disorder, social anxiety disorder, specific phobia, depressive disorder or bipolar disorder, and some kinds of impulsive disorders and behaviors.[23]

Not wanting to further jeopardize her job, Carla waited until she arrived home that evening to think through the research carefully. Certain characteristics were clearly a part of her life, but others were not. Could it be that she had Obsessive Compulsive Disorder (OCD)? Marcia had recommended that Carla see a certified Christian counselor who had good biblical training. She was certain that the Bible had answers for this condition, but she knew Carla needed someone more qualified to help her. After contacting their church, Carla was put in touch with a woman counselor who was ready and willing to help her.

Weekly counseling sessions began soon after. Never had anyone taken such an intense interest in helping her through such a difficult problem and especially using the Bible in such a practical way. Her parents' influence had engendered independence and self-sufficiency in the past, and as a result, Carla often resisted letting anyone help her. However, she found this counselor, Sheila, was a tremendous help to her in both understanding what was happening to her and in showing how she could take reasonable steps to overcome these repetitive compulsive behaviors.

By asking good questions about Carla's upbringing, Sheila was able to show how Carla's response to her parents' high expectations had contributed to her present-day difficulties. Sheila's confidence in God's Word conveyed much hope. Carla learned that she did not have an incurable disorder, but that her repetitious behaviors flowed from the thoughts and intentions of her heart—her thoughts about herself and God. Her thinking and behavior would change by addressing the fears she had hidden within her. She had begun to think she was alone in having these episodes of abject fear and habitual behaviors, but that wasn't the case (1 Corinthians 10:13). Her counselor went on to explain four characteristic descriptions of a person who is experiencing uncontrolled episodes of compulsive behavior:

1. There are a preponderance of recurrent and persistent inappropriate thoughts, impulses, or even images experienced at some time during such an episode, causing a considerable amount of anxiety or distress.

2. These thoughts or images are so excessive and commanding that they go beyond common concerns about normal life problems.

3. Usually the person experiencing these dominating thoughts tries unsuccessfully, or with limited success, to suppress or even neutralize these thoughts by focusing upon other more pleasant thoughts.

4. There is always a recognition by the person experiencing these episodes that these obsessive thoughts are coming from their own internal thought processes and not from some external source.

Carla could personally relate to all four observations. Her repetitive thoughts and episodes had been dominating every aspect of her life and controlling nearly every waking moment. She described them to Sheila as "addictive canyons of thinking" because they created furrows in her thinking, draining every thought in her mind into one deep channel. No matter how hard she tried to think about other less anxious thoughts, her mind would rebel and her compulsive behaviors would repeat themselves. Sheila reassured Carla that she had known other Christians to struggle with similar behavioral patterns caused by unexpressed anxiousness and fears.

Compulsive thoughts of fear are the source of compulsive behaviors. There is no doubt that for Carla, many of the seeds of these thoughts were sown in her early childhood fears of disappointing her parents and others. Two common observations come from extensive studies of people who exhibit compulsive behaviors:

1. These repetitive physical behaviors (e.g., hand washing, ordering, checking) or mental behaviors (e.g., praying, counting, mouthing repeated words quietly like a mantra) occur because the person feels driven to perform them. This is often self-inflicted due to self-appropriated rigid rules or in response to an obsession.

2. Both the recurrent physical and mental behaviors have a purpose or goal of either eliminating or reducing personal distress, or possibly preventing some dreaded future event. Yet both the physical and mental behaviors are not realistically connected to the very things they are attempting to prevent or neutralize.

As Carla was learning more about her compulsive behaviors, she realized she had a hidden behavior she had revealed to no one. Before leaving her apartment in the morning, she would stand in front of her mirror and brush her hair more than 200 times with a plastic-tipped wire brush. In her anxiety, she had allowed the intensity of this activity to become so excessive that parts of her scalp were now raw and bleeding. Knowing this was shameful behavior, lately she had been wearing fashionable hats and beanies so she could hide the disgraceful sores and bald spots on the crown of her head. Why would she do such awful things to herself?

Looking back, one of Carla's most pleasant childhood memories was of a tradition her mother had each evening before Carla went to bed. Her mother would come to her room and brush her hair in front of her vanity mirror. This was so relaxing that eventually she got to the point she could not go to sleep without this routine. When her mother stopped brushing her hair in her early teens, it had become more difficult for Carla to fall asleep. She now realized why she did this: It made her feel relaxed and at ease before going out in public. But it also had the unwanted opposite effect of making her feel ill-at-ease because of the embarrassment the habit caused. What had started as a comfort measure had turned into an anxiety-producing activity.

Carla and Sheila spent a considerable amount of time discussing insights into Carla's pattern of thoughts and behaviors given the four observations about those who exhibited compulsive behaviors. Carla finally realized that what she was experiencing was not strange or unusual. Earlier, she had begun to question her sanity because of her inability to stop certain invasive thoughts and stubborn behaviors. But others had faced similar challenges and had been able to overcome them with God's help.

Carla also began to fully comprehend how her patterns of fearful thoughts went back into her childhood. Knowing this was helpful because it enabled her to see why her pervasive anxious thoughts were not something she could easily change by sheer willpower. They had deep historical roots in her thinking with years of reinforcing and rehearsing. She was encouraged to learn that her behavioral repetitions were not random, but had a purpose—they were attempting to relieve the anxiety and distress she was experiencing. However, instead of bringing relief, they only served to magnify her fears with greater intensity and frequency. What was once a mysterious anomaly to Carla was now beginning to make sense as she gained a better understanding of herself and the role her thoughts and fears played in these behaviors.

Although Carla had already been a Christian for a few years, her habitual compulsive behaviors had been brought over into her Christian walk and now were directly affecting her testimony before others, especially her unbelieving parents. She needed to see these behaviors as part of the continuing presence of the sinful condition of the flesh. This is referred to in Romans 6:19 as the lingering condition of the believer's "natural limitations" (i.e. "weakness of your flesh"). No person becomes perfect or sinless when they repent and believe in Jesus Christ. Sinful tendencies and habits are brought into the Christian life from one's days as an unbeliever and may still cause a person to stumble and fall long after she has become a believer. The difference, however, is that the Christian now possesses the ability to radically change through obedience to the Word of God and the enabling power of the Holy Spirit (15:13).

Although Carla was more than willing to work on changing her bad habits with the help of Scripture, she was concerned that a possible biological abnormality in her brain was causing her compulsive thoughts and behavior. She asked Sheila, "If this were true, then how could I be held responsible for my thoughts or my actions?"

Sheila confirmed that this was a valid question which needed an answer. Although she was not a neurological expert on the brain or the nervous system, she produced from her files a helpful article by Dr. Jeffrey Schwartz, one of the world's foremost authorities on the underlying mechanisms of obsessive compulsive disorder. He wrote,

The cause, at a neurological level, is hyper-connectivity between two brain regions, the orbitofrontal cortex and the caudate nucleus, creating a tidal wave of unfounded mortal fear and triggering habitual response as the only way to attain calm. But the worst part is that, despite recognition that all these thoughts and behaviors are irrational, the OCD sufferer feels driven to obey them, nonetheless.[24]

Schwartz's studies used Positron Emission Tomography (PET) scans on OCD patients to find the critical regions of the brain that were affected. Sheila went on to explain that he also found that for those patients who practiced a "mindfulness-based" treatment strategy (a form of verbal therapy and not chemical therapy), structural changes were observed in the brain. Mindfulness-based meditation encourages OCD patients to stand back dispassionately from their compulsive thoughts and impulses.

If a patient suffered from a constant obsession with dirty hands and a compulsion to wash them, Schwartz advised his patient to think: This is not an urge to wash my hands, this is a bothersome thought brought about by my OCD.[25]

Schwartz says that even mature adult brains have a considerable amount of "neuroplasticity." Most adults still possess a lot of flexibility to change even deeply engrained thought patterns. This treatment relies on a radical refocusing of thoughts away from the impulses and urges to a dispassionate recognition that it is the OCD producing them. Post-therapy PET scans showed a considerable change in the brain of the OCD patient who followed the treatment. Such non-chemical treatments have evidenced a high degree of success.

Sheila explained that if unbelievers with OCD thoughts and

behaviors could enjoy this type of success, then how much more should that be true of a believer who possessed the authority of God's Word and the power of the Holy Spirit (Romans 8:2-4). Carla was in full agreement, eager to pursue a biblical solution to her problem. They began with a biblical process that involved four major steps toward durable change. These steps were similar to those applied through "Mindfulness Meditation," but they involved a radically different "Christ-focused" redirection of thoughts. Each step is redefined by biblical truth.

• • • • •

Here are the four steps critical for changing compulsive thoughts and behaviors for the Christian:

1. *Repent*—This includes identifying and confessing all the obsessive fearful (un-Christlike) thoughts which control you because they sinfully deny the goodness of a sovereign God, and because they presume on your own self-righteous ability to abide by rigid rules of thoughts and behaviors that are unbiblical and supposedly will provide you with peace and joy (Romans 14:17; 1 John 1:9-10).

2. *Relabel*—All of these anxious and fearful thoughts are to be labeled as the chief source of your sinful condition (recurrent thoughts and behaviors); choose to fear only the Lord, because sinful thoughts elevate earthly concerns over heavenly concerns. They exalt the creature over the Creator; they are self-centered, not Christ-centered (Psalm 34:9; Proverbs 1:7, 29; 29:25; Luke 12:4-5; 2 Corinthians 5:9).

3. *Replace*—Substitute anxious and fearful thoughts with thinking that fully trusts your future welfare into the hands of a good and loving God in whom your life is hid. He is your Redeemer, Lord, Rock, Shield, and Sovereign (Psalm 18:2; 119:114; 144:2; 2 Corinthians 4:5; 1 Timothy 6:15).

4. *Refocus*—Devote yourself to loving God and others; don't feed the human tendency to love yourself (Matthew 22:36-40; James 2:8; 1 John 4:18).

• • • • •

Carla began by making an exhaustive list of all of her compulsive fears. Anything that caused anxiety in her life was placed on this list. Her lists included anxiety over going out in public; her deep-seated fears of disappointing other people, especially her boss and her parents; her fearfulness of not being exceptional in everything. Together, Carla and Sheila discussed the steps above and how each one would be applied to her particular compulsions. Sheila cautioned that change would take time, but for most people who daily practice these steps, there is significant improvement within six to ten weeks. Carla was grateful to learn that other believers had been freed from such dominating fears (Proverbs 1:33; Romans 8:15). Whenever these fears arose in her own life, she needed to repent and determine how she could grow in her trust of the Lord (Psalm 23:1-6; Proverbs 3:5-8).

First, Carla wrote out the list of rigid rules that had governed her compulsive thoughts and behaviors—rules that she had believed were the answer to her distress and her pursuit of a better life full of ease and comfort. Instead, they had been deceptive slave masters, ingraining within her cyclical and unprofitable thinking that had caused even greater despair. When her list was complete, Carla and

Sheila had an extended time of confessional prayer, during which Carla *repented* of her fears that had become idolatrous substitutes for the fear of the Lord and obedience to His Word (Psalm 32:5). For the first time in a long time, Carla experienced the joy found in forgiveness.

Then Shelia encouraged Carla to carefully *relabel* each of her fears using a sheet of paper divided into two columns. On the left side she wrote all her fears and rules. On the right side she wrote all the ways those fears and rules failed to trust God or bring glory to Him (1 Corinthians 10:31; 1 Peter 4:11). In addition, for each item listed, she was to find as many Scripture passages as she could that pointed out the consequences of failing to trust the Lord (Proverbs 22:8; Hosea 10:12-13; Galatians 6:7-8). Not used to thinking biblically, this took quite a long time for Carla to do, but she found the exercise extremely beneficial.

Now it was time for Carla to implement *replacement* in this process of change—an important step in looking to the Lord for His help. For every specific way she had responded to life with sinful fear and rules, Carla was to write out a specific plan for how she now intended to trust the Lord, including verses that spoke of God's goodness and promises to her (Psalm 37:3, 5; Proverbs 3:5-6; Jeremiah 9:23-24). When this step was completed, Sheila carefully reviewed Carla's plan and encouraged her to memorize Scripture passages that would remind Carla to trust God in various situations. Memorization was important because it was these verses that would replace her fearful thoughts of the past. The more Carla practiced right thinking and trust in God, the more compulsion's grip on her life was slowly released. Carla found that biblical truth and obedience truly do change thinking *and* brain chemistry.

Compulsive fears make us intensely self-centered, not Christ-centered, which creates idolatrous cravings in the heart. An idol is anything you become obsessed with other than God Himself. Carla's desires had been for others to see her as exceptional, be in awe of the quality of her work at the office, and be impressed with her dedication at Bible studies. In addition, she had created rigid standards for herself to meet—and they were exceptionally high standards. Those elevated standards demonstrated how highly she thought of herself—how much she was filled with pride and self-righteousness. Repetitious thinking and behaving fed this idol of wanting to be pleased with herself, of longing for others to be pleased with her.

Through the years, Carla's pride had become a harsh taskmaster. She could not bring all of her expectations to pass at all times no matter how gifted, talented, and intelligent she was. By the time she realized this, the obsessive/compulsive patterns had become well established in her life. And the solution was to *refocus* her thoughts on loving God and others!

There had been a little change in Carla's thinking and behavior when she became a Christian while attending the university, but now she needed to appropriate all the blessings of being "in Christ" (Romans 8:2, 10). This change had to penetrate into every area of her life. Together with Sheila, she studied Scripture and read theological articles that explain what it meant to be "in Christ."

The truth that Christ had lived and obeyed God the Father perfectly *on her behalf* was very helpful in refocusing her thought life. Carla's motivation for doing all things with excellence—which a Christian should be committed to doing—changed from doing these things for the praise of man and her own prideful satisfaction to doing these things out of love for Christ. One of the most practical results of understanding her undeserved position of being "in Christ" was the new energy she had toward loving God and others. She also discovered that where genuine grace-driven Christian love abides, there is no room for fear: "There is no fear in love, but perfect love casts out fear. For fear has to do with punishment, and whoever fears has not been perfected in love" (1 John 4:18).

As the counseling sessions proceeded, Carla become increasingly aware of how little she loved God and others. Obsessive-compulsive living was wasting her life on herself. One of the most helpful assignments Sheila gave was for Carla to carefully identify how she had failed to love God in her disobedience. What were some of the tragic consequences of this failure? She knew her testimony to her parents had been harmed. She realized that her ministry in the Bible study group failed to glorify God because she was so focused on being seen doing her best. Even her own personal worship was affected because her mind was so preoccupied with her own self-accomplishments that her ability to fully acknowledge and grant to the Lord His worth and worthiness was stilted. In short, her love for God was pitifully deficient (John 14:15; 15:10).

With Sheila's help, Carla developed a daily schedule of personal worship. It was not long before she realized how much this helped to enhance her experience of public worship at church. This motivated her all the more to make this a daily routine. She became personally consumed with worship, and her love for God grew.

Carla's obsessive behavior also revealed her lack of love for others, which was often due to neglect. She was so consumed with herself she had no time to think about others and their welfare, much less do helpful things for them. She began volunteering more at church, offering to cook meals for the sick and shut-ins. She began to reach out to other women at the office, inviting them to her home for dinner and using the opportunity to share the gospel. Her efficiency at work greatly improved, and within a year her boss had gone from almost firing her to giving her a promotion. In fact, she became regarded as one of the most valuable employees at her law firm.

But the great difference this time around is that her behaviors were not motivated by a desire to please people. Rather, she was doing these things to show love to them. She saw everything she did as being a service to Christ and a means of bringing glory to Him. She was no longer focused on what she could receive, but on what she could give.

The changes in Carla were striking, and her parents wanted to know what had brought about such a radical transformation. One day she was able to sit down with them and share her whole story. They saw how Jesus Christ meant everything to her and witnessed her unwavering confidence in Him. That same afternoon, both her parents humbled themselves and asked Jesus Christ to become their Lord and Savior.

Carla had thought she would never see the day when her two proud university professor parents would surrender their lives to the Savior. But Christ had made it possible. There were many tears shed that day, and it was a day that Carla would never forget. Jesus Christ had changed her life, and He had used this change to bring her parents to Himself. This made her realize all the more just how much she could trust God and His desires for her life.

Questions for Discussion

1. Describe the effect that Carla's parents' expectations had on her thinking about herself and her performance in the eyes of others. How can godly parents carefully set the bar high enough for their children so as to discourage laziness and encourage a good work ethic and, at the same time, not place too much pressure on them? In your response, consider what Ephesians 6:1-4 and Proverbs 3 have to say.

2. Children naturally want to please their parents and make them proud. How can they be raised to please their parents

in the proper way so that they (a) learn a healthy response to disappointment when they fail, and (b) do not develop a slavish dependence on their parents? In your answer, take into consideration how the gospel can free children from slavish dependence—see Acts 4:12, Matthew 22:37-40, and Colossians 3:17.

3. A diagnosis like OCD—Obsessive Compulsive Disorder—can lead a Christian to believe that the only one who can be of help is an expert in the field of psychology. Explain why this is not the case, and how God's Word speaks to the issues that this person is facing.

4. Describe how Carla's uncontrolled thought life turned ordinary fears turned into compulsive fears.

5. Why is learning to love others a key part of overcoming compulsive fear?

13

Panic Attacks

Do not be afraid of sudden terror or of the
ruin of the wicked, when it comes.

PROVERBS 3:25

It happened in the grocery store, of all places—Valerie's first *public* panic attack. That growing sense of impending doom, her heart rate increasing, her breathing accelerating, pressure building in her chest, nausea, cold and clammy hands, and the feeling she was about to faint had all become familiar sensations as her "at home" panic attacks had become more frequent over the past year. *What is happening to me?* she wondered. *Am I having a heart attack? Am I dying?* As she began trembling all over, Valerie's appearance drew the attention of the store's manager. Despite her protests that she was fine, he called 9-1-1, and she was taken away in an ambulance to the nearest hospital.

As soon as Valerie was in the ambulance, her symptoms began to abate. Between the emergency personnel listening to her heart, taking her blood pressure, and giving her oxygen, Valerie was quite embarrassed. How could she convince them that she now felt fine? No one listened to her objections, and upon arrival at the emergency

228 • The Biblical Counseling Guide for Women

room (ER) of the hospital, the medical staff ordered several tests to check out her heart.

A few hours later, the medical tests revealed no serious problems. Still, the ER physician was concerned about the intensity of Valerie's episode. Lately she had been having two or three panic attacks a week. They had been increasing in intensity, and this one had been the worst yet. The doctor discussed with her some common treatment options for panic attacks, including selective serotonin reuptake inhibitors (SSRIs) or antidepressants. [26]

The doctor went on to explain that these medications treat the symptoms of panic disorder, and that within a few weeks the number and severity of the attacks should decrease as well as the fear and anxiety that often accompanied her attacks. Valerie stared at the small white prescription sheet in her hands. Was this the course of action she wanted to take? The doctor did make it clear that the medications would not cure the problem; they would simply address the symptoms. Valerie knew this meant the medication would only serve to mask the cause of the panic instead of addressing it. What would get at the core of her problem?

After her release from the ER, Valerie waited for her husband, Steve, to arrive. He had just finished work and arrived at the hospital with concern written all over his face. He was relieved to hear that all the tests were negative, but he recognized that his wife of eight years needed help. Unable to have children up till this point, Valerie worked very hard in her career as a physician's assistant. Perhaps the pressure from her job was bringing on the attacks—after all, the other attacks had happened in the evenings after a long day of work. Steve gave his wife a long embrace. "How are you doing? I was worried about you!"

As devoted Christians, Steve and Valerie had prayed together about her attacks several times, but the problem only got worse.

Steve's concern was justified because there were times when her home panic attacks would put her into an almost full-catatonic state for several minutes. This could not continue, as it was beginning to take control of her life. Something had to change. And they both had agreed that the real answer to her problem was not going to come from psychiatric medication.

Valerie herself worked in an emergency room as a highly trained physician's assistant. Almost every day she was called upon to perform life-and-death medical procedures, having to making quick judgments in order to try to help save the life of a patient. Routinely she would see people who had been mangled in an accident, or had been shot, or had suffered from some type of heart attack or stroke. She was good at what she did, and everyone who worked with her spoke highly about her job performance.

Amazingly, there was never a time when Valerie suffered from a panic attack on the job. She recognized this as the grace of God. But with the frequency and intensity of the attacks increasing, as well as this public attack at the grocery store, Valerie realized that it was very possible her next attack could happen at work—when the lives of others were dependent on her.

Valerie was thankful that, after her attack, she had been taken to a hospital across town, where none of her coworkers would be able to witness her weakness and inability to handle herself in the moment of an attack. Desperate for release from the growing bondage of panic, Valerie was ready to seek help from a Christian counselor. Steve called their church office and set up an appointment for her to meet with one of their well-trained biblical counselors. Husband and wife were filled with hope and anticipation.

Dana listened carefully to Valerie as she shared her history with panic attacks. Normally a stable person, it was the unexpectedness of the episodes that was so puzzling. They seemed to happen at arbitrary and random times, during which she would lose all sense of control. She could not think of any reason these panic attacks should be happening. At the time they occurred, her thinking was not focused on anything threatening or fearful, so what was triggering them? What disturbed Valerie most was the increasing intensity of the attacks. Her experience with each new attack seemed to so overpower her that she began to wonder if there was some demonic power in play. With all that in mind, Valerie lived in dread of the next attack.

Dana brought up the question of a medical difficulty: Might Valerie have an undiagnosed medical problem? There are some physical diseases and disorders that can produce symptoms of panic attacks. Most of these organic problems are easily diagnosed or discovered through fairly common medical tests and procedures. Valerie had already gone through a list of them carefully and discussed them with her doctor:[27] Here were the possibilities they ruled out:

Cardiovascular

- Angina pectoris
- Myocardial infarction (heart attack) and recovery from
- Arrhythmia
- Postural orthostatic hypotension
- Coronary artery disease
- Congestive heart failure
- Stroke and transient ischemic attack
- Hypertension
- Tachycardia
- Mitral stenosis or mitral valve prolapse

Respiratory

- Asthma
- Emphysema
- Bronchitis Hypoxia
- Collagen disease
- Pulmonary fibrosis, embolism, or edema

Endocrine/hormonal

- Carcinoid tumor
- Pheochromocytoma
- Hyperthyroidism
- Premenstrual syndrome
- Hypoglycemia
- Pregnancy

Neurological/muscular

- Compression neuropathies
- Myasthenia gravis
- Guillain-Barre syndrome
- Temporal lobe epilepsy

Aural

- Benign positional vertigo
- Meniere's disease
- Labyrinthitis

- Otitis media
- Mastoiditis

Hematic

- Anemia: iron deficiency, Vitamin B-12, sickle cell, folic acid

Drug-related

- Stimulant use: alcohol, prescription or illegal drugs or withdrawal
- Withdrawal: drugs, alcohol, prescribed medication
- Side effects of many medications

Miscellaneous

- Caffeinism
- Head injury

Dana was relieved to hear about how thoroughly Valerie had ruled out any real physical problem along with her medical doctor. It was time to turn to Scripture to diagnose the source of her panic and discover the biblical remedy. Opening their Bibles to 2 Peter 1:3, Dana asked Valerie to read the verse out loud: "His divine power has granted to us all things that pertain to life and godliness, through the knowledge of him who called us to his own glory and excellence."

This means that God has provided answers for people experiencing *all* types of spiritual problems, including panic attacks. Fear and anxiety are inevitable because we live in a sin-cursed world. Rational fear will lead us to feel anxious when we walk down inner-city streets at night or we're confronted by a wild animal. We often experience anxiety before having a medical procedure, taking an exam, or while standing on the edge of a high cliff. Such anxiety is useful because it can make us more cautious and careful. God created us with a degree of fear so that we would not do anything unnecessarily dangerous or foolish.

A person who does not like heights, spiders, germs, large bodies of water, or flying in airplanes will experience panic on account of their specific fear. And when that person is taken away from whatever caused the panic, their fear will subside. But for some people, episodes of panic can occur without any perceived threat or cause. What makes their situation worse is that the anxiety from the attack doesn't usually go away after a while. It usually increases over time, to the point the fearful person becomes afraid of fear itself. Valerie could relate to that.

In the Bible, there is a type of anxiety that is good. Paul used the Greek term μεριμνάω when describing the "anxiety" or care that Christians should have for one another (1 Corinthians 12:25). This form of anxiety is a deep concern and constructive care believers should possess for one another. This is the type of anxiety Valerie demonstrates on the job in the ER. She is anxious to do a good job and save lives.

But using the same Greek word, Paul also warned that there is a sinful form of anxiety that is destructive and unproductive (Philippians 4:6). This is not an anxiousness to do good; rather, it is a fear that is overly focused on things that are beyond our control. When the mind and body have been subject to an intense form of anxiety over a long period of time, the result is an enslavement to autonomic-like reactions and responses that produce involuntary episodes of overwhelming fear-like experiences which are often called panic attacks. With this simple clarification, Valerie was ready to begin to take inventory of how she was processing her stressful life, especially on the job.

Dana assigned Valerie the task of keeping a thought journal to record each time she began to feel anxious or fearful. It consisted of answering four important questions:

1. What was happening when she realized she was anxious or fearful?

2. Where did her thoughts go when she became anxious or fearful?

3. What did she want when she became anxious or fearful?

4. What does God say about her anxious and fearful thoughts and desires?

The journal was helpful because it enabled Dana and Valerie to see that Valerie's anxiety stemmed, in part, from a conscientious and caring heart. Valerie really cared for the people under her watch, she cared deeply for her husband, and she put a lot of effort into caring for their home. There was no doubt these self-imposed pressures brought an intensity to her life that was difficult to maintain, taking a toll on her mind and body over time.

It also became clear from the thought journal that Valerie's good thoughts and intentions had begun to rule her spirit, producing worry and anxiety. Dana assured Valerie that giving her time, attention, and energy to the proper care on her job and in her home was not the same thing as worry. In addition, it was not an anxiety issue to be a good planner who looked ahead to future events and challenges. But Dana wanted Valerie to see that her thought life was focusing too much on the fearful possibilities in the future and her inability to control the outcomes. Her thought life was so given over to these things that she had begun to worry and fret over them.

Worry becomes sinful when the Christian becomes overly anxious about the future as well as the welfare of people and important things. In Matthew 6:25, Jesus said, "I tell you, do not be anxious about your life, what you will eat or what you will drink, nor about your body, what you will put on. Is not life more than food, and the body more than clothing?" The worrier tries to take God's place and control the outcomes. She needs instead to rely upon God's sovereign goodness, even though He may ordain what she considers to be unfavorable circumstances (1 Samuel 2:6-7; Ecclesiastes 7:14; Isaiah 45:7; Lamentations 3:38).

The Christian can trust God's wisdom and faithfulness to her at all times (Proverbs 3:5-6). The etymology of the Greek term having to do with worry emphasizes the *actions* and *effects* of worry. The New Testament term translated "worry" means "to divide, part, rip, tear apart, be anxious, distract your attention" (see Matthew 12:25; Mark 4:19). When the believer worries about future circumstances, her attention is drawn away from her priorities and responsibilities in life, and eventually she will become unproductive.

Valerie began to realize that a large portion of her daily thoughts were filled with worrisome expectations. How would she ever handle the death of a patient in her care? What would she do if Steve somehow lost his job? Surely she must work harder and save more money in case that happened. She tried to justify this intensity by telling herself she was just doing her best, but her journal revealed that her thoughts had gone way beyond a mere dedication to her responsibilities. This is where counseling was helpful for her. Dana helped Valerie to discern when genuine concern had in fact become sinful worry:

1. When her thoughts were focused on changing the future.

2. When her thoughts became cyclical and unproductive.

3. When concern controlled her instead of her controlling it.

4. When concern caused her to neglect other godly responsibilities and relationships.

5. When concern began to damage her body.

6. When she lost sight of God and the hope He provides instead of seeking good, godly answers.

7. When it paralyzed her and she ceased to function.

Sinful anxiety and worry are centered on the self. They ask, "What can *I* do to bring about good and meet *my* expectations?" In contrast, righteous concern focuses on seeking to benefit others while trusting in God's work to produce what *He* perceives to be good (Matthew 22:37-40).

Eventually Valerie came to see that self-centered thinking had marked her thought life long before her first panic attack. This self-centered thought life had not prevented her from doing good to others, but it did reveal how her good intentions gradually turned into unbiblical expectations. She began to assume that she controlled much of her own life and its outcomes. As time passed, circumstances proved her wrong over and over again. Her inability to control so much of what happened in her life took its collective toll on her entire outlook. It also served to become fertile ground that nurtured many of her fears.

Just as there is a righteous side and an unrighteous side to anxiety, there is also a righteous side and an unrighteous side to fear. The Bible speaks about a godly fear and an ungodly fear. The fear of the Lord is a righteous fear that all believers should possess (Psalm 112:1, 7-8; Proverbs 1:7; 9:10; 2 Corinthians 5:11; 1 Peter 2:17). This does not mean that a Christian should be terrified by the Lord or be in deep dread of Him. Rather, this kind of fear is a deep, reverential respect for the Lord's sovereignty and goodness as He exercises His omnipotent will. It recognizes that He is in control of all things and everything is subject to Him (Psalm 33:11; 115:3; 135:6; Lamentations 3:37-38; Daniel 4:35).

Valerie soon realized that during her panic attacks, she lost sight of God and His purposes for her. When she began to reflect upon her thinking during the midst of a panic attack, it became clear to her that in her fright she forgot God and began to think and react like an unbeliever. Dana pointed out that, according to Scripture, the ungodly have "no fear of God before their eyes" (Romans 3:18). This was a sobering wake-up call for Valerie. She had no difficulty trusting God when life was going smoothly, but when panic surged through her body, she abandoned her Lord by surrendering to her fears.

There is also a sinful side to fear. Any controlling fear that takes over a person, dominating their life and replacing the fear they should have of God alone, is ungodly and sinful. The dominant nature of these fears can be seen in the physiological reactions that occur during panic episodes—the heart palpitations, sweaty palms, lightheadedness, etc. They are also seen in the terrorizing thoughts of hopelessness that flood the mind. In order to address Valerie's fears, Dana and Valerie carefully studied seven theological observations in the Bible concerning fear. They studied and discussed each passage in order to determine what it meant in its original context, and then what it meant to Valerie in her situation.

1. Ungodly fears were directly related to what she was thinking (Genesis 12:11-13; Proverbs 4:23; Philippians 4:8).

2. When sinfully fearful or panicked, she was focused on the circumstances rather than on God (Genesis 32:7-12; Numbers 13:25–14:5; Psalm 55:22; 77:4-14; Mark 4:35-41).

3. When she panicked, she was focused on herself (Deuteronomy 7:17-18; Isaiah 51:12-13; Philippians 2:4).

4. When she was engaged in a panic episode, she was fearing something else more than she was fearing God (Job 1:13-20; 3:25; Proverbs 14:26-27; 29:25; Matthew 6:31-33; 10:28; Galatians 1:10; 2:12; Hebrews 13:5-6; 1 Peter 3:13-14).

5. When she succumbed to ungodly panic, it would most likely motivate her to commit other sins (Genesis 26:7; 1 Samuel 15:24; Matthew 26:69-70; Galatians 2:12).

6. Ungodly fear and panic accomplish absolutely nothing worthwhile (Proverbs 13:15; Matthew 6:27).

7. Not being right with God can lead to anxiety, fear, and panic (Psalm 38:17-18; Proverbs 28:1; Hebrews 9:27).

A careful study of God's Word was exactly what Valerie needed. Having been Christians for several years, she and Steve had faithfully prayed together, studied God's Word, and were involved in regular ministry at their church. Although she had heard many good sermons, she had seldom allowed God's truth to change her outlook on life; consequently, over the years, her thinking had not been disciplined by the Word.

As a result of the counsel she received, Valerie began to understand that the Christian life is not a static existence. One of the most memorable verses Dana shared with her came from the book of Proverbs: "Cease to hear instruction, my son, and you will stray from the words of knowledge" (19:27). There is a natural drift to the human heart, and it is a sinful drift away from the truth. Over the years, Valerie's heart had drifted from the truth, even though she was an active Christian.

Now things were beginning to change. As she studied Scripture and worked at living it out in her thoughts and actions, the panic attacks began to decline both in frequency and intensity. She could relate to the words of the apostle Peter: "For you were straying like sheep, but have now returned to the Shepherd and Overseer of your souls" (1 Peter 2:25).

Dana knew that Valerie's battle with panic attacks was going to need an effective biblical strategy. First, it needed to be *biblical* to work and bring about lasting change. Second, this strategy needed to be *practical* in order to be effective. Over several sessions they focused on a strategy that applied the truths of Philippians 4:6-9:

> Do not be anxious about anything, but in everything by prayer and supplication with thanksgiving let your requests be made known to God. And the peace of God, which surpasses all understanding, will guard your hearts and your minds in Christ Jesus. Finally, brothers, whatever is true, whatever is honorable, whatever is just, whatever is pure, whatever is lovely, whatever is commendable, if there is any excellence, if there is anything worthy of praise, think about these things. What you have learned and received and heard and seen in me—practice these things, and the God of peace will be with you.

This biblical strategy included three essential phases in conquering these panic attacks: the Readiness Phase, the Resistance Phase, and the Review Phase. Valerie needed a solid plan that would help her before (readiness), during (resistance), and after (review) a panic attack. All three phases were based upon the transformational truths of Philippians 4:6-9. After they studied the context and meaning of each scriptural reference, Dana had Valerie write out each point of her strategy and her plan for implementing it. She encouraged Valerie to give much thought and effort to this biblical strategy for bringing about real and lasting change.

Readiness Phase: How she can prepare before a panic attack strikes again

1. She needs to make sure her salvation is settled and repent of any known sin in her life (Psalm 32:5; 1 John 5:10-13).

2. She needs to confess and repent of her sins of mistrusting God and surrendering to panic and fear. This may include reconciling with people whom her sins have affected (Psalm 50:1-4; Matthew 5:23-24).

3. She needs to ask God to work in this area of her life and help her to put forth full effort toward change (2 Corinthians 9:8).

4. She needs to determine the right thoughts and actions to combat the ones she had wrongly assumed during past panic attacks. She should make her thoughts thankful, hopeful, trusting, and loving while using appropriate scriptures. Then she needs to turn these thoughts into prayers (Psalm 119:59-60).

5. She needs to memorize verses that will help her to renew her mind. These verses should be kept with her at all times, either written upon index cards or typed on an app in her cell phone, so that she has access to them in a moment's notice (Psalm 119:9-10; John 17:17).

6. She needs to do a careful study of God's sovereignty (Genesis 50:20; Isaiah 46:9-11; Jeremiah 32:27; Romans 8:28).

7. She needs to do a careful study on God's sufficient grace

(help) in times of trouble (Isaiah 41:10; 2 Corinthians 12:9; Hebrews 4:16).

8. She must daily choose to fear the Lord (see Proverbs 1:29) by studying, praying, and committing to loving God with all her heart (Deuteronomy 10:12-13, 20; Psalm 119:2).

9. She needs to be alert and ready to use grace-enabled self-control to defeat her fearful thoughts (James 1:13; 1 Peter 1:13).

Resistance Phase: What she must do during a panic attack

1. She needs to immediately and earnestly seek the Lord and His gracious help (Psalm 34:4; 46:1-3; 2 Corinthians 1:3-4).

2. She must *put off* fearful, God-dishonoring thoughts of panic (Isaiah 12:2; Ephesians 4:22-23; Colossians 3:8-9).

3. She must ask herself: "What am I fearing more than God?"

4. She must ask herself, "Are my thoughts headed in the wrong direction? Are they on the future? Are they on temporal things that pass away with time? Are they focused on untrue things? Are they focused on me? Are they devoid of God's hope and truth?"

5. She must *put on* trust, responsibility, and love (Ephesians 4:24; Colossians 3:10-11).

6. She must focus on God and His promises (Psalm 18:1-2).

7. She must make herself dwell on right thoughts and her memory verses. This will keep her focused on God's supply of grace in the present and not whatever the

future might hold. It will keep her focused on true, honorable, just, pure, lovely, commendable, excellent, and praiseworthy thoughts. It will enable her to have productive and not paralyzing thoughts.

8. She needs to ask herself, "How can I do what is right for this moment? What is the responsible thing to do right now? What is a loving thing I can do right now? What constructive things would God want me to do about this panicked situation?"

9. She must be willing to endure the physical sense and experience of panic, if necessary, in order to love God and others (2 Corinthians 4:17-18; 5:10-11).

Review Phase: What she can do if she fails and gives in to her panic and ungodly fears

1. She must ask herself, "How did I surrender to these fears and sin?" She must be specific about her thinking and how her frightful feelings controlled her.

2. She must ask herself, "If this were to happen again, what would I think and do differently next time?"

3. She needs to confess and ask forgiveness of God, as well as anyone else who was negatively affected by or a witness to her panic episode (James 5:16; 1 John 1:9).

Just having this biblical plan ready for use gave Valerie a great sense of relief. She knew the battle was not an easy one, and she also knew it was not going to be won quickly. Dana had warned her there would be setbacks. She needed to aim at growth, not perfection. But she took great comfort and security in knowing she had an effective strategy for combatting her panic attacks.

Valerie discovered, with the help of her thought journal, that her most vulnerable times were when she was relaxed and off guard. These were the times she was most subject to a panic attack. That's why her attacks hadn't occurred at work, but instead, took place in the evening or when she was doing something relaxing, like shopping. Knowing this helped Valerie to be more prepared.

Within a year, Valerie's panic attacks were completely gone. She was enjoying life again and greatly rejoiced in her Savior. Steve was delighted over her strong faith in God and the new confidence she exuded in her life. Others noticed too. She even had women in her church begin to come to her with their own fears and struggles over episodes of panic, asking for her help. She was able to share with them how the Word of God had dramatically changed her life and she encouraged them to seek biblical answers. Valerie personally understood—and had memorized—the apostle Paul's words about affliction and the help that the Lord supplies:

> Blessed be the God and Father of our Lord Jesus Christ, the Father of mercies and God of all comfort, who comforts us in all our affliction, so that we may be able to comfort those who are in any affliction, with the comfort with which we ourselves are comforted by God (2 Corinthians 1:3-4).

Questions for Discussion

1. As in Valerie's case, panic attacks often happen even when people are not feeling fearful, leading them to believe they have a medical problem. After ruling out a medical condition, why should a Christian look at this as a spiritual problem? Consider what Psalms 56 and 57 have to say as you give your answer.

2. Because Valerie was very confident in her job, she didn't consider herself a fearful person. Describe how Valerie's thought journal was helpful in identifying her fears even though her panic attacks happened when she wasn't feeling fearful.

3. The fear of the Lord is not the same thing as the paralyzing fear we experience when things look uncertain. Read Deuteronomy 10:12-13, then describe what it looks like for a Christian to live in fear of the Lord.

4. Explain why is it helpful for a person experiencing a panic attack to ask herself, "How can I do what is right at this moment? What is the responsible thing to do right now? What is a loving thing I can do right now? What constructive things would God want me to do about this panicked situation?"

5. Review this excerpt from the chapter. "Having been Christians for several years, she and Steve had faithfully prayed together, studied God's Word, and were involved in regular ministry at their church." With that in mind, how is it that panic attacks can happen even to faithful Christians?

14

Post-Traumatic Stress Disorder

My soul continually remembers it and is bowed down within me.

LAMENTATIONS 3:20

Trish bolted upright in bed, her heart pounding and her hands clenched. The terror within made her feel like she was suffocating. When would the nightmares stop? Would she ever forget?

For more than two years, Trish had kept her secret. She worked hard to avoid any conscious thought about the incident, but it was always lurking in the recesses of her mind, ready to raise its ugly head anytime a memory was involuntarily triggered. Today was such a day—her whole day colored by the nightmare that had awakened those horrible memories. But it wasn't always a nightmare. Sometimes it was a color, sometimes it was a smell, and sometimes it was someone who appeared to resemble him. Panic would grip her and she would stare into space, thinking that perhaps her silence and motionless body would somehow drive the fear out of her.

During such catatonic-like episodes, Trish would relive the unthinkable incident all over again, remembering and rehearsing all the gruesome details. Over the past 24 months, she must have relived it a hundred times over. Each flashback seemed more traumatic than the last. No one knew—not even her family or her friends. She kept this secret all to herself.

Just a few days after the incident, Trish had experienced her first dissociative episode. It was very traumatic, but lasted for only a couple of minutes. Over the past several months these flashback episodes of dissociative behavior had been growing in severity and length—now lasting nearly an hour. Reliving such a horrible event repeatedly was beyond terrifying; she was beginning to think that she was losing touch with reality. The strong emotions kindled with each flashback left her thoroughly exhausted and mentally drained. Nothing she did seemed to help, not even praying. Trish knew she could not continue to live at the mercy of such terror, especially as the effects seemed to be increasing in intensity.

The rape had changed her on a fundamental level. As a young teen, Trish had always thought herself to be tough—never turning down an opportunity to prove herself. But the vicious assault of her rape had weakened her considerably. In her behavioral studies class she had learned that according to statistics kept in the United States, every six minutes a woman reports being raped. That had been a mere statistic to her—until now. Her perspective forever changed, rape had become something that was disgustingly personal.

The attack happened when she was 17, while she was with her family on a camping trip with other members of the extended family. One morning while everyone left the campsite for a day hike, Trish stayed behind to catch up on her schoolwork. An hour after the family left, while she was settled into a comfortable lawn chair with her books, her uncle showed up unexpectedly. Uncle Ted had recently gone through a nasty divorce after being married for less than five years. No one knew he was coming on the camping trip, so Trish was quite surprised to see him. She cautiously welcomed him, but could tell he had been drinking.

Once Uncle Ted discovered everyone else was a long way off, he began to act inappropriately familiar with his niece. His eyes taking in her youthful form, with a smirk he remarked that she had grown up to be a *"fine* looking" young lady. Suddenly uncomfortable, Trish moved away from him and tried to change the subject, but he continued to pursue her, moving ever closer. In an instant he quickly pulled her close and gave her a long, passionate kiss.

Filled with fear, adrenaline kicked in and Trish tried to free herself from his strong grip. Enraged at her resistance, Ted reacted, "You're just like my ex-wife! You flaunt your 'attributes' and then act surprised when men accept your invitation!"

Still struggling to free herself, Trish shot back, "I did *not* give you an invitation!"

"Oh, so you really think you are better than me, don't you? You and your Christian 'holier than thou' attitude—I'll show you who is better!" Increasing his grip on her, he dragged her into one of the nearby tents. She landed on a pile of sleeping bags and, in an instant, he was on top of her. He was so much bigger and stronger than her. Even though she tried to fight him off, she could not.

The horrible feeling of utter helplessness was something she had never experienced before. It was so humiliating. She tried to scream, but he covered her mouth. In muffled words she kept saying, "Uncle Ted, don't! Uncle Ted, don't! This is not right!"

The whole event lasted only a few minutes, but to Trish it was as if time had stood still. Every movement, every feeling, every smell, and every expression on Uncle Ted's face was magnified many times over. It was all so repulsive and disgusting to her. It made her so sick to her stomach that she felt like throwing up. A gag reflex overcame her as he finished his nasty deed and left the tent. Uncle Ted then disappeared into the woods, and never returned to the campsite.

Trish laid in the tent for an hour, sobbing in humiliation and shame. She was thankful there were no other campers near their campsite. Fearing that Uncle Ted might return, she considered taking the family car and fleeing back to the city alone. But then she would have to reveal what had happened. As a Christian, she had been saving herself for her future husband, and in a brief few minutes, all of that had been stripped away. What would she say to her family?

They all knew Uncle Ted had serious problems, but she doubted anyone would believe her if she reported what had happened. She knew how much her mother loved her only brother and would often excuse his foolish behavior. If her dad believed her, he would probably overreact and do something violent to Uncle Ted. Then *he* might end up spending the rest of his life in prison!

Trish was unsure of what to do. She greatly feared disappointing her parents, who were so pleased that she had maintained her virginity all through high school when so many young girls her age had willingly given it away. She did not want them to look at her as damaged goods. In her confused thinking, she concluded it would be best not to say anything at all. She had to protect her family from this crisis. This was her personal cross, and she would bear it alone. She cleaned up the camp, took a long shower to scrub the vileness off her body, changed her clothes, and opened her books in a difficult attempt to get her mind back on her studies.

Late that afternoon, the family returned to the camp excited and hungry. She was so happy to see them, but felt awkward, as if they could see through her façade. But she also felt a warm and comforting security in their presence. Her father built a fire, and her mother prepared hot dogs for roasting. Everyone was laughing and joking, telling stories around the fire of that day's adventures, except Trish.

Noticing she was quiet and reserved, her mother asked, "Are you all right, Trish? Your eyes are bloodshot!" Trish quickly dismissed it. "I guess I overdid it with the studies today. I'm fine, really. I'm enjoying listening to all your stories. I wish I could have joined you on the hike today—it sounds like it was a lot of fun. As for my eyes…maybe my allergies have kicked up."

Trish's mother gazed at her for a few uncomfortable seconds, and then turned her attention back to the lively discussion around the fire. Trish had passed her first big "cover-up" test with her mom without breaking into tears.

That night, Trish got very little sleep. The next morning, she told her dad she was tired of camping and wanted to go home. He was surprised, because in the past, she had loved camping and hated it when they had to leave. He reassured her that they would return in two more days.

For Trish, those two days were torturous because the tent where she was raped was a constant reminder of those hideous few minutes with Uncle Ted. Almost everyone in her family noticed that she was acting uncharacteristically distracted and nervous, leaving her studies behind to go on every hike. But they attributed it to typical teenage moodiness and instability.

Returning to school and church, Trish had plenty of things to occupy her mind. Several weeks went by, and she came to believe she had truly put the Uncle Ted assault behind her. Everything seemed to be going well until one day she overheard her mother announce to her father that Uncle Ted was coming to visit for a day. Trish instantly felt a rush of panic wash over her like she had never experienced before. Her heart raced furiously, and she stood stunned and motionless for several seconds, a sense of impending dread swirling around her.

This was the worst possible news. How could Uncle Ted be so arrogant and unfeeling? Didn't he know what he had done was wicked and contemptible? All the ugly memories returned to her mind of those torturous moments of horror with him. How he had betrayed her trust, violated her, and showed no remorse! A wave of nausea swept over Trish and she ran to her room to hide her reaction from her parents. She determined to be away at a friend's house the entire time Uncle Ted was visiting.

Soon afterward, Trish began experiencing recurring nightmares. She would wake up several times a night, sweating and terrified, recalling the vividness of the rape that haunted her night after night. She was not sleeping deeply, and it was taking a toll on her patience and concentration. Her family noticed that she was acting uncharacteristically irritable. In addition, her grades were beginning to suffer. She had always been a good student, but now she was barely passing her courses. This was not good, especially as she approached graduation and looked forward to going to college.

Months passed with no improvement. Trish believed that she was losing her grip on reality and occasionally experienced bizarre hallucinations. Lack of sleep over an extended amount of time will have that effect. After four days of total sleep deprivation, most people will have a psychotic break. Psychosis is believed to be a serious mental condition featuring impaired thinking and emotions—so much so that the psychotic person loses contact with reality to one degree or another. Trish knew she was beginning to experience some of these symptoms. Although she was frightened by the persistence of these experiences, she still resisted talking with her parents.

One Sunday at church, Trish ran into one of the youth leaders, a woman who had noticed the changes in her and determined to reach out to her. Barbara wisely engaged her in some friendly and comfortable conversation, ending with the offer to disciple Trish if she would be interested. Barbara's kindness hit Trish at a vulnerable moment, and with tears beginning to form in her eyes, she agreed to begin meeting with her.

Later that evening, when Trish told her parents she would need the car to go meet with Barbara, they were relieved that she would be getting some help. They had been at a loss to know how to help their daughter, who had grown increasingly silent and sullen. They knew Barbara to be a gracious and knowledgeable woman. She knew her Bible well, and she was even a certified biblical counselor who had helped many women over the years. Trish knew this as well and was hopeful that she could share her secret with someone who could help pull her out of this living nightmare.

At their first meeting together, Trish arrived nervous and apprehensive. She was about to reveal something that she had never told anyone, not even her best friend. Thankfully, Barbara's compassionate demeanor made it easy for Trish to share what had been troubling her for so long. As Trish began to share her story, she was not prepared for the flood of emotions and tears that would accompany her revelation. It was like a dam had broken as she choked her way through her story—alternating between anger at her uncle, and shame and grief over her lost virginity.

As Trish wiped away her tears, she felt a wonderful sense of relief that finally, someone knew her secret. Trish was surprised at how emotional Barbara had become as she recounted the details of what had happened. Barbara cried with Trish and hugged her tight.

Trish had felt so filthy after the rape and she had wanted nothing more than to forget it had ever happened. But when she poured out her heart to Barbara, she knew this was the right thing to do. Trying to bury the memories had only produced recurring flashbacks, nightmares, and hallucinations—reliving that horrible day over and over again. Robbed of all her joy, she no longer had any interest in celebrating family birthdays or holidays. Fear, anger, and shame had been her constant companions. Where once she was a very happy and positive young lady, now she was uncharacteristically pessimistic about almost everything and everyone. She did not believe she could trust anyone anymore. She even secretly wondered whether she could trust God again with her life.

252 · The Biblical Counseling Guide for Women

Barbara was a good listener. Her tenderheartedness toward Trish was unmistakable and reassuring. She gently reminded Trish that the Bible says we live in a wicked and selfish world of sin and sometimes really bad things do happen to people (Jeremiah 5:26). Even though this is alarming, it is what God has said will happen because of the prevalence of wicked people with evil desires (Galatians 5:19-21). As well, God hates rape and condemns it as a sin of perverse wickedness (Judges 19:22-26; 2 Samuel 13:1-19).

Barbara further explained that God did not blame Trish for what happened. The rape was forced on her against her will, and God would judge Uncle Ted for his selfish wickedness (Proverbs 13:15, 21; 17:13). She then asked Trish to read aloud the following passage:

> If in the open country a man meets a young woman who is betrothed, and the man seizes her and lies with her, then only the man who lay with her shall die. But you shall do nothing to the young woman; she has committed no offense punishable by death. For this case is like that of a man attacking and murdering his neighbor, because he met her in the open country, and though the betrothed young woman cried for help there was no one to rescue her (Deuteronomy 22:25-27).

They both paused for a moment to think about what they had just read. In explanation, Barbara commented that in ancient Israel, betrothal was a binding contract between two families, often with an exchange of gifts, for their respective son and daughter to marry one another. During this time the couple would not live together or have sexual relations. To have a sexual relationship during this time was a sin similar to adultery. Because Trish had been a virgin and was reserving herself for her future husband, even though she was not engaged or betrothed, she too was innocent like the betrothed virgin woman. And under the Old Testament covenantal system, what

Uncle Ted had done required capital punishment. This shows how seriously God took this type of sin (Proverbs 6:30-33; 22:8).

The counsel that Trish was receiving from Barbara was beginning to make a lot of sense, helping her understand the confusion of feelings and emotions she'd been struggling with—especially her anger toward Uncle Ted. However, the trauma of the rape had caused her to question what God was doing in her life. Where was God when Uncle Ted had appeared? Why didn't God, who knows everything and is all-powerful, step in and stop the rape before it happened? How could anything good ever come from such evil?

Barbara reassured Trish that these questions were natural, since, as finite human beings, we have a very limited perspective on what God is doing in our lives. Trish's questions were similar to the ones Job asked after a great tragedy came upon him and his family. Job lost almost everything—his children, his wealth, and his health. Even his wife turned upon him, saying, "Do you still hold fast your integrity? Curse God and die" (Job 2:9). She gave up on God in response to great calamity, which revealed her weak faith in God.

But Job would not turn his back on God. He said to his wife, "You speak as one of the foolish women would speak. Shall we receive good from God, and shall we not receive evil?" (verse 10). We are told that "in all this Job did not sin with his lips" (verse 10).

We live in a sin-cursed world, and there will be times when God will permit His people to go through serious suffering and loss (Ecclesiastes 7:14-15; 1 Peter 3:13-14). This does not mean that God does not care. Not only does He care, but He is sympathetic to the suffering of His people.

Barbara invited Trish to read Hebrews 2:17-18 along with her:

> Therefore he had to be made like his brothers in every respect, so that he might become a merciful and faithful high priest in the service of God, to make propitiation

for the sins of the people. For because he himself has suffered when tempted, he is able to help those who are being tempted.

Tears returned to Trish's eyes. She remembered memorizing those verses along with Hebrews 4:15-16 when she started high school, and now they took on a completely new significance. She knew that her Lord not only saw her suffering, but had suffered an even greater indignity than she had. Jesus was totally innocent and did not deserve any of the suffering He endured (1 Peter 2:21-22). That means all the suffering He experienced in this world was unjust. Trish knew she was not perfect like Him, and that not all of the suffering she experienced in this world was unjust, even though the rape was a great injustice. Her eyes were now opened to the travesty that Christ had suffered at the hands of sinful man, and she humbly began to ask different questions.

"What is God up to when these injustices occur?" she asked.

Barbara responded with a question: "What do you believe is the greatest crime in all of human history?"

After careful thought Trish said, "I suppose it had to be the crucifixion of Jesus Christ, because He was both God and an absolutely perfect man who died for transgressions He never committed." Acknowledging that she was right, Barbara emphasized the fact that the Bible says the greatest crime in human history was all part of "the predetermined plan and foreknowledge of God" (Acts 2:23; 4:28). This was hard for Trish to comprehend, even though she fully trusted the Word of God.

However, it was important for Trish to believe in both the absolute sovereignty and goodness of God with regard to her suffering. God took the greatest evil in human history—the murder of Jesus—and turned it to the greatest good, eternal life for His people. It was *because* of the suffering and death of Jesus Christ that redemption was made possible for people.

Barbara wanted Trish to see that God could take this great evil in her life and turn it around for good (Genesis 45:4-9; 50:20; Romans 5:3-5; James 1:2-4). As devastating as the rape was, as well as the residual suffering, Trish was beginning to understand how God could take this evil perpetrated upon her and turn it around to be an asset in her life. Like affliction did for Job, this severe trial could strengthen her faith in God as she experienced His comfort and grace in a way that she would never understand when her life was going favorably. Furthermore, she would likely have opportunities to help and encourage other victims of wickedness with the comfort God provides (2 Corinthians 1:3-7).

Rather than growing in bitterness, self-pity, and unbelief, it was time for Trish to look forward to how she can view this as a way to become a stronger Christian woman. Barbara explained that *humble receptivity* is a heart attitude that can be cultivated by any Christian, but is most often developed in someone who has suffered greatly. Many Christians do not become truly open to spiritual change at the heart level until a major affliction comes into their life. Before difficulty arises, the perception of spiritual growth is usually limited to the practice of godly disciplines such as Bible reading, prayer, church attendance, etc. Adversity, on the other hand, often propels the Christian toward even greater trust in God and His Word.

The psalmist spoke clearly on this, saying, "Before I was afflicted I went astray, but now I keep your word" (Psalm 119:67), and "It is good for me that I was afflicted, that I might learn your statutes" (119:71). When a true Christian goes through such a traumatic event and asks the hard questions already mentioned, her search for answers should drive her toward greater faithfulness to study God's Word. It is in the pages of the Bible that she will learn God's character: that He is good and without sin (119:68), that He never tempts His children to sin (James 1:13), and that He is the protector and refuge of all who call upon His name in saving faith (Psalm 125:4-5).

"Many believers who have endured great hardships have often spoken of a new appreciation for the rich and robust nature of God's enabling grace and goodness," said Barbara. Trish listened carefully to all that Barbara was teaching her about God in relationship to her adversity, and wanted to ask God for humble receptivity so that she might honor Him in her life in spite of the difficulty she had faced.

A serious issue had yet to be addressed, and that pertained to Trish's age when the rape occurred. At age 17, she was considered by law to be a minor, placing the rape in the category of child abuse. Even though Trish was now an adult, as a counselor in her church, Barbara was required by law to report this abuse to the state authorities. This was hard for Trish to accept, because it meant that she would now have to tell her parents what had happened.

Because both Barbara and Trish wanted to be obedient to the law as Scripture commands (Romans 13:1-7; 1 Peter 2:13-14), they worked together to develop a plan to tell her parents. When the time came to let them know, Barbara was present along with Trish, who then shared with her mother and father all that had happened. Many tears were shed, but the meeting went much better than anticipated. No longer was it necessary for Trish to live a lie before them, and she felt as if a heavy weight had been lifted off her shoulders.

As a result, Uncle Ted was arrested, tried, and convicted of child molestation and rape. He was sentenced to prison for 20 years, and his name was placed on a child sex offenders list, where it would appear for the remainder of his life. God's Word had a softening effect on Trish's heart, and the anger she had formerly felt toward her uncle gradually changed to genuine concern for his soul (Proverbs 24:17). She and her parents covenanted together to pray for Uncle Ted, sending him a Bible and gospel tracts.

Although Trish began to sleep better with the biblical help of her counselor, she was still experiencing traumatic flashbacks and nightmares. She was manifesting classic symptoms of what is often referred to as Post-Traumatic Stress Disorder (PTSD), triggered by a memory, feeling, sight, or a sound. The nightmares came because of her unconscious fears that dominated her thought life. Scripture speaks to such episodes being so dramatic that they produce engrained automatic fearful responses.

Barbara helped Trish gain a practical approach from Scripture for dealing with these horrible recurring episodic events. First, Trish needed to cultivate her confidence in the Lord and His sovereign purposes. Without such confidence, she would continue to be subjected to her free-floating fears. The two chief characteristics of these sudden bursts of fear were that they were seemingly automatic and unconscious. Barbara and Trish began to study how the Christian should learn to trust God and fear Him during crisis events instead of fearing people and circumstances (Psalm 37:3,5; 91:1-16; Proverbs 3:5-6; 22:17-19; Luke 12:4-5). There is evil everywhere in this world where Satan asserts his will and, except for the restraint of the Holy Spirit, the whole earth would crumble into complete chaos and anarchy (2 Thessalonians 2:6-7).

Barbara shared with Trish a keen observation made by a Christian military chaplain after working with hundreds of soldiers who had returned from various war zones with PTSD. He said, "I can always tell a distinct difference between those who have a solid theological background and those who do not after witnessing firsthand the horrors of war. The Christians with a good background, coming from solid homes and churches, are deeply bothered by their experiences in war and for a time experience terrible flashbacks and nightmares, but they are quicker to return to normal than those without a good theology."

What was it about their theological training that helped them recover faster? They knew that the natural depravity of man that drives him to do wicked and hurtful things is not to be unexpected. During wartime, wickedness is unrestrained and mankind sinks to its lowest state because of sinful depravity. Those who are well-grounded in the teaching of God's Word understand that. But a person reared with the worldview that people are essentially good by nature ends up witnessing the opposite before his very eyes. He cannot make sense of the death and destruction that he sees, and having no hope, he spends the rest of his life reliving these unforgettable horrors, perpetually shell-shocked, and his worldview in shambles.

Trish did not want to live the rest of her life as a victim of PTSD, recycling the agonizing memories of her rape. She knew that a biblical worldview would not only help her rightly interpret her past, but it would also enable her to be released from its mind-numbing captivity. As Trish poured herself into Bible study with Barbara, she found great help in Proverbs 3:25-26: "Do not be afraid of sudden terror or of the ruin of the wicked, when it comes, for the LORD will be your confidence and will keep your foot from being caught" (see also 1 Peter 3:14). She committed these verses to memory so that each time a flashback occurred, she would instantly remember them rather than dwell on the vivid memories of the past. As a result, the intensity and frequency of her flashbacks began to diminish.

Trish eventually came to realize that her recurring flashbacks and nightmares were driven by a fear deep in her heart. Fear is a God-given capacity to be able to avoid possible danger (Psalm 56:3; Matthew 14:26-27). God created the body so that it experiences fear during times of distress through the way chemicals and hormones are regulated in the brain. These hyperarousal symptoms were a part of Trish's episodes and included feeling tense, being startled easily, and having trouble sleeping. As her episodes continued on over time, fear began to habitually enslave her thoughts.

The world then labels a person like this as having PTSD. The most common treatments for PTSD are extended psychotherapy and antidepressants.[28] It is important to understand that these psychopharmacological medications can only treat the symptoms, and not the underlying causes. From a biblical perspective, a person who has suffered a horrific event has been marked, not simply in their body/brain, but deeply in their soul. Their whole worldview is shattered. No medication can treat or heal a wounded soul. That's why Barbara wanted to get to a deeper level with Trish than just addressing repetitious symptoms. When the cause is properly addressed, the symptoms will naturally fade.

Trish's continual rehearsing of the rape in her mind showed that she was permitting those wicked memories to rule her thinking, as opposed to focusing on thoughts that would guard her heart and mind (Proverbs 4:23; Philippians 4:8). It demonstrated how she was focused on her losses in this world instead of the richness of her gains in Christ (Psalm 55:22; 77:4-14; Mark 4:35-41). When Trish recognized that the driving compulsion of her heart had become personal protection, then she clearly saw how fixated she had become on her own welfare as opposed to focusing on God and others (Deuteronomy 7:17-18; Isaiah 51:12-13; Romans 15:1-4; Philippians 2:4).

As long as this god of self-protection ruled her heart, there would be no place for the proper fear of God (Proverbs 1:7; 9:10-11; 29:25; Matthew 6:31-33; 10:28; Galatians 1:10; 2:12; Hebrews 13:5-6). Worshipping this god of self-protection had become a means of remaining vigilant, lest this should ever happen again—yet it was completely fear-driven and actively denied the promises and faithfulness of God. It was also a fear that resulted in other sins, like lying to her parents in order to cover up her sense of shame or giving lame excuses for allowing her grades in school to drop. Ungodly fears always lead to other closely associated sins like lying, cheating, irresponsibility, irritability, impatience, false accusations, hateful reactions, lack of prayer, and failure to trust the Lord (Genesis 26:7; 1 Samuel 15:24; Matthew 26:69-70; Galatians 2:12).

For two long years, Trish had allowed the trauma of the past to define her. She had come to view herself *only* as a victim, which left no room in her thinking for her true identity: beloved child of the Most High God. When she looked at herself in the mirror, she saw a "rape victim." She was sure that everyone around her saw the same thing, as though she had a huge *R* emblazoned on her forehead. Now that she was looking to Jesus Christ to help her overcome the life-dominating flashbacks and anguish, Trish began to ask some very important questions: "Who am I really? What does it mean to be a redeemed and beloved child of God? Can a Christian truly begin to rejoice in such a trial and see God work in it for her good?"

Trish carefully weighed her options: She could either continue to live as a rape victim—living at the mercy of flashbacks, sleeplessness, and hallucinations—or she could agree with Scripture that her identity as a Christian is firmly rooted in Jesus Christ. The difference that Jesus makes is that through His death, burial, and resurrection, He broke the power that sin once had over us—even sin that others commit against us. He gave us a new identity by adopting us as His children (Ephesians 1:3-14). Therefore, sin can no longer utterly destroy the child of God. Although we will sin and be sinned against, the power of sin to crush us is gone. Through the help of the Spirit of God, as we read His Word and obey it, we learn how to leave the past behind—free from enslavement to fear and sin (Psalm 23:1-6; 34:4; Isaiah 41:10; 61:1-8; Matthew 11:28-30; 1 Peter 5:7).

Because this trauma had come about due to someone sinning against her, Trish needed to learn the biblical concept of genuine forgiveness. She and her parents had been praying that Uncle Ted would repent and come to believe in Jesus Christ. But she also had to forgive Uncle Ted in her heart, which is what Jesus commands in Scripture (Matthew 6:12-14; Mark 11:25; Luke 11:4; 23:34). This might seem to pose a problem, because Uncle Ted was not repentant and didn't want to have anything to do with God or forgiveness. How could Trish go about forgiving him? In this case, Trish was to have a "ready to forgive" attitude toward Uncle Ted.

Each one of the passages listed above is taught within the context of prayer, where the offended party is praying to God. The one who sinned against her is not present. It is clear that this is not a time of reconciliation, where forgiveness is being granted to the one who sinned against the other. Rather, the emphasis of each text is upon the offended person making sure her heart is right before God, so that there is no longer any room for lingering bitterness, anger, or hatred. Theologians call this *attitudinal forgiveness* (Psalm 86:5).

Scripture is also clear that Trish should not say "I forgive you" to Uncle Ted until he has repented to God and to her (Luke 17:3-5). To offer him forgiveness without his repentance does not take sin seriously. It is critical for Uncle Ted to see the seriousness of his sin, first against a holy God, and then against Trish. As long as he continues in a state of unrepentance there will always be a barrier between him and Trish. If she happens to see him in the future, it will be important for her to bring up his sin against her as an opportunity to turn his attention to a far greater sin—his sin of failing to repent and surrender his life to Jesus Christ as his Lord and Savior.

Within a year, Trish was no longer having flashbacks or nightmares. Her symptoms were gone. This did not mean they would never return, but if they did, she was more than ready to battle them with biblical help. Before God, she was a restored virgin. Actively involved in her church, she had begun dating a Christian young man. If you asked her the secret of her dramatic change, she would give all the credit to her Lord Jesus Christ and the help He provided her through His Word and through a loving Christian counselor in her church.

Questions for Discussion

1. If you were trying to help a rape victim, how would you answer her question, "Where was God when I was being raped? Why didn't He protect me?"

2. Discuss why you think it is that "humble receptivity is a heart attitude that can be cultivated by any Christian, but is most often developed in someone who has suffered greatly." What heart attitudes tend to exist in Christians who have not suffered? Can you think of any examples where these attitudes are prevalent?

3. The secular counseling culture encourages rape victims to always view themselves as a victim. Discuss why this need not be true for the Christian, with consideration for what is said in Romans 8:18-39 and 1 Peter 4:12-19.

4. If Trish had chosen to be continually bitter against Uncle Ted, how would her unwillingness to forgive affect her walk with Christ and her relationships with others around her?

5. Because there are no assurances that a repeat offense will never happen, what Scripture would you share with Trish so that she might be free from terror and live in the light of God's love and care for her?

15

Schizophrenia

You keep him in perfect peace whose mind is stayed on you,
because he trusts in you.

ISAIAH 26:3

Sitting on the couch in her living room, Mary was engaged in quite an in-depth conversation. As she talked, her movements were animated and yet natural, and she seemed completely at ease. There was only one problem: she was completely alone in the room.

Mary's husband, Thomas, watched silently from the doorway, desperate to know how to help his wife of five years. Just the day before he had found her standing at the kitchen sink, holding her hands out in front of her and staring blankly at them. She kept repeating, "My hands are different than they used to be. One of them is larger than the other." Other unpredictable behavior and unusual comments from her were becoming commonplace, such as imagining things that were not there and acting surprised when other people could not see what she was sure she was seeing.

Thomas and Mary were in their early thirties, but had no children. They both longed for a baby, but had experienced three miscarriages. Recently Thomas had lost his job due to a corporate merger, and they had moved into her parent's large home while he looked for work.

The effects of these difficulties weighed heavily on them both. The economy was depressed, and no one was hiring for his skill set. The most recent miscarriage left Mary seriously depressed and withdrawn. For days afterward she would not eat and lost a lot of weight. Thomas tried his best to encourage her, but to no avail. Both he and her parents became so deeply concerned about her that they began to keep a list of her unusual behaviors, using it as a prayer list when they prayed for her together. Here is a composite sample of their prayer lists:

- This week Mary has been sleeping excessively, although the previous week she had hardly slept at all.

- She is beginning to isolate herself from friends and loved ones, sometimes being crassly indifferent to people and important events.

- We are noticing a significant personality change characterized by sustained bouts of depression at times, hyperactivity at other times, and occasional uncharacteristic hostility.

- She seems to have lost her ability to concentrate or deal with simple problems.

- Mary has become increasingly stubborn and inflexible.

- We are alarmed to observe unusual accidents or self-injuries; yesterday it appears that she was cutting her forearms.

- Usually so sharp in her thinking, Mary is becoming forgetful.

- Physically, Mary is not taking care of personal hygiene like she once did and has lost interest in eating. She is becoming dangerously thin.

- Her behavior is becoming more bizarre: she will stop whatever she is doing and begin hopping on one foot; she will burst out in laughter at the most inappropriate times; she will blink her eyes excessively when we try to talk with her; she will stare at an object for a several minutes without responding to anything else around her.

- Mary is filling up journal after journal with meaningless writing. We can't make sense of what she is saying.

- If we try to talk with Mary about her behaviors, she accuses us of not accepting and loving her. In fact, she is suspicious that we are talking about her all the time.

Mary's family understood that although some of these behaviors by themselves could be viewed as "normal," collectively they were alarming, especially since they were becoming increasingly habitual. She was quickly changing into a completely different person than the woman Tom had married.

Mary came from a good background—she had grown up in a family full of love for God and one another. Attending a Bible-teaching church with her parents, Mary had committed her life to Jesus Christ as her Lord and Savior when she was 16. Her father had been an elder in their church for almost 20 years, and her mother was very active in teaching a girls' seventh-grade Sunday school class and a women's Bible study.

Mary had met Tom on a mission trip to South America while she was in college. He too was a Christian and desired to marry a young lady with the same passion for Christ that he possessed. Mary seemed to be that kind of girl. But now something had changed in Mary on a most fundamental level. In spite of her surroundings, loving parents, and a husband who loved both her and the Lord, her grasp on reality was quickly slipping away. Tom had been somewhat discouraged by their recent setbacks with the loss of his job and their attempts to start a family, yet he believed they still had good reason to press forward with their lives in serving Christ. This new situation with Mary was perplexing beyond imagination.

Getting medical help for Mary seemed the wisest course of action. Although she was hostile to the idea, she eventually consented after gentle prodding from her family. Tom was eager to rule out any possible undiagnosed medical condition, like an aneurysm, brain cancer, or a tumor. After all the standard tests came back negative, Dr. Simon said that physically, Mary was perfectly healthy. After listening carefully to Tom describe the various changes in her behavior, her doctor recommended she be admitted to the psych ward of the local hospital for further observation and tests. He diagnosed her as having classic schizophrenia and provided a description of her disorder from the National Institute of Mental Health (NIMH):

> Schizophrenia is a chronic and severe disorder that affects how a person thinks, feels, and acts. Although schizophrenia is not as common as other mental disorders, it can be very disabling. Approximately 7 or 8 individuals out of 1,000 will have schizophrenia in their lifetime.
>
> People with the disorder may hear voices or see things that aren't there. They may believe other people are reading their minds, controlling their thoughts, or plotting to harm them. This can be scary and upsetting to people with the illness and make them withdrawn or extremely agitated. It can also be scary and upsetting to the people around them.
>
> People with schizophrenia may sometimes talk about strange or unusual ideas, which can make it difficult to carry on a conversation. They may sit for hours without moving or talking. Sometimes people with schizophrenia seem perfectly fine until they talk about what they are really thinking.[29]

Tom immediately recognized Mary's symptoms in this description. Dr. Simon carefully explained the definition to Tom and Mary and answered all their questions. Mary was noticeably agitated during the entire discussion and definitely did not want to be hospitalized for her condition. She openly argued with Tom and Dr. Simon, then broke down in tears.

Tom had some questions: "Was this a physical condition? What was the actual cause of her schizophrenic symptoms? Could Mary's condition be corrected?"

Dr. Simon explained that there is no definitive cause for schizophrenia, although many top researchers believe that many different genes tend to contribute to an increased likelihood of having the problem—even though no single gene has been proven to be a direct cause for it. Some of the best research suggests that schizophrenics have a higher incidence of rare genetic mutations involving hundreds of different types of genes. This, in combination with changing environmental factors, could contribute to schizophrenia in some people.

Other research points to abnormalities in brain chemistry, which may mean that imbalances in neurotransmitters—such as dopamine and glutamate—disrupt the brain's ability to process information or deal with reality. Still other top researchers note certain abnormalities in the structure of the brain that contribute to schizophrenia, which have been discovered through autopsy after the death of a schizophrenic.

Dr. Simon then read from the NIMH pamphlet, "For example, fluid-filled cavities at the center of the brain, called ventricles, are larger in some people with schizophrenia. The brains of people with the illness also tend to have less gray matter, and some areas of the brain may have less or more activity." [30]

Any or all of these theories may explain schizophrenia from a

268 • The Biblical Counseling Guide for Women

physiological viewpoint. Biological science seems to be getting closer to a reasonable scientific explanation. However, at this point, no one knows with absolute certainty its actual cause.

Tom pressed for additional information. "What is the standard medical treatment for schizophrenia?"

Dr. Simon explained that most schizophrenic patients are prescribed psychotherapy, which usually continues through the remainder of the person's life, as well as antipsychotics.[31] These drugs, however, do not cure the problem. They are simply used to alleviate the symptoms and to improve the patient's quality of life. Tom and Mary wanted to know if there were side-effects to antipsychotics, and Dr. Simon confirmed that yes, there were. Many of the drugs used have common side-effects such as drowsiness, dizziness when changing positions, blurred vision, rapid heartbeat, sensitivity to the sun, skin rashes, and menstrual problems for women.

Typical antipsychotic medications can affect physical movement, rigidity, persistent muscle spasms, tremors, and restlessness. Atypical antipsychotic medications can cause significant weight gain and increase the risk of diabetes and high blood cholesterol. Anyone who takes these drugs needs to be monitored by a qualified physician or psychiatrist in order to assure that there are no additional complications.

After hearing all this, both Tom and Mary were distressed and considerably bewildered over their limited options. Hospitalization, antipsychotics, and lifelong therapy were difficult conditions to accept. They informed Dr. Simon that they would get back to him after they had a chance to thoroughly discuss his recommendations and pray about them.

As Mary left the office to go to the front desk, Dr. Simon pulled Tom aside privately. He said that Tom should expect Mary's condition to deteriorate, that she would likely lose more and more touch with reality, and that Tom might have to make the decision of hospitalization against her will. Tom was taken aback by this possibility. He and Mary had always made major decisions together, and he was resistant to forcing her against her will. He hoped that day would never come.

Mary's doctor was right. Her condition did worsen. One day a counselor at their church suggested to Mary's mother they watch a documentary about a very intelligent woman who lived during the 1940s and 50s. The film chronicled the adult life of Brenda, who had been diagnosed with paranoid schizophrenia. As time went on, Brenda continued to slip deeper and deeper into her schizophrenia in spite of heroic methods used by psychiatrists to treat her. They even attempted insulin shock therapy, which was experimental and dangerous. Insulin shock therapy was an aggressive approach used exclusively from the 1940s through the 1960s as a form of rebooting the neurological system of schizophrenics in the hopes of returning their minds to normal.

The idea for doing this was based upon empirical observations that patients with epileptic seizures never seemed to experience schizophrenia. However, too many patients suffered devastating effects and even death from this form of radical shock therapy; it was eventually outlawed and replaced with neuroleptic drugs. Mary's family shuddered as they viewed what might have been her treatment had she been alive several decades earlier.

An observation made by Brenda's psychiatrist was enlightening. "This is the horror of schizophrenia, a person's inability to know with certainty what is real. Suppose you were to suddenly realize that everything and everyone that was so important to you was false and never true. The shock to your system would be almost unbearable. This is what Brenda is experiencing!"

Unfortunately, the shock treatments Brenda had received did

not bring her back to reality as hoped; in fact, they drove her deeper into her deception. Realizing that society did not approve of her imaginary life, she learned how to better disguise her schizophrenia from family and friends. Tom and Mary's parents realized that as Mary slipped into her alternate reality that she would always be confused about what was real and what was not. After reviewing Brenda's story, Mary's family wondered if the antipsychotic medications Mary would receive would encourage the same thing in her: leading her to be more deceptive with her imaginary world as well. She would likely not be helped at all with this type of treatment.

Tom and Mary, as well as Mary's parents, were decidedly against seeking this kind of medicinal and psychotherapeutic treatment. None of them were convinced that it would really help. Sitting in church that next Sunday morning, they noticed an announcement in the weekly flyer inviting anyone who needed counseling and specialized support to sign up for help from the biblical counseling ministry. They all agreed that this was the next step to take. Their request was answered by a woman named Connie. She and her husband, Jim, had counseled people in their church for more than 20 years using the Word of God. Connie was a certified biblical counselor and a registered nurse who worked in the cardiac unit of a nearby hospital.

After Connie met with Mary and her family, collecting as much background information as she could, she agreed to begin helping Mary. Because of Connie's years of experience, she knew that the best way to help would be to have the whole family involved in the counseling process. The plan then was for everyone to meet with Jim and Connie every other week. During the intermediate weeks, Connie would meet with Mary alone.

At the outset of counseling, Jim and Connie introduced the family to a process they called "Five Critical Components." In order for the counseling to be effective, everyone had to agree to implement these components throughout the counseling process. The counselors explained that each was very important in helping Mary change, and that they were to be carried out simultaneously. That's because schizophrenia is a difficult problem that involves a complexity of physiological and spiritual dimensions. The disposition of the soul directly affects the physiological condition of the body (brain) and vice-versa (Proverbs 3:7-8; 14:30; 15:30; 17:22; Ecclesiastes 8:1; Acts 6:15). Therefore, this would require a considerable amount of faithfulness to each component from everyone involved in Mary's life and even Mary herself. Because of their love for Mary, the family agreed to commit themselves to the entire process. Mary was reluctant at first because the prospect of change was intimidating, but she eventually agreed.

Tom asked, "Will antipsychotics need to be used?" The simple answer was, "Only as a last resort." They would be needed only if it became impossible to counsel Mary because of her detachment from reality. Hospitalization might also be necessary then, but only if she became physically uncontrollable. Psychotropic drugs and the hospital psych ward can be helpful as a measure of God's common grace to restrain evil and promote what is good in the world (Psalm 145:9; Matthew 5:45). They can keep people like Mary from severely hurting themselves or someone else. In this case of last resort, the drugs would be like chemical handcuffs. As hopeful as the counselors were, they knew there was no guarantee that Mary would listen and turn her back on her delusions. At the point that she chose her delusions over reality, then she would cease to be a counselee and instead become a patient.

There is this potential in every human heart. Ecclesiastes 9:3 is a good reminder: "This is an evil in all that is done under the sun, that the same event happens to all. Also, the hearts of the children

272 · The Biblical Counseling Guide for Women

of man are full of evil, and madness is in their hearts while they live, and after that they go to the dead." Medications can sometimes help to gain control of confused thoughts if the help they give outweighs the negative side-effects. But if Mary were to place her hopes primarily in the medication, that would not be good. Because she felt a little better and functioned better in the real world, she could wrongly think that everything was well in her life, when in reality the medication was merely enabling her to be a higher-functioning weak or sinful believer. Biblical counseling seeks to address the whole person, soul as well as body.

Component #1: Personal Counseling

Connie and Mary began meeting three times a week in order to establish the direction of change in her thoughts and behavior early on. There were five areas of biblical focus in the personal counseling component that were addressed with Mary concerning her schizophrenic-like symptoms. If a person manifesting schizophrenic-like symptoms is not a genuine believer in Jesus Christ as her Lord and Savior, then these areas of biblical focus will not be helpful to her. This is because the Holy Spirit is not present in her life, enabling her to make the internal changes that must be made. The Spirit's role is to authenticate the truth of Scripture and empower the believer toward living it out. But to the unbeliever, the Bible looks like merely one more book among many human ideas. In contrast, a Christian possesses the indwelling Spirit of God, and thus is able to recognize the authority of God's Word (2 Peter 1:20-21) and bear the fruit of the Spirit (Galatians 5:22-23).

Looking back to the documentary they had watched, Connie helped Mary evaluate why psychiatric treatment failed to help Brenda. They recalled that when all the drugs and shock therapy failed, it was the love of her husband and family that drew her back to reality. Then Connie said to Mary, "If the love that a family has for their wife and mother can help to deliver her from her schizophrenia, how much more can the love of your Savior, the Lord Jesus Christ, help to deliver you from your schizophrenia!"

She then had Mary open her Bible and read Romans 8:35-39 out loud:

> Who shall separate us from the love of Christ? Shall tribulation, or distress, or persecution, or famine, or nakedness, or danger, or sword? As it is written, "For your sake we are being killed all the day long; we are regarded as sheep to be slaughtered." No, in all these things we are more than conquerors through him who loved us. For I am sure that neither death nor life, nor angels nor rulers, nor things present nor things to come, nor powers, nor height nor depth, nor anything else in all creation, will be able to separate us from the love of God in Christ Jesus our Lord.

After reading the text, Mary sat silent for a few minutes with tears in her eyes. She said to Connie, "Do you suppose what verse 37 says about us being 'more than conquerors through him who loved us' is still true for me today?"

Immediately Connie responded, "Yes, I do! If the love of Christ is greater than severe persecution and death, then it is greater than your schizophrenia. This is where hope and change begins!"

Here is a summary of the five areas of focused concentration Mary and Connie explored together from Scripture.

Reality

Mary relied upon her own feelings and experience to determine her reality, and it was destroying her life. Feelings do not determine ultimate truth or what is real, and personal experience is unreliable and subject to false impressions and subjective interpretations. These can lead to mysticism and pseudo-experiences that appear real, but are not. A person like Mary can begin to believe things that are not true and imagine things that are not there, much like one of Job's counselors, Eliphaz the Temanite. His source of truth came from mystical encounters and words spoken in his own mind:

> Now a word was brought to me stealthily; my ear received the whisper of it. Amid thoughts from visions of the night, when deep sleep falls on men, dread came upon me, and trembling, which made all my bones shake. A spirit glided past my face; the hair of my flesh stood up. It stood still, but I could not discern its appearance. A form was before my eyes; there was silence, then I heard a voice: "Can mortal man be in the right before God? Can a man be pure before his Maker?" (Job 4:12-17).

This voice and Eliphaz's visions were a product of his own depraved imagination or some sort of demonic visitor. They did not come from the God of heaven. This demonic visitor used this esoteric experience to falsely accuse Job of having committed some unconfessed sin that brought on his great tragedy and loss. In a similar way, Mary's suspicious attitudes and actions toward members of her family and friends can result in false assumptions and accusations that are hurtful and not helpful.

Connie knew that Mary had allowed her personal experiences to become her chief authority. Her interpretations of reality were becoming the only authoritative truth she recognized as relevant to her. By contrast, the apostle Peter, one of the disciples who was closest to Jesus, did not allow his own *personal experiences* of walking next to Christ to be elevated to a level of final authority in his life. One of those experiences was "transcendent" in nature, meaning it was beyond what any ordinary man would see and hear. Mary and Connie turned their attention to Peter's words in 2 Peter 1:16-18, where he talked about his extraordinary encounter on the Mount of Transfiguration:

> We did not follow cleverly devised myths when we made known to you the power and coming of our Lord Jesus Christ, but we were eyewitnesses of his majesty. For when he received honor and glory from God the Father, and the voice was borne to him by the Majestic Glory, "This is my beloved Son, with whom I am well pleased," we ourselves heard this very voice borne from heaven, for we were with him on the holy mountain.

Peter was saying that if you want to talk about the reliability of personal experience, it doesn't get any better than this. He saw Jesus Christ transfigured before his very eyes, Jesus' face shining like the sun and His clothes dazzling white. He also heard the voice of God speak audibly. What he saw and heard was unmistakable. However, even though this was his personal experience in the flesh, he spoke of something far more reliable in 2 Peter 1:19-21:

> We have the prophetic word more fully confirmed, to which you will do well to pay attention as to a lamp shining in a dark place, until the day dawns and the morning star rises in your hearts, knowing this first of all, that no prophecy of Scripture comes from someone's own interpretation. For no prophecy was ever produced by the will of man, but men spoke from God as they were carried along by the Holy Spirit.

Even though Peter's encounter was supernatural, he made it clear he trusted God's Word more than his experience. As great as this phenomenon was that he witnessed on the Mount of Transfiguration, it was the Word of God that was more fully confirmed (verse 19). He did not trust his experience as much as he trusted God's Word. Connie and Mary spent a considerable amount of time studying this passage and discussing its implications for Mary. Connie made sure that Mary kept detailed notes throughout the sessions.

Another biblical example comes from the life of the apostle Paul. He too was a dedicated apostle of Jesus Christ to whom God had entrusted the "surpassing greatness" of special revelations (2 Corinthians 12:7). Yet he understood the fallacies of his own perceptions and judgments. He wrote in 1 Corinthians 4:4, "I am not aware of anything against myself, but I am not thereby acquitted. It is the Lord who judges me."

Paul's conscience was not his guide, but it was his guard. In other words, the human conscience can be misinformed, full of bias, and limited in its understanding—but God is not. His will and His Word are always reliable. Therefore, as Paul said, it is not the conscience that is the final judge, it is the Lord.

With that in mind, Mary had to learn to mistrust her own judgments. What was going to define reality for her? Was it going to be her personal experiences and feelings, or was it going to be God's Word? A schizophrenic is ready to change when she learns to mistrust herself and trust God's truth instead (Proverbs 12:15; 16:2; 21:2; 30:12).

Mary and Connie also did a careful study of Psalm 36, noting how the Bible describes human judgment as untrustworthy, and noting in contrast how loving and trustworthy is God's care for His people. They also memorized Proverbs 30:5-6 together and would quote it before every counseling session. "Every word of God proves true; he is a shield to those who take refuge in him. Do not add to his words, lest he rebuke you and you be found a liar."

Humility

For Mary to learn to mistrust her perception of reality was a necessary prerequisite to attaining humility. Humility is greatly lacking in schizophrenics like Mary. They become stubborn and obstinate because prideful and self-centered thoughts consume their thinking. Connie and Mary spent several weeks discussing and studying the biblical importance of cultivating humble thoughts and attitudes in her life. Pride can be such a destructive force in a believer's life and can even distort her view of circumstances and people. Scripture speaks of...

- pride of position (Matthew 23:6-12; 1 Peter 5:3)

- pride of ability or achievement (1 Corinthians 4:6-7; 2 Chronicles 26:15-16)

- pride of possessions (1 Timothy 6:17)

- pride of knowledge (Isaiah 47:10; 1 Corinthians 8:1; James 3:13-18)

- pride of spiritual attainment (Luke 22:24-30)

God hates pride, calling it a self-destructive sin (Proverbs 6:16-17; 16:5; 21:4). Pride is the essence of foolishness that leads to madness (Ecclesiastes 7:22-25). Mary slowly began to recognize how her thinking had been consumed with arrogant and self-righteous thoughts. For example: *People are out to hurt me. They are always talking about me. They don't understand me or care about me. I have to look out for myself. I will only listen to voices that tell me how to protect or hide myself. My secret and imaginative world is a safe place, everywhere else is dangerous.* Mary then began to capture those thoughts and label them as sinful as she learned to trust God's Word over her own perceptions and judgments.

Then Connie and Mary turned to studying the biblical concept of humility and how she could incorporate its truth into her daily thought life. This is where counseling turned to considering and modeling the life of Jesus Christ. Schizophrenics are ruled by self-importance; Jesus Christ demonstrates self-denial. If Mary was going to follow Christ, then she had to learn the spiritual discipline of self-denial (Luke 9:23).

Together Mary and Connie dug into Philippians 2:1-13, observing how Jesus had no selfish ambition or conceit, but took upon Himself the appearance of a slave, even though by nature He was God (verse 7). This was the attitude and approach that Mary needed in her life. The argument from the greater to the lesser says this: If Mary's Lord and Savior was willing to be a slave among men, then how much more—as His subject—should she be ready to assume the same attitude and role. Mary was startled to realize how lacking her life was when it came to humility. No wonder she was having so many hardships and difficulties (Matthew 11:29-30; James 4:6). This marked the beginning of some substantial changes in her life.

Joy

Humility and joy are closely related in Scripture. Humble people are joyful people because they have few or limited expectations for their life. Their cravings and desires are simple because their chief joy is bringing pleasure and glory to God (Proverbs 10:28). Mary had not experienced genuine Christian joy for some time. She was too wrapped up in her own fears and worries. Whatever made her feel safe or secure was her main focus. Sometimes her alternate reality centered on pleasing imaginary friends because it was easy to do that, and she was fearful of rejection from the real people in her life.

A contributing factor to Mary's lack of joy was the disorganized way she went about her everyday responsibilities. The more tasks that she failed to complete, the more withdrawn and joyless she became. Daily living became a chore. She found herself sitting motionless in a catatonic-like state for extended periods of time, doing nothing productive. As her irresponsibility increased, so did her joyless experience of life.

Joyful people sing (Psalm 68:3; 89:1), and Mary didn't sing anymore. She had a beautiful voice and, in the past, she loved to sing during the worship services at church. Now silent, her body was present in the pew, but her soul was distracted with self-interest. Rather than enjoying the experience of worship among God's people, she was disconnected and suspicious concerning the intentions of everyone around her. They made her uncomfortable and apprehensive.

After King David confessed his sin of adultery and murder, he cried out to God, "Restore to me the *joy* of your salvation, and uphold me with a willing spirit" (51:12). In this psalm, David was repenting of his own transgressions. Repentance is the beginning of finding joy again. If Mary wanted to have her joy restored, she too would need to repent.

- She will need to repent of allowing her feelings and experiences to create an alternate reality for her, rather than living in God's reality (Psalm 63:6-7; 84:1-4).

- She will need to repent of suspicious attitudes toward her friends and family—attitudes that reveal her self-centered and prideful heart (Psalm 131:1-3).

- She will need to repent of being consumed by her fears and failing to take refuge in the Lord (Psalm 5:11).

Following her repentance, Mary was reminded of the joyful news that God had saved her, though she was an unworthy sinner (Isaiah 12:3; 29:19). Together Mary and Connie studied the first two chapters of Ephesians. They carefully noted, verse by verse, the goodness of God's grace in saving her. She also was once "dead in the trespasses and sins…carrying out the desires of the body and mind, and [was] by nature [a child] of wrath, like the rest of mankind" (2:1, 3). She had been made alive in Christ—"by grace you have been saved"—totally apart from any worthiness of her own (Ephesians 2:5). Mary was able to look at these verses with fresh eyes, fully aware of how marvelous God's gift of eternal life was:

> By grace you have been saved through faith. And this is not your own doing; it is the gift of God, not a result of works, so that no one may boast. For we are his workmanship, created in Christ Jesus for good works, which God prepared beforehand, that we should walk in them (Ephesians 2:8-10).

As these words took on a new and deeper meaning for Mary, her heart was filled with joy! Connie brought a hymnal to their counseling sessions and they began to spend a portion of their time together singing choruses and hymns that spoke of the wonders of redemption in Christ. Mary was awakened anew to the joy of singing about her Savior. It was not long before she was looking forward to Sunday worship services again, joining the entire church family in exalting the Savior through song.

Fear

One of Mary's symptoms was a severely distressed mood that was evidenced in an unusually heightened form of anxiety. That meant that often she would be restless and active at night and then sleep during the day. It was at night that Mary would be alone with her own thoughts, and subsequently her mind would pulse with fears about her health, her safety, or her mental stability. Once her thoughts were racing, adrenaline was stimulated, which caused persistent insomnia.

She would be up all night pacing the floor while she talked to herself or imaginary people.

The biblical truth Mary learned about her fears was that they were a sinful lack of trust in the goodness and faithfulness of God. She believed her fears more than she believed that God was good and faithful to her, as promised in His Word. Trusting in His goodness did not mean that her life would be trouble-free, but it did mean that she had to recognize that God would not allow anything into her life that would be more than she could bear (1 Corinthians 1:9; 10:13). Mary began to memorize many Scripture passages concerning the faithfulness of God. Meditating on these truths slowly changed her thinking and helped her turn away from her fears.

There were seven theological principles concerning fear that Connie and Mary explored together while Mary took careful notes:

1. Controlling fears come directly from her own thoughts (Genesis 12:11-13; Proverbs 4:23; Philippians 4:8).

2. When sinful fears take command of her thoughts, she is focused on her circumstances and not on God (Genesis 32:7-12; Numbers 13:25–14:5; Psalm 55:22; 77:4-14; Mark 4:35-41).

3. Sinful fears reveal she is self-centered and not God-centered (Deuteronomy 7:17-18; Isaiah 51:12-13; Philippians 2:4).

4. When she is controlled by ungodly fear, she cannot be controlled by a fear of the Lord (Job 1:13-20; 3:25; Proverbs 14:26-27; 29:25; Matthew 6:31-33; 10:28; Galatians 1:10; 2:12; Hebrews 13:5-6; 1 Peter 3:13-14).

5. Ungodly fears will lead her to commit other sins (Genesis 26:7; 1 Samuel 15:24; Matthew 26:69-70; Galatians 2:12).

6. Ungodly fears will destroy any worthwhile productivity in her life (Proverbs 13:15; Matthew 6:27).

7. When she fails to repent of sin in her life, it can lead to ungodly fears and anxiety (Psalm 38:17-18; Proverbs 4:23; 28:1; Hebrew 9:27).

Connie encouraged Mary to keep a Bible and a journal next to her bed. In this journal she would have notes she had taken during their counseling sessions, prayer lists, and references to passages on the faithfulness of God. Each night, when she went to bed, she was to read through her notes and look up the passages in her Bible. She was to fill her mind with the promises and presence of God in her life. After she finished reading she could listen to some recordings of hymns from her cell phone. This would help to focus her thoughts on wholesome, righteous things rather than on fearful, ungodly things.

Gradually, as a result of doing these things, Mary began to sleep longer and deeper. This rewarded her with better mental dexterity and acuity during the day. Slowly she was able to become more focused and concentrate on her responsibilities during the day.

Anger

One of the most uncharacteristic features of Mary's schizophrenia was the anger and hostility. Previously she had been an even-tempered, caring person. Now, although she never became aggressive, she would often become inappropriately angry at the most awkward times. She had developed a social cognition deficit, especially in relationship to her ability to assess the intentions of people around her.

Sometimes Mary's inability to interpret her environment did not involve people, but irrelevant events or arbitrary stimuli. Whatever the case, Mary would lose her temper. When her inappropriate anger was directed at people, they were surprised and taken aback, not knowing what they had said or done to provoke such a strong reaction. Her family learned to approach her gently in order to calm her down. If they later confronted her about her explosive reaction, she would become embarrassingly uneasy and could not recall why she had reacted that way.

These ten theological truths concerning anger were instrumental in helping Mary return to her calm, loving self:

1. Sinful anger is a deed of her flesh (Galatians 5:19-20).

2. Anger is natural to the sinful human heart (Genesis 6:5; Matthew 15:18-19; Titus 3:3).

3. Anger always involves her thoughts and intentions (Proverbs 4:23; Ephesians 4:17-18).

4. Sinful anger is directly caused by not being able to attain her prideful and selfish goals (James 4:1-3).

5. Sinful anger never accomplishes God's righteous purposes (Proverbs 11:23; James 1:20).

6. Sometimes her anger will point to something good and right that should be done about a problem (Psalm 119:4, 9, 15-16; Proverbs 14:8).

7. Anger is expressed in a person's thoughts, body language, speech, and actions (Psalm 19:14; Romans 6:12-13).

8. Sinful anger involves a lack of mental self-control (Proverbs 17:27; 25:28; 29:11; 2 Peter 1:6).

9. Sinful anger is often accompanied by other sins when she allows it to be tolerated (Proverbs 29:22).

10. When she allows sinful anger to continue, it will eventually become something worse (Ezekiel 18:30; Hosea 8:7; 10:13; Galatians 6:7).

Having had much difficulty with concentrating, it seemed impossible for Mary to concentrate on these truths about anger. But the more she focused her thoughts and practiced mental self-discipline, the easier it became. Mary was discovering that she had more neuroplasticity than she knew.

Component #2: Family Counseling

Helping a person like Mary requires the investment of almost everyone in her life who is close to her. Studies have indicated that when the family of a schizophrenic is involved with their recovery, the success rate is much higher. This was certainly true for Mary. When the family met together with her in counseling, they learned how to think and behave around her in ways that were both biblical and helpful to Mary's progress. They gained insight into the hard work that Mary was putting into changing from someone controlled by schizophrenia to someone controlled by the Spirit of God. This was greatly encouraging to Tom and Mary's parents.

These sessions also provided a considerable amount of time for reviewing the most effective ways to help Mary when she retreated into her old symptoms. Stress was placed on the virtues of patience and gentleness, because the road to recovery could be long and hard (Galatians 6:1-2; Ephesians 4:1-3; 1 Thessalonians 5:14-15). But it was their genuine love for her that would make the difference, as well as their encouragement for her to be faithful to what she was learning through her personal counseling.

Component #3: Problem-Solving and Skills Counseling

Mary's church was able to get involved in her recovery as well. Connie invited two Christian ladies who were former schoolteachers to help Mary with her reasoning skills. They were able to supply problem-solving exercises for Mary to do, sometimes with pencil and paper, and sometimes using computer games. She met with them once a week over a ten-week period, and they were able to gradually increase the complexity of the exercises they gave to Mary as her problem-solving skills improved.

The two schoolteachers started slowly, testing Mary's ability to recognize details. Then they moved to more difficult problems as Mary became more proficient. Early in these sessions they asked Mary to copy, by hand, specially selected verses from Scripture onto paper. Many of these verses were the same ones Connie had used in her counseling sessions with Mary. The teachers then evaluated how well Mary copied and spelled each word.

Later they had Mary write brief personal comments about some of the verses. She eventually graduated to copying whole paragraphs and then entire chapters from the Bible. Included in these sessions were simple mind puzzles, computer programs that emphasized matching, and picture puzzles—moving from simple to complex. At times, some of the exercises were frustrating for Mary, but as her mental acuity developed she began to look forward to the challenges. Her ability to concentrate grew from a span of only a few minutes to more than 30 minutes before they were finished. Mary's husband and parents were extremely pleased with her progress.

Component #4: Journaling and Organizational Counseling

After a month of counseling, Mary was given an assignment: She was to journal her thoughts every day. Anytime she became angry or fearful, she was to answer four questions in her journal:

1. What was happening?
2. What did you say or do?
3. What were you thinking, and what did you want?

286 · The Biblical Counseling Guide for Women

4. What should you be thinking and wanting, according to Scripture?

Even if Mary did not know what Scripture said about her thoughts or responses, she was still supposed to answer question 4 as best as possible, knowing that Connie would assist her at the next counseling appointment. At first the notes in Mary's journal were very scattered and garbled. But as time went on, her sentences became more coherent and her reasoning improved. Through all this, Connie was gaining a much clearer picture of how Mary's thinking was developing.

Another assignment given to Mary was for her to develop a daily organizational planning guide. Each evening before she went to bed, she was to make a chart of the things she needed to accomplish the next day. Then she was to prioritize each item on her list from the most important item to the least. This required abstract thought, which had been difficult for her to do when she began coming to the counseling sessions.

Whenever Mary had problems organizing the items on her charts, Connie would help her think through the reasons for prioritizing some items over others. This was extremely helpful to Mary, and her reasoning abilities gradually developed and became more sophisticated.

Component #5: Weekly Worship and Group Bible Study

After only two sessions, Mary was required by Connie to begin attending church again. At first she was to attend only the Sunday service each week. But later, Sunday school class was added, and then a Bible study group. This was important not only for the social-relational skills Mary needed to relearn, but so that she could sit under the teaching of God's Word again and participate in corporate worship. In time, Mary's love for singing and for hearing the Word of God preached returned. It was a gradual process, but God was gracious to her each step of the way.

Eventually Mary overcame her schizophrenia completely. God used her to bless other women, and she went on to become a teacher in the women's group in her church. The women loved her teaching because they could see how personally committed she was to the sufficiency of God's Word to change lives.

Questions for Discussion

1. Many people, when they hear the term *schizophrenia,* immediately associate it with an incurable brain disorder that can be handled only by psychological professionals. Describe how Connie was able to help Mary with God's Word.

2. What difficult life circumstances triggered Mary's schizophrenic behavior? What was it about her perception of these experiences that led her down this path?

3. "Mary relied upon her own feelings and experience to determine her reality, and it was destroying her life." Many women who are not schizophrenic also see life solely through their feelings and experiences, which leads them to make decisions based on those feelings and experiences. Although these women will not necessarily exhibit schizophrenic-like behavior, they are still failing to let God's Word determine what is real and what is not. Read Psalm 103, and explain how it would help a woman to anchor her life in the truth of who God is and what He does for us.

4. Explain how a schizophrenic response to life's difficulties reveals self-centeredness.

5. What is the role of pride in the thinking of the schizophrenic? How would you counsel a person toward humility?

16

Transgenderism

If anyone would come after me,
let him deny himself and take up his cross daily and follow me.

LUKE 9:23

The phone rang in Jon's office immediately after he returned from lunch. The unfamiliar voice at the other end of the line was the guidance counselor at the high school where his daughter Patricia was a student. A mild panic rushed through him, for he couldn't recall ever having been contacted by a school administrator. Reports of school shootings were becoming more frequent, and he couldn't help but think about the potential danger that Patricia faced each day.

The guidance counselor asked Jon, "Would you and your wife be available to come by the high school today, say around 2:30, to meet with myself and a couple of our staff?" Taking a deep breath, Jon replied, "Is anything wrong with Patricia?" Mrs. Smith reassured him, "No, there is nothing wrong at all. This is just an important informational meeting." A bit apprehensive, Jon agreed to pick up his wife, Teresa, and meet them at the school.

On the short drive from their home to the school, Jon and Teresa speculated about the subject and importance of this meeting. Their 16-year-old daughter was a bright student and excelled in sports.

Perhaps this meeting was about Patricia receiving some academic or athletic award. Graduation was just 18 months away, and any scholarship would be helpful as she was making decisions about which universities to send applications to.

When Jon and Teresa arrived, they were ushered into a small administrative boardroom where five school officials were sitting across the table and their daughter was seated off to one side. Patricia was looking at the floor and made no effort to make eye contact with her parents, which made Jon and Teresa's hearts sink within them. The whole scene appeared to be somewhat awkward and contrived. There sat the high school principal, the school counselor, a school board member, and two teachers. It would not require such a formal group of the high school staff to inform them of an award for academic or athletic achievement. Jon and Teresa had obviously mistaken the purpose of this meeting; something *was* seriously wrong.

The guidance counselor, Mrs. Smith, proceeded to thank Jon and Teresa for coming because they were about to witness an important and serious transition in Patricia's life. Their role in this change would be critical to the continuing success of their child. Without further preliminary remarks, she then announced that Patricia no longer wanted to be known as Patricia. Instead, from this day forward, she wanted to be identified as a male. *His* name was not Patricia, but Patrick.

Jon and Teresa felt as if all the oxygen had been sucked out of the room. They were completely bewildered. The very idea that this was happening with their daughter seemed to come out of nowhere. Emotional shock set in as Mrs. Smith continued. "As a public high school we intend to be completely supportive of Patrick, providing all the encouragement and help he will need in order to establish his own masculine identity. We believe that the exploration of one's gender identity is crucial to our students' ability to find themselves, and thus to be able to make their way in the world—both here at the high school and beyond. This is a necessary part of their development into young adults. Some of our students identify as they always have from birth; others strongly object to the gender identity they have lived with and choose another. Neither is right or wrong; it is simply a choice and each student is autonomous—completely free to choose whatever makes the most sense to them. We want our students to be happy, to be comfortable in their own skin."

Sensing the shock and resistance that was clearly registering on Jon and Teresa's faces, Mrs. Smith took a deep breath and proceeded to lay out the parental role in this process. She made it clear that this transition for Patrick would be much easier if his parents would agree to be supportive and helpful. To be the greatest support, they would need to set aside any preconceived notions of right or wrong they might have with regard to transgenderism.

There was a tacit acknowledgment of the adjustment that they as parents would need to make in their own thinking about their child, but the expectation from the school personnel was that Jon and Teresa would encourage and support Patrick's freedom to make this choice. Just as the school was "on board" with this change, so the parents would be expected to be in full agreement with their child's decision.

Both Jon and Teresa suddenly realized this was more than an informational meeting; it was intended to imply a warning and a threat if they were not in agreement. Mrs. Smith concluded by stating, "Young people need to be true to themselves, and if that means that your daughter feels more comfortable being a boy, then we are here to be sure that nothing stands in his way of making that identity change and that you are supportive of this fact." Shock quickly turned to anger as Jon and Teresa witnessed the public school system turning on them with implicit bullying tactics.

Before anything further could be said, Jon decided to take the initiative. With marked self-control, he stood to his feet and kindly thanked each of them for sharing this information. Then he carefully remarked, "You have given us a considerable amount of information to think about and discuss. I think it is time for my wife, my daughter, and myself to go home and discuss this further."

Everyone heard Jon refer to *his daughter* and not his son. The counselor immediately interrupted him and said, "I think I could be helpful during this discussion if you permit me to come with Patrick."

"No," Jon responded quickly, "this is something we will discuss as a family—thank you!"

Teresa then looked at the counselor and said, "I am sure you mean well, but you must understand we have spent the last seventeen years rearing our daughter, and the information you have provided for us today is important to our family, and we will lovingly discuss it as a family."

Patricia looked over at Mrs. Smith, who nodded her assent. Then with shoulders slumped, she joined her parents—eyes still downcast—as they left the school building. Jon and Teresa wanted to enfold her in their arms, but she seemed stiff and resistant, sporting a new attitude of bold independence they had not noticed before.

Arms folded across her chest, Patricia sat in silence in the back seat of the car. Tears streamed down her mother's face as her mind raced with unanswered questions. Her father broke the silence by assuring Patricia of their love for her in the past, in the present, and in the future as well. Their love was a reality that would not change. He went on to say that this came as a complete surprise to him and her mother. They had no idea she was struggling with her femininity. But before they talked at length with her about it, they wanted to spend time discussing and praying about it as her parents. Jon and Teresa were faithful Christians who were committed to rearing their children in a godly home. Patricia had made a profession of faith in Jesus Christ when she was seven, and the whole family faithfully attended a local Bible-believing church where they were members.

Although Patricia was thoroughly convinced of her "maleness," she also knew this news would be hard for her parents to receive, much less accept. Knowing what she would face at home, her counselor at school had advised her to insist that everyone call her Patrick, not Patricia, and if *he* had any problems at home, *he* was to call the counselor, and she would intercede on Patrick's behalf to ensure *his* rights were not denied. The counselor had even suggested that if his parents failed to be supportive of Patrick as his real identity, he could possibly report them for child abuse because their failure to provide emotional support was a form of parental neglect.

Patricia loved her parents and did not want to get them in trouble, but she was also determined to see this change come about. She was convinced that she was doing what was right and comfortable for *her*. Now it was time to see just how this was going to play out.

After arriving home, Patricia's parents asked her to go to her room and they would return soon and discuss this with her. She was reluctant, but complied. Jon and Teresa went to their bedroom and closed the door. After the door shut, Teresa broke down sobbing. "What has happened to our daughter, and what are we going to do?"

As Christian parents they never imagined they would ever face such circumstances. Was their daughter genuinely serious about wanting to become a boy? They did not know any other parents who had faced this difficulty. Where could they find help for their daughter? For more than an hour they talked and prayed together. At the end, they resolved to call their pastor after talking with Patricia.

Their conversation with Patricia was difficult, to say the least. She demanded that they call her Patrick and refused to respond to the name Patricia. Why had she kept this from them? Because she believed they would not accept her and would try to change her mind! The school counselor had warned her this would happen. Her father responded by saying, "We fully accept and love you, but not a redefinition of you!" Patricia went on to explain her dissatisfaction with femininity, that she did not like having breasts, which was why she always wore a sports bra.

"I am a boy trapped in a girl's body! It doesn't feel like my body, and I want to be seen as a male," she announced boldly. She said she had agonized for several years over having a girl's body, even though her parents could not recall any significant signs of her anxiety until now. The school counselor had explained that she could have a gender dysphoria because of her dislike of appearing like a girl. She had always admired the things that boys do: competing in contact sports, driving trucks, and working at dirty outdoor jobs. Ever since she was a little girl she had despised makeup, dresses, perfume, and all the frilly things girls like. As time went on, however, her clothing choices became less feminine and more masculine, with a preference for athletic attire over just about anything else. Any feminine dressing in the past was merely to please her parents, not because it was what she liked or wanted.

Patricia went on to explain that she did not like the restrictions of being a female either. "Girls are treated differently than boys. Women do not have true equality the way that men do; even the Bible treats them differently. Besides," she remarked to her father, "you now have the boy you always said you wanted. Before this, it was only me and my two sisters."

Jon remembered having expressed the desire to have a son around, and a sudden sense of shame overwhelmed him. Teresa looked at him with disappointment. Jon admitted, "I did want a boy, but I didn't want any boy that would replace my beautiful daughter! I love you and I would not trade my daughter for any boy!"

Patricia calmly sat in silence with a sense of relief and satisfaction. Her secret was now out! She did not have to pretend anymore. "Do you still trust Jesus Christ as your Lord and Savior?" her father asked. Quiet but agitated, she responded, "I am still a Christian, Dad! I just believe that God somehow made a mistake when He put me in a girl's body."

Her parents were surprised by the arrogance of her answer, especially how she elevated her own opinion over God's creation. Jon opened his cell phone Bible app and read Psalm 18:30 out loud: "'This God—his way is perfect; the word of the LORD proves true; he is a shield for all those who take refuge in him.'"

"God does not make mistakes," said Jon. "He always acts perfectly, and He did not cease from acting perfectly when He made you as a girl."

Patricia thought for a moment about what her father said. "Then why did God give me the desires and feelings of a boy and put me into a girl's body?"

Her mother responded, "Why do you assume that it was God who gave you those boyish feelings? There are other explanations for how you feel."

"But being a boy feels natural to me!" Patricia continued. "I have to be true to myself! This doesn't have to be such a big deal. I learned in school that gender is a socially constructed concept and it is not something that is fixed by your biology."

Then Patricia added angrily, "Only a patriarchal system like the church would force me to be a girl when I know I am a boy. I am free to be able to think about myself in a nonbinary way now."

Both Jon and Teresa were grieved to hear their daughter express such criticism of God and His church. She was so different from the little girl they remembered who used to love to go to church, read the Bible, and sing in the choir. Patricia was evidencing attitudes and opinions they had never seen or heard before. It was as if they did not know their own child sitting in front of them. She had obviously mastered the art of deceit—forming opinions and a worldview contrary to her upbringing without giving a hint as to what was going on inside. Jon and Teresa knelt down next to her, pulling her into a group hug and praying for her.

Within the hour, Jon called their pastor and explained the unexpected events of the day, seeking his counsel. Pastor Steve recommended they remove their daughter from the public school system and begin to homeschool her or send her to a nearby Christian school, regardless of her protests. Not all public schools are so heavy-handed with parents about how to rear their children, but this high school and its guidance counselor appeared to be especially militant when it came to gender identity.

Pastor Steve concurred with Jon and Teresa's assessment that the school administration had tried to bully them into agreeing with their transgender ideological doctrine. He noted that the effect on Patricia's thinking was similar to that of brainwashing, with the administrators convincing her that it was her highest moral responsibility to be true to herself in rejecting her femininity. This was a frontal assault upon Jon and Teresa's most basic Christian values and their freedom to raise their children according to God's ways.

Pastor Steve also recommended their family get some biblical counseling. He agreed to counsel Jon and Teresa and their other two daughters, but he believed that Patricia was going to need to receive counsel from a more experienced biblical counselor. He knew a woman from a nearby church who was a certified biblical counselor and had several years' experience working with young women like Patricia. Her parents thought this was a wise course of action in moving forward.

When Patricia heard that her parents were removing her from her high school, she was not happy. They explained to her that they were appreciative of the education she had received, but when a school actively undermines biblical values and parental authority, it has ceased to be an educational institution and has become an advocacy organization dedicated to reconstructing social values. These values are based upon an anti-Christian notion that gender is a socially contrived idea and is not fixed at conception.

For the Christian, however, gender is fixed from the time a person is conceived with either female homogametic chromosome (XX) or male heterogametic chromosome (XY), and it is fixed by God.[32] As parents, they could no longer in good conscience send any of their children to a school system that denied clear biological evidence in order to promote a false social construction of reality theory.

Not only were Jon and Teresa removing Patricia from the school system, they were removing their other two daughters as well. For the rest of the school year they would homeschool their daughters. Then the following school year, they would consider sending them to the local Christian school.

At first Patricia was angry and even hateful in response to her parents. Her volatile temper was well-known to her parents, and it was especially bad now. After unleashing a stream of unfounded accusations upon them, she ran to her room, slammed the door, and collapsed on her bed in tears.

After several hours of intense anger and prolific tears, Patricia was exhausted. Although she had just accused her parents of not loving her and not accepting her for who God made her to be, deep in her heart, Patricia knew they loved her. She also knew they were right—that she had been born a girl by God's wisdom and loving design; that her boyish inclinations and feelings, although strong, were not able to determine who she really was.

Patricia had meant it when she told her parents she was a true

298 • The Biblical Counseling Guide for Women

Christian, and slowly she became ashamed of the way she had high-handedly accused God of wrongdoing in creating her a girl. Patricia reasoned rightly that her mom and dad were making decisions with her best long-term welfare in mind and that she had no power to change their minds, especially when it meant compromising their commitment to biblical truth.

Genuinely grieved over the difficulty she had caused them, Patricia began reconsidering her demands and decided to go to her parents and seek their forgiveness. She would no longer demand they call her Patrick, but she struggled over what to do about her boyish feelings. She knew she was doing the right thing in reconciling with her parents, but she had a hard time sorting out all the confusion in her mind. There was her love of masculine clothing, sports, and lifestyle that seemed to fit her—what was she to do with that? There were her feelings of being ashamed of her feminine-looking body and her dislike of girly clothes and appearance—what was she to do with that?

Patricia had been listening to the wrong people, of that she was sure. Her guidance counselor at school had told her to follow her masculine feelings, and in that way, she would be true to herself. But as she thought about Jesus' teaching, she couldn't remember Him ever directly teaching or even implying that a Christian should be true to oneself. In fact, she kept remembering Luke 9:23: "If anyone would come after me, let him deny himself and take up his cross daily and follow me." Somehow that didn't sound like being true to self.

To make matters worse, Patricia had become so fascinated with the possibility of a gender change that she was becoming well-known for her views and popular with many of her fellow students. Her English literature teacher had her read several books about young girls who wanted to be boys. Her friends talked about sex reassignment surgery and how it was now fully covered under many medical insurance programs. Patricia had relished her celebrity status as a "transgender pioneer." She had successfully hidden these things from her parents for a time, knowing they would be very displeased if they ever found out. But now she was beginning to realize that her deception had caused both herself and her parents a lot of grief. What was she going to do now?

Jon and Teresa cried and hugged Patricia as she confessed her elaborate deception that went back over a two-year period. When she was finished, they knelt by their living room couch and prayed with her for more than an hour. She fully repented and asked God to forgive her for her deception and her willingness to accept worldly counsel. She asked Him to help her learn how she could be content and happy with her femininity.

There was never a time where Jon, Teresa, and Patricia were closer as a family than that day when they were on their knees before God. Afterward, her father shared their pastor's recommendation for Patricia to see a qualified biblical counselor. This time she willingly consented. If he had forced her to go and see a counselor against her will, it would have only served to make her angrier. But now she was receptive to hearing what the Bible said about how to deal with her transgender thoughts and feelings. That night, Patricia slept better than she had for more than two years. Her conscience was no longer riddled with the guilt of her deception or the deceitfulness of her desires.

In less than a week, Patricia was able to meet with her counselor, Stacey. She was pleasantly surprised how knowledgeable Stacey was concerning the issue of transgenderism and the Bible. Stacey was a young woman, almost 30 years of age, and also a fully certified high school teacher as well. But unlike Patricia's other teachers, Stacey was a committed Christian. She understood the unique pressures of being a student and a faculty member in a public school system. There was a time when school systems supported Christian values without endorsing them, but public schools like this were quickly vanishing.

Stacey helped Patricia to understand that public schools and universities were undergoing a revolution to normalize transgenderism in society and culture, and this revolution still had a long way to go. This is the reason the Bible clearly warns the believer about what to avoid while living in an ungodly world.

Stacey and Patricia discussed together the relevance of Psalm 1:1-2: "Blessed is the man who walks not in the counsel of the wicked, nor stands in the way of sinners, nor sits in the seat of scoffers; but his delight is in the law of the LORD, and on his law he meditates day and night." To walk, stand, and sit among ungodly counselors implies that a person has become comfortable with their sinful ways of thinking and acting. Eventually such a person will scoff at the biblical worldview.

What's more, to the ungodly, the biblical worldview is patriarchal, oppressive, and an imposition on what they really desire. Patricia could see how her thinking, attitudes, motivations and behavior had been affected by her high-school friends and faculty. She had allowed their paganism to dramatically influence her Christian worldview and, in the process, she had become increasingly critical of her parents as well as of all Christians. Even the restrooms and locker rooms of her high school had become gender-neutral, a fact that did not bother her until now. The more she and Stacey discussed these things, the more her eyes were open to how she had been inoculated against the importance of gender distinctiveness as stated in God's Word.

Stacey began each counseling session with an extended time of prayer for Patricia and herself as they opened the Word of God, looking for authoritative answers to Patricia's questions. Beginning with their first session together, Stacey wanted to build a solid friendship with Patricia and understand what she was facing in her struggle with transgenderism. So she asked her many probing questions about her life, her likes and dislikes, as well as the feelings and thoughts she was experiencing.

Patricia was grateful that Stacey was not judgmental with her, but really evidenced a genuine love and deep concern for her struggle. She told Stacey that she had grown up in a home with two sisters and she always knew from the time she was a little girl that her parents also wanted a son, but they were never able to have one. Her father had spent a lot of time with her playing sports in the same way a father would spend with a son.

Over the years, Patricia had come to really enjoy the special relationship she had with her father—a relationship that her sisters did not possess. They both loved doing guy-things. Because of this, many of Patricia's girlfriends had called Patricia a tomboy. But she said they did not really fully understand her.

"The difference between a tomboy and a transgender is that a tomboy is completely happy with her body as a female and a transgender is not," said Patricia. "Most tomboys would be repulsed by a sex change, but the transgender has a dysphoria—an unhappy restlessness that develops into a rebellious perversion concerning her body, and many would welcome a sex-change to resolve the uneasiness and sexual awkwardness."

"I think I understand," Stacey remarked. "A tomboy enjoys *acting* masculine, but a transgender enjoys *being* masculine."

"Yes, a tomboy acts like a guy, but still considers herself a girl in her mind," said Patricia. "A transgender is a biological female on the outside, but considers herself a male on the inside. I started out with a love for boyish things and playing the part of a son to my father as a young girl. But I got caught up in the educational culture of self-realization and autonomy—you know, from kindergarten, you're told that you can be whatever you want to be. This has come to mean you can be whatever gender you want to be, and I was buying into that. The popularity I gained only fueled my desire to be true to myself, and I wrongly thought that meant I was to turn myself into a guy."

Patricia had shared those exact same thoughts with her high school guidance counselor when she was a freshman. Mrs. Smith had encouraged her to follow her feelings to be the person of authenticity she needed to be in order to be happy with herself. She had also said that anyone who denied her the right to be the male she wanted to be was prejudiced and intolerant of transgenders.

Mrs. Smith had also rearranged Patricia's class schedule so she could take a course from the literature teacher who would guide her in reading books and articles about females who desired to be males. Patricia was told that this was all worthwhile in finding relief from her gender conflict. Patricia was told that the federal government considered this to be so important to the health needs of average citizens that even Medicare was now covering sex-reassignment surgeries. She was told the issue was a significant part of her civil rights—to be the gender she wanted to be.

Mrs. Smith's input had its intended effect in making Patricia feel not so isolated with her masculine-like longings, amd helping to legitimize her rejection of her female body. At first, Patricia's Christian conscience had been plagued with a sense of guilt. She knew that her parents and other believers at her church would not approve of a sex change. But she couldn't think of why it was so wrong to do something that felt so right. She reasoned that God, in creating her, must have given her a female body with a male soul. Since she couldn't find any verses in the Bible that forbid a sex change operation, she rationalized that this was part of her freedom in Christ to choose the gender of her preference.

Any time that doubts came to Patricia's mind, she told herself this was a civil rights issue and should not be looked at as anything that should be forbidden. She became convinced that it was simply a medical problem: having been born different on the outside than the inside, this condition was easily correctable with surgery. She had even gone so far as to research her father's medical insurance plan, hoping it would cover the costs of a sex-change surgery for her.

Stacey had done extensive research on the long-term effects on transgenders who had chosen to be surgically altered. She wanted Patricia to know that biological reconstruction offered short-term relief but long-term regret. The tragic consequences of such radical procedures were often premature mortality, persistent depression, unrelenting sorrow, and in many cases, suicide. It is a permanent procedure that is unnecessary and destructive. To help to illustrate this to her, Stacey read from an article concerning definitive research on transgenders and sex-reassignment surgery:

> You won't hear it from those championing transgender equality, but controlled and follow-up studies reveal fundamental problems with this movement. When children who reported transgender feelings were tracked without medical or surgical treatment at both Vanderbilt University and London's Portman Clinic, 70%-80% of them spontaneously lost those feelings...A 2011 study at the Karolinska Institute in Sweden produced the most illuminating results yet regarding the transgendered, evidence that should give advocates pause. The long-term study—up to 30 years—followed 324 people who had sex-reassignment surgery. The study revealed that beginning about 10 years after having the surgery, the transgendered began to experience increasing mental difficulties.

Most shockingly, their suicide mortality rose almost 20-fold above the comparable nontransgender population…At the heart of the problem is confusion over the nature of the transgendered. "Sex change" is biologically impossible. People who undergo sex-reassignment surgery do not change from men to women or vice versa. Rather, they become feminized men or masculinized women. Claiming that this is a civil-rights matter and encouraging surgical intervention is in reality to collaborate with and promote a mental disorder.[33]

It was important for Patricia to know there are reliable and authoritative studies that question transgender claims and the long-term devastating consequences of sex-assignment surgery. This research was particularly interesting to her because of her background with the Debate Club. Thinking like a debater, Patricia reasoned that if between 70 to 80 percent of transgenders eventually revert to their original sex, then it should give a person, especially one who claims to be a Christian, pause before taking such a life-altering step.

Stacey then had Patricia read 1 Corinthians 6:19-20 out loud: "Do you not know that your body is a temple of the Holy Spirit within you, whom you have from God? You are not your own, for you were bought with a price. So glorify God in your body." For a Christian woman to permanently mutilate the genitalia of the body that God has given her is to do violence to something that God considers sacred. It is His temple! Her body belongs to the Lord, and it is not something to be treated in a cavalier fashion as a personal possession. And if God considers her body sacred, it is a sin to view it with disgust and disdain. With all that in mind, Patricia realized it was her thinking that needed changing, and not her body.

Beyond research and statistics, Stacey knew it was time to help Patricia find the source of her interest in transgenderism. As she carefully listened to Patricia's story, she realized how influential her past experiences were in forming the way that she viewed her life and her body. From her earliest childhood memories, her father's verbal expressions of wanting a son had fueled Patricia's love of sports and all-things-boys, to the point that she eventually became discontent and unthankful for her God-created femaleness. As her boyish feelings increased and her body reached puberty, she felt increasingly uncomfortable with who she was.

At the same time, Patricia found it difficult to fit in with most of the girls at school, so she had very few friends. That all changed with the second formative influence: her introduction into the world of transgenderism through her high school teachers and counselor. Not only did she begin to buy into the worldly unbiblical philosophy, but she found a place for herself—a place of comfort and acceptance. In her sophomore year she had joined the Debate Club, which gave her a place to express her newly formed opinions about transgenderism. It also gained her acceptance among many of her peers; because although most of the students remained comfortable with their own genders, they verbally praised her for her liberal stand on this "hot topic" social issue.

To help Patricia overcome her attachment to the idea of being male, Stacey introduced a Bible study on the word *thanksgiving*. Far from being merely associated with a national holiday, Patricia learned that giving thanks to God is an integral part of being a Christian—a child of God. This is particularly true in the life of the believer as it relates to sexuality. Those who are discontent and unthankful for how God has made them will often be greatly tempted to indulge in sexual deviancy.

One passage Stacey and Patricia studied together that was particularly helpful was Ephesians 5:1-21. Here, Paul instructed Christians as follows:

Sexual immorality and all impurity or covetousness must not even be named among you, as is proper among saints. Let there be no filthiness nor foolish talk nor crude joking, which are out of place, but instead let there be *thanksgiving*. For you may be sure of this, that everyone who is sexually immoral or impure, or who is covetous (that is, an idolater), has no inheritance in the kingdom of Christ and God (Ephesians 5:3-5).

They also looked at Colossians 3:5-17, where Paul instructed Christians to put off all kinds of sin, including sexual immorality, and to put on compassionate hearts, kindness, humility, meekness, and patience. He concluded this passage by calling Christians to be *thankful* (verse 15) and by admonishing them: "Whatever you do, in word or deed, do everything in the name of the Lord Jesus, giving *thanks* to God the Father through him" (verse 17).

Patricia had never realized how her unthankful heart had led her to listen to the errors of the world. This new revelation became a foundation for change in how she viewed the body and life God gave her, and thanksgiving became a regular part of her prayer life and attitude each day. The result was that she was increasingly less drawn to her boyish thoughts and interests, and more interested in feminine characteristics. And she became more convinced of the errors of transgenderism as she had been taught. A humble heart of thanksgiving was transforming her life into one of peace, acceptance of herself as a girl, and a determination to live her life based on the truth of her creator God. The more she gave thanks to God, the less she was interested in finding acceptance among her peers. She began to live, as the Bible states it, in the proper fear of the Lord and not the fear of man (Proverbs 9:10; 29:25).

As Stacey and Patricia continued to meet weekly, Patricia brought a Bible and notebook to each session and took copious notes on the texts they studied together. God's Word began to radically change her view of her conceived feminine gender. There were ten transforming truths about transgenderism she learned from her biblical counseling that greatly helped her thinking.

1. Biblical counseling's ultimate goal is not to convince you to accept your physical gender, but to help you know Jesus Christ and His gospel.

Stacey explained to Patricia that to merely convince her to accept her female body was moralistic and would not change her heart. Whereas moralism condemns, it is biblical grace that forgives. Moralism is a false gospel that advocates a Christianized form of morality because it reduces Christian truth to improvements in her behavior. As a biblical counselor it was not Stacey's purpose to try to straighten out Patricia's bad behavior so that she no longer told lies, read the wrong books, or talked or acted like a male. Biblical counselors do not practice any type of conversion therapy that is used with homosexuals, neither do they practice techniques of behavioral therapy with transgenders. Such approaches reduce Scripture to a rule book!

Instead, biblical counselors seek to help their counselees understand justification by faith. In Galatians 2:16, the apostle Paul rejected moralism by declaring, "We know that a person is not justified by works of the law but through faith in Jesus Christ, so we also have believed in Christ Jesus, in order to be justified by faith in Christ and not by works of the law, because by works of the law no one will be justified." When the Christian sins, she misrepresents the gospel, and it is not a mere matter of behavioral adjustments to make it right. Changing the external behavior of a person who claims to be transgender is pointless because the real problem is not the body; rather, it is the heart.

As a Christian, Patricia was justified by faith alone and she was saved by grace alone. Her redemption came as a result of the redeeming work of Jesus Christ alone. Real change, then, must come through a godly repentance of her heart that is in keeping with her undeserved standing by grace in Jesus Christ (2 Corinthians 7:10). In the same way that she had exercised faith in Jesus Christ when she was saved, now she would need to exercise the same faith in Christ and His Word to see lasting change. Living by the law can never impart life. This is why the apostle Paul wrote, "So then, the law was our guardian until Christ came, in order that we might be justified by faith" (Galatians 3:24).

Patricia came to recognize that real change begins with an inward change of heart. Whereas mere moralism may help sinners behave better, it is the gospel of Jesus Christ that genuinely transforms a woman into an adopted daughter of God. Transgenderism says, "My body is the wrong gender"; Christianity says, "My view of my gender is wrong thinking."

Galatians 4:4-5 says, "When the fullness of time had come, God sent forth his Son, born of woman, born under the law, to redeem those who were under the law, so that we might receive adoption as sons." It was time for Patricia to bring her thinking in line with her redemption.

2. Your body is not the prison of your soul so that your goal becomes escaping the body.

Stacey explained to Patricia that during the first and second centuries AD, there was a Hellenistic view known as Gnosticism. One notable aspect of Gnosticism was Docetism. The Docetists believed that the physical world was full of imperfections and innately sinful, but the spiritual world of the inner soul was perfect and sinless. They could trust their inner soul and its inclinations. Therefore the Docetists taught that Jesus Christ could never have come in the flesh because that was a sinful form. He only *seemed* to have come in the flesh.

But, if this were true, it would negate the gospel because if Jesus came only in spiritual form without a real human body, then He was merely a phantom. Therefore, He did not suffer in the flesh, or die a physical death. Nor was He raised bodily from the dead. Such a clear denial of Christ's body destroys the claims of the gospel and makes Christianity worthless (1 John 4:2; 2 John 7). The apostle John recognized Docetism as a dangerous philosophy that was contrary to what Scripture taught about Christ and created reality. However, many early Christians were influenced by this teaching. They came to believe that the created world was essentially evil, including their own bodies, and that their goal was to escape the body and become what they believed was more perfect in the inner man.

Transgenderism is not Docetism, but much of the philosophy is similar. The outer body is wrong, and the inner person's view of themselves is the greater reality. To the transgender female, salvation comes by liberating her soul from the prison of her female body by becoming physiologically male through sex-reassignment surgery and hormonal therapy. This is not the way a biblical Christian thinks; rather, it is more in line with eastern religions. For example, the goal of Buddhism is liberation from the cycles of aimless drifting in this mundane world. Jainism seeks to escape the cycle of rebirth and death through moralistic behavior. But the Christian does not view this physical world or their body as evil—something to escape. On each day of creation, God saw what He had created and He called it good. This means the physical body is good as well.

Stacey pointed out to Patricia that it wasn't until the sixth day of creation that God created the female body. Giving Eve life was God's final act, and He called all that He created "very good" (Genesis 1:31). How then could Patricia continue to believe that God had made a mistake by creating her with a female body? The psalmist says, "O LORD, how manifold are your works! In wisdom have you made them all; the earth is full of your creatures" (104:24). Among other things, this means the wisdom of God was reflected in the way that God created Patricia's body.

Later the psalmist said about God, "You are good and do good; teach me your statutes" (119:68). Then five verses later, after stressing the goodness of all that God does, he said, "Your hands have made and fashioned me; give me understanding that I may learn your commandments" (119:73). God had not only created something good when He created Patricia's female body, but He had given her good health and strength as well. Instead of being resentful, Patricia should be rejoicing.

Part of Patricia's assignment was to memorize these important verses and be ready to explain what they mean within the context in which they were given in Scripture. This memorization was crucial toward helping to change Patricia's thought life. One verse that she found particularly helpful was 1 Timothy 4:4: "Everything created by God is good, and nothing is to be rejected if it is received with thanksgiving." This was the verse Patricia careful inscribed on parchment paper in calligraphy and hung on the wall of her bedroom and mirror in her restroom. She knew she had to refuse to believe the false philosophy of transgenderism and replace it with thankful thoughts concerning her female body.

3. You must reject the ungodly notion that the highest good of life is driven by the moral imperative to be true to oneself.

This moral imperative is radically divergent from the thinking of previous generations. Stacey helped Patricia see that previously, people had lived by the ideal of "do your duty." But this is no longer the goal in today's generation. Instead, it is "express your true self." Such an ideal reveals a serious falsehood: You can and should trust in self as a reliable guide to truth and happiness. A resulting philosophy is that to be true to yourself means you are acting in accordance with who you are—the essence of being genuine or authentic.

In contrast, to deny your feelings and personal impressions and live by a standard external to yourself is viewed as disingenuous. Such insincerity is not tolerated in the transgender world. If you lack the courage to accept who you think you are, regardless of your female chromosomes and genitalia, you will never be true to yourself. And if you cannot be true to yourself, you will never be true to anyone else. This is what Patricia had been taught in her high school classes and her sessions with her guidance counselor. On the surface such thinking seemed reasonable, but it is full of falsehoods and misleading assumptions.

"Such ideas are not only false, they are anti-Christian," Stacey said to Patricia. "They are based on two dangerous misconceptions. First, the fact that self can be trusted. Second, you cannot trust anything outside of yourself."

Stacey went on to explain that in order to trust self, you must believe that self is essentially trustworthy or good. But the Bible teaches that self is untrustworthy and essentially evil in its thoughts and desires (Genesis 6:5; Psalm 14:1-3; 36:1-12; Proverbs 6:18; 16:2; 21:2; Matthew 15:19; Romans 1:28-32). This is still true even *after* a person becomes a Christian; all personal thoughts and desires still need to be held subject to the critique of God's Word. Even the apostle Paul revealed mistrust of himself as a Christian when he said, "I am not aware of anything against myself, but I am not thereby acquitted. It is the Lord who judges me" (1 Corinthians 4:4; see also Psalm 143:2; Ecclesiastes 7:20). The apostle John includes himself in this declaration and confirms the fact that sinful thoughts, motivations, and actions are a factor for the believer: "If we say we have no sin, we deceive ourselves, and the truth is not in us" (1 John 1:8).

Self cannot be trusted. Self is not something to be loved or esteemed. In fact, Jesus taught that self must be treated like a vile criminal. "He said to all, 'If anyone would come after me, let him deny himself and take up his cross daily and follow me'" (Luke 9:23; see also Matthew 16:24; Mark 8:34). During the first century, the Romans hung only the worst of criminals on crosses. Jesus said that anyone who follows Him must deny *self* and hang *self* on the cross—not just once, but daily!

When self is set aside willingly, a person is ready to turn her trust to someone external to her. Stacey reminded Patricia of a verse she had memorized as a young girl: "Trust in the LORD with all your heart, and do not lean on your own understanding. In all your ways acknowledge him, and he will make straight your paths" (Proverbs 3:5-6). This was something Patricia had failed to do when she allowed the influence of her friends and her high school administrators to turn her reliance over to self-trust. She had to learn the trustworthiness of God's Word anew. It was a righteous standard that she could depend upon with absolute certainty. The trusted Word of God had to be the light of truth that would mold her decisions and direct her life (Psalm 119:42, 105).

4. You must reject the pseudosophisticated cultural norm of the "self-defining self" and learn to be grateful for the way God has created your body.

The epistemological approach of letting one's self define self is a form of extreme egocentrism. It is called *solipsism*, and means that self is the only true and reliable existent thing. It says that a person's mental states are the only mental states that exist. It involves a preoccupation with personal feelings, desires, and thoughts.

Solipsism is a word that comes from the Latin *solus* ("alone") combined with *ipse* ("self"). This was new to Patricia; she had never heard this before. But Stacey's explanations made a lot of sense. Solipsism was actually an extreme form of self-absorption that enables a young girl like Patricia to define her own reality. Her solipsismal reality had granted her the liberty to define her own gender. She was her own god; she was her own source of truth.

Back in ancient Israel, during the time of the Judges, Scripture says, "In those days there was no king in Israel. Everyone did what was right in his own eyes" (Judges 17:6; 21:25; see also Deuteronomy 12:8). There is no god to answer to in the mind of the solipsist, except for the god of self. The cry of emergent transgenderism is "self alone" (*solus ipse*), but the cry of the Protestant Reformation was the five solas: "faith alone" (*sola fide*), "Scripture alone" (*sola Scriptura*), "Christ alone" (*solus Christus*), "grace alone" (*sola gratia*), and "glory to God alone" (*soli Deo gloria*). It was becoming obvious to Patricia that she had been influenced by very ungodly thinking.

While the world loves to speak of being free to be true to oneself, the Bible says following self is a type of bondage and enslavement. Self is a deceptive slavemaster. Solipsism is a miserable myth. Transgenders are subject to much higher rates of depression and suicide than the average population.

Stacey helped Patricia to see that all approaches to life that reject biblical truth end in bondage and misery. "They promise them freedom, but they themselves are slaves of corruption. For whatever overcomes a person, to that he is enslaved" (2 Peter 2:19). Stacey went on to point out this passage as a descriptive analysis of how false teachers "entice by sensual passions of the flesh" (2:18). They teach people to follow the passions of the flesh—that is, whatever feels right to them, rather than following truth. But in so doing, they actually put people into captivity to their desires.

This can especially be true of those who claim to be Christians. But those who persist in following their fleshly passions (2:20-21) demonstrate they had a "knowledge of our Lord and Savior Jesus Christ" (2:20) but were not true believers. "What the true proverb says has happened to them: 'The dog returns to its own vomit, and the sow, after washing herself, returns to wallow in the mire'" (2:22; see also Proverbs 26:11). Why does the dog return to its vomit or the sow to the mud? Because their essential natures have never changed.

By contrast, when a person is genuinely saved, her essential nature has fundamentally changed, and she will not return to or remain wallowing in the ways of the world. Following transgender's solipsism elevates personal feelings and desires over God's faithfulness and desires.

Discontentment and ungratefulness are the critical factors that contribute to the transgender's personal anguish. It begins with discontentment, wishing to be another gender, and leads to a settled ungratefulness, an overall miserable and depressing outlook on life. *I hate my body* was a disturbing thought that had replayed itself countless times in Patricia's mind. This was not something that came from a poor opinion of self. Nor was it a lack of self-love. On the contrary, it was already clear to both Stacey and Patricia that Patricia greatly esteemed herself. What had happened was this: Patricia had elevated self to an ungodly level of importance. It was a high view of herself that caused her to have a low view of one aspect of her life: her body. Patricia believed she needed a better body, a masculine body. The fact that she *believed* she needed a better body came from the assumption that she *deserved* a better body. This reveals an intense love of self, not a diminished view of self. She loved her *self*—just not her body.

Jesus warned this would be the great struggle of man when He reviewed the great commandment in God's law. Man would be prone to love self: "And [Jesus] said to him, 'You shall love the Lord your God with all your heart and with all your soul and with all your mind'" (Matthew 22:37). It is love for God that should draw out a woman's full affections and passions.

Jesus continues by saying, "This is the great and first commandment. And a second is like it: You shall love your neighbor as yourself" (22:38-39). To "love your neighbor as yourself" does not mean you need to love self. If Jesus was saying that people needed to love God, their neighbor, *and* themselves, He would have said there were three commands. But in verse 40 Jesus made it clear He was speaking of only two commands, not three: "On these two commandments depend all the Law and the Prophets."

Jesus was saying that a person must learn to love God and her neighbor with a greater love than the natural tendency to love self. Patricia quickly understood how her affections had changed to a deep love of herself instead of a deep love of God and others. Furthermore, she realized how this deep love of herself had produced in her a miserable discontentment and ungratefulness for her body.

Stacey and Patricia spent a considerable amount of time developing a "Personal Thanks List," which would be in line with the exhortation in Philippians 4:6 to give thanks "in everything." This was an exhaustive list of the many ways God had blessed Patricia with a good life and good body. Patricia used a special cell-phone app and developed electronic flash cards listing all the things she needed to be grateful for. They would pop up randomly on her cell phone throughout the day to remind her to thank God for the way He had created her.

Patricia also memorized Colossians 3:16 and would repeat it to herself whenever she become discouraged: "Let the word of Christ dwell in you richly, teaching and admonishing one another in all wisdom, singing psalms and hymns and spiritual songs, with thankfulness in your hearts to God." As Patricia faithfully committed herself to renewing her mind, her discontentment was replaced with joy.

5. You must be fully committed to the truth that your created biological gender glorifies God.

Transgenderism denies the goodness of God's creation. God created both genders as valid and good. He does not create junk, and He does not make mistakes (Romans 3:4). Again Scripture clearly says, "For everything created by God is good, and nothing is to be rejected if it is received with thanksgiving" (1 Timothy 4:4). Patricia acknowledged to Stacey that this was one of the most difficult assumptions to change in her thinking, especially when she had read so many secular books on transgenderism and had listened to former teachers and friends for so long. Essentially, they did not openly deny God or His existence, but they did question His goodness. How could a good God put a male like Patrick into a female body and name her Patricia? Either He had made a terrible mistake, or He enjoyed seeing Patrick suffer. Even though Patricia could now see the foolishness of this assumption, it was still going to take a serious effort to remove its lingering effects in her thinking.

Stacey realized it was important to effectively address this struggle in Patricia's thought life. So she had Patricia turn in her Bible to Psalm 119:73: "Your hands have *made* and *fashioned* me; give me understanding that I may learn your commandments." She went on to explain the verse by having Patricia look carefully at its wording. The psalmist speaks of God's personal act of creation: "Your hands have made...me." In the original Hebrew text, the statement about God's personal act of creating a person from conception is stated in the *past tense* (see also Psalm 100:3; 138:8; 139:15).

But God was not finished—the psalmist then said, "Your hands...fashioned me." This is a different Hebrew tense, the imperfect tense, meaning that God *continues* to fashion him. In other words, God was not finished with Patricia, but He was continuing to use a variety of circumstances in her life to mold her into a woman who would bring Him glory. After creating her, His continuing work in her life was seen in saving her. After saving her, His continuing work in her life was seen in sanctifying her. In fact, God had saved her and sanctified her for good! "For we are his workmanship, created in Christ Jesus for good works, which God prepared beforehand, that we should walk in them" (Ephesians 2:10). God's purposes go beyond just being content with your gender. He desires for you to be an asset for goodness and glory.

While transgenderism reaches for personal contentment and satisfaction, God was calling for Patricia to focus on the good of others and to glorify Him (1 Corinthians 10:31; Colossians 3:17; 1 Peter 4:11). Personal contentment and satisfaction are fleeting goals that were never intended by God to be the focus of anyone's pursuit. In fact, the more they are sought after, the more elusive they become.

True personal contentment and satisfaction are the by-products of seeking first God and His kingdom (Matthew 6:33). As Stacey had mentioned earlier, the question was not whether Patricia loved herself. Rather, the question was how much she loved God and others. If her love for God and others had been where it needed to be, then her attention would no longer have been on herself and her desires. Instead, it would be on God and caring for others in order to honor Him (Isaiah 8:13; John 5:23; Revelation 5:13).

6. God-designed "binary gender distinctiveness" models an even greater spiritual reality that must not be lost with transgenderism.

There is an intentional design by God within creation. A binary (twofold) genderism is embedded within the very nature of creation and mankind. Man was created as male and female (Genesis 1:27; 2:22-23), a fact that has been obscured by the sexual redefinitions of today's generations. God created Adam masculine on a chromosomal level (XY) and with external male genitalia. He created

Eve feminine on chromosomal level (XX) and with external female genitalia.

Stacey wanted Patricia to understand that this binary design actually serves greater purposes in God's cosmic plans than merely providing for human marriage and procreation. God's binary gender design is simple, strong, and clear. Nonbinary gender speculation, by contrast, is confusing, debilitating, and misleading. In essence, God's uncomplicated binary design is intended to bring more complex and elusive spiritual realities into greater clarity.

This is best seen in God's relationship to His people. The depth of love and intimacy God enjoys with His own is best illustrated in the male-female relationship in marriage. There is no greater level of intimacy enjoyed on a human level than that of a husband and wife. They were originally created as gender complements, a male and female in a covenantal relationship of marriage. God's close intimacy with His people can be more fully understood because of the male-female bond in marriage.

In Jeremiah 31:31-32, God said to Israel, "Behold, the days are coming…when I will make a new covenant with the house of Israel and the house of Judah, not like the covenant that I made with their fathers on the day when I took them by the hand to bring them out of the land of Egypt, my covenant that they broke, *though I was their husband*." God's love for His people is more clearly understood because of the binary relationship of the genders. Even God's grief and anger is better understood when Israel's failure to be faithful to her divine Husband is revealed through the relationship that the prophet Hosea had with his adulterous wife, Gomer (Hosea 1–4).

Later in the New Testament, the male-female analogy is used again when describing the church's relationship to Jesus Christ. For example, the apostle Paul wrote, "The husband is the head of the wife even as Christ is the head of the church, his body, and is himself its Savior. Now as the church submits to Christ, so also wives should submit in everything to their husbands" (Ephesians 5:23-24). Then later in the same chapter, Paul wrote, "'Therefore a man shall leave his father and mother and hold fast to his wife, and the two shall become one flesh.' This mystery is profound, and I am saying that *it refers to Christ and the church*" (verses 31-32). God used the distinctiveness of male/female genders as a means of describing the nature of His close relationship with His people (see also Revelation 19:9).

When the binary nature of the two genders is confused or obliterated by lesbian, gay, bisexual, and transgender ideologies, then we lose a critical and experiential point of reference to God. As Patricia took notes during her discussion with Stacey, she observed, "It is as if Satan has provided a counterfeit delusion with transgenderism in order to destroy our knowledge of God." She herself had been seduced by such a delusion.

7. It is imperative you acknowledge that everything God created is good and to be enjoyed, which includes the gender-specific attributes of your body.

Patricia's brain kept telling her that she was male, while her body kept reminding her that she was female. It was the disparity between the two that caused her so much anguish. But it was not her body that needed to be fixed, it was her thinking. It adversely affected the way she thought about God and whether He had erred in making her the way He did. Her counselor, Stacey, knew that part of her complete transformation had to involve a new understanding of the goodness of God. Patricia needed to resolve in her mind the Lord was good and had always done good for her.

Stacey and Patricia committed themselves to a thorough understanding and study of the attributes of God, especially His goodness. Stacey sent Patricia home with some work to do on several passages that spoke of the goodness of God. She was to look up each passage and answer the following questions:

- What is this text saying within the context in which it was given? (Patricia needed to carefully study the surrounding context in order to be sure she understood the verses correctly.)

- What circumstances (societal, cultural, covenantal) were different in Bible times than they are today? (Not everything referred to in the text is meant to be applied today.)

- What universal truths found in this text are applicable to me today? (These truths should be stated in such a way that they are true for any believer, at any time in history, and for any situation.)

- How does my heart and thinking need to change so that I become more biblical in my thoughts, motivations, desires, and expectations? (This is the level where true biblical change occurs.)

Here is a sampling of the many Bible passages Patricia and Stacey studied together:

> *Psalm 16:2*—"I say to the LORD, 'You are my Lord; I have no good apart from you.'"
>
> *Psalm 25:8*—"Good and upright is the LORD; therefore he instructs sinners in the way."
>
> *Psalm 34:8, 10*—"Oh, taste and see that the LORD is good! Blessed is the man who takes refuge in him…The young lions suffer want and hunger; but those who seek the LORD lack no good thing."
>
> *Psalm 84:11*—"The LORD God is a sun and shield; the

Lord bestows favor and honor. No good thing does he withhold from those who walk uprightly."

Psalm 100:5—"The Lord is good; his steadfast love endures forever, and his faithfulness to all generations."

Psalm 106:1 (see also 107:1; 118:1)—"Praise the Lord! Oh give thanks to the Lord, for he is good, for his steadfast love endures forever!"

Psalm 119:68—"You are good and do good; teach me your statutes."

Psalm 135:3—"Praise the Lord, for the Lord is good; sing to his name, for it is pleasant!"

Once Patricia had studied what Scripture said about God and His goodness, then she needed to carefully identify those times when she started falling back into her negative and pessimistic thoughts about God. She learned that no matter what her view was concerning the difficulties of her life, God was always good. His goodness was the very essence of His nature (Psalm 119:68).

When was Patricia most tempted to deny God's goodness? This question went way beyond her battle with transgenderism. She noticed she was tempted to deny God's goodness when she relished her coveted position as her father's "son." She was also tempted to deny God's goodness when she struggled with dressing in a feminine way.

Stacey helped Patricia develop a plan to identify times of struggle as times when she was failing to see the goodness of God. Patricia learned how to put off ungodly thoughts and desires, and to put on godly thoughts about her body and God's goodness in creating her as a female. She also began to see that when she struggled, it was not God who had failed her, but it was she who had failed God. So her struggles were not occasions to question the goodness of God, but rather, to question her own goodness (139:23).

8. Being resistant to transgenderism is a matter of purity, not prejudice.

Patricia's high school counselor had told her that anyone who was opposed her wish to be masculine was bigoted, intolerant, prejudiced, and even hateful. Even at the time Patricia received this advice from her high school counselor, it seemed rather judgmental of her to paint all people who objected to transgenderism with such a broad brush. Patricia knew there were many who weren't intolerant or hateful—including her parents, whom she knew loved her and wanted to do what was best for her. So Patricia had chosen to believe that her parents were ignorant and unenlightened, not intolerant or prejudiced. Such labels appeared to be extreme and unjust, and this was especially so now.

Stacey explained that to be bigoted, intolerant, and prejudiced is to be obstinate, ignoring obvious facts in order to hold a firmly believed opinion. However, it is not the Christian who is ignoring obvious facts, it is the advocate of transgenderism. From the perspective of chromosomes and genitalia, transgenders are one definitive gender. But they decide, for whatever reason seems persuasive to them, that they do not want to be the gender of their body, and no amount of factual evidence will change their obstinate view. It would seem that the greater amount of opinionated bigotry, intolerance of alternative views, and prejudicial conclusions actually lies with them.

From an informed Christian perspective, a woman could think she can decide to be anyone or anything she wants to be, especially if she is not a Christian. For example, some people choose to live their lives as a dog or a cat. They don't view themselves as human beings because they want to be an animal. Such people are free to do so and are not under any coercion from Christians to be anything they do not want to be (1 Peter 4:3). However, for the Christian, this is not so. Why? Because Christians should not deny truth and reality (Romans 1:20). Instead, they should believe that God's creation of their gender is good, and that binary genders are good (Mark 10:6).

Stacey went on to say that there is even a greater reason for believers to respect their God-given gender: When a woman becomes a Christian, she surrenders all of herself to God. Christians do not own their own bodies, God does; and they are to commit themselves to doing God's will with their bodies (1 Corinthians 6:19; 1 Peter 4:1-2). They cannot deny the reality of their gender and do anything they wish with their bodies. In submitting to the lordship of Christ, a true Christian is happy with the sex of her body; her attitudes, behaviors, and thoughts remain pure and contented with this reality (Matthew 5:8; Philippians 4:8).

9. Susceptibility to the errant transgender assumptions should show you how broken your life is when not relying upon Jesus Christ.

Shortly after Patricia had confessed her feelings to her high school counselor, the counselor had begun to pressure her to see a gender psychologist. The high school counselor was able to arrange a meeting with this psychologist at Patricia's high school without her parents knowing.

During the first session with this psychologist, Patricia was diagnosed with a gender dysphoria, and a medical procedure was recommended to change her sex. The psychologist assured her that this would be the cure. At first Patricia was open to the idea; surely this would be the answer to bring her feelings and her body together. But, the more she considered the reassignment surgery, the more she became uncomfortable with the idea. Both her high school counselor and the school psychologist were persistent in pressuring her to move forward with the procedure. However, her conscience would not permit her to do this, even though she came dangerously close to doing so.

As Patricia looked back upon this experience, she could see how the Holy Spirit had been working in her life to keep her from taking such a drastic step. She tearfully confessed to Stacey that she could now see how God had been merciful to her even in her rebellion (Psalm 86:15; 103:8; 116:5; 145:8). Patricia went even further and acknowledged that the realization and confession of her sinfulness proved to her how much she needed to rely upon Christ.

Such a critical lesson concerning daily reliance upon Christ was important for Patricia to grasp. She had been self-reliant, not Christ-reliant. It was during her two years of high school that her personal relationship with Jesus Christ had waned. At that time, she believed she could maintain the spiritual status quo and still pursue her own desires, but she realized that this made her highly vulnerable to wicked persuasion and belief.

Stacey pointed Patricia to Proverbs 19:27: "Cease to hear instruction, my son, and you will stray from the words of knowledge." Patricia's spiritual standing with the Lord was never a static thing. Either she was progressing or declining. Like a ship without its moorings, her heart would naturally drift away from God and His Word if she was not purposeful in her devotion to Christ.

Patricia had gone through a rebellious period of her life during which she had drifted and the sinfulness of her own heart was carried away by the currents of a worldly cosmology. It was a cosmology that taught her that the created binary genders were a mistake and the addition of a host of nonbinary genders was necessary. But God was gracious to her and saved her from this wicked belief system that would produce nothing but a life of hardship and misery. And thankfully, she repented before permanent damage was done.

With Stacey's help, Patricia identified an idol that had directed her heart to demand, "I must be masculine!" She asked God to forgive her and then sought the forgiveness of her parents. In the words of the apostle Peter, Patricia's turnaround was like that of the early Christians: "You were straying like sheep, but have now returned to the Shepherd and Overseer of your souls" (1 Peter 2:25).

10. When you fail to follow God's truth, it results in incalculable human suffering and personal misery.

Only hypermodernity would superimpose upon mankind a confusing and judgmental nonbinary transgender cosmology—*confusing* because gender identity is subject to the vacillating impressions of human feelings and emotions, and *judgmental* because anyone who refuses to accept the "normality" of transgenderism is labeled a narrow-minded bigot.

But there is always a price to pay when people decide to rebel against God's created limits. The result is incalculable suffering and pain. Listen to the testimony of a 56-year-old man who had undergone sexual reassignment surgery to become a woman: "I knew I wasn't a real woman, no matter what my identification documents said. I had taken extreme steps to resolve my gender conflict, but changing genders hadn't worked. It was obviously a masquerade. I felt I had been lied to. How in the world had I reached this? How did I become a fake woman?"[34]

This man, in his desperation and despair, eventually surrendered to alcohol abuse and contemplated suicide until he became whole again as a man. There is a growing awful legacy of other tragic testimonies describing the personal havoc that transgenderism has caused in the lives of many.

Scripture warns believers that those who willfully practice ungodliness will reap what they sow (Proverbs 22:8; Hosea 10:12-15;

Galatians 6:7). Stacey helped Patricia see that this is the way that God has designed all of life. Open rebellion results in inevitable miserable consequences.

However, the reverse is just as true. When a person like Patricia decides to follow the path of righteousness, then it can be said that good consequences will follow. Solomon affirms this in Proverbs 13:21: "Disaster pursues sinners, but the righteous are rewarded with good" (see also 13:15). This does not mean that every righteous person has a good and carefree life, nor does it mean that every wicked person will have a difficult and miserable life. This proverb is a broad generalization that indicates that in most cases, this is what happens to the righteous and the wicked, even though there are exceptions to this principle, and God is in control of those exceptions.

What we do know with certainty is that eventually, those who pursue wicked ways will all receive divine judgment (Hebrews 9:27). They will face an eternal misery. On the other hand, those who repent will escape judgment and find mercy, grace, and peace (Ezekiel 18:21-23).

Questions for Discussion

1. Read through the first two chapters of Genesis. Write, in your own words, a description of God's creation of male and female—what the world calls "binary gender."

2. Read Psalm 18:30-31, Deuteronomy 32:3-4, Isaiah 45:5-6. Think about the perfections of the Most High God, both in what He created (male and female) and in His essence and character. How would you answer Patricia's objection, "Then why did God give me the desires and feelings of a boy and put me into a girl's body?"

3. Frequently, Christian women have a hard time relating to someone who has transgender or homosexual tendencies. It seems so foreign to their thinking and experience that they are reluctant to befriend them. Read through Colossians 3:12-17 and write down three practical ways that you could befriend a Christian who is struggling with transgender or homosexual tendencies. Include the ways in which your own thinking would need to change with regard to compassion, humility, meekness, etc.

4. Again reading Colossians 3:12-17, describe ways in which a Christian woman can encourage the parents of a child who is struggling with transgenderism.

5. In what ways can you encourage a Christian mom to influence her daughter toward a godly view of femininity? Provide examples of how to handle clothing choices, domestic involvement in the home, and the influence of social media.

17

Victim of Abuse

Let all who take refuge in you rejoice; let them ever
sing for joy, and spread your protection over them, that
those who love your name may exult in you.

PSALM 5:11

Amanda cowered in fear behind the large wingback chair, hoping
he would not see her. If she could hide long enough—just until he
fell asleep, exhausted from his latest binge and angry tirade directed
at anyone who got in the way...well, then maybe she would escape
the abuse...this time...

Amanda had gotten married at 18 years of age. Life was good! Justin had a job, and although he was 9 years older than she, they were
happy together. It had taken her several months to convince her parents that she was ready for marriage, but they finally gave in and she
had the wedding of her dreams. She couldn't understand why her
dad seemed so reserved around Justin. It was true that Justin had
been married before, and that his first wife had divorced him not
long after they had gotten married. But Amanda didn't see how that
affected her. She was blissfully in love with her man, and he seemed
happier than she had ever seen him.

A few weeks after their wedding day, Justin came home late from
work looking red in the face and not too steady on his feet. Amanda

smelled alcohol and turned away from the nauseating odor. Angered at her response, he shoved her aside. "What's the matter, don't you want a kiss from your hard-working husband?" He slumped down on the couch and picked up the TV remote. "Why isn't dinner ready? Can't you find the time to think about me for a change?"

And thus began a new life for Amanda. Instead of a loving, hard-working, supportive husband, Justin became more selfish and abusive as the days progressed. She kept quiet about the unwelcomed changes in their marriage, but her family could see that she was quiet and withdrawn most of the time. When her mom tried to ask her about how things were going, Amanda just said "Fine" and quickly changed the subject. Fear lurked in her heart that opening up to her family would mean more abuse than ever.

Amanda had grown up in a close, loving family. Always faithful to attend church, Amanda had heard the truth of the gospel of Jesus Christ from her earliest days. At age 12 she recognized her sinfulness before a holy God and cried out to Him in repentance and faith. Grateful for God's mercy, she began to read her Bible and pray. Her mother was there to help Amanda's 12-year-old mind grasp the truth about sin and judgment and undeserved grace.

The teen years are always challenging, especially when boys start noticing girls. Amanda was growing into a cute young lady, and the guys were paying attention. She enjoyed their flirtatious comments and had a few boyfriends. Then when she was 17 she met Justin. Tall, blonde, and very handsome, he swept her off her feet. He had started attending church with some guys he knew from work. Age-wise, Justin was well past high school, but that didn't faze Amanda. He identified himself as a Christian, carried a Bible to church, and prayed earnestly. Amanda was smitten!

And now this: abuse. The word sounded foreign to her. Never had she imagined she would be facing constant fear and terror. Wincing in pain from Justin's most recent blow, Amanda had come to know the physical pain of abuse. But she also knew another pain as well—a relentless terror along with an agonizing, emotional shredding of the soul. The unanticipated betrayal of the one whom she had once trusted seared her innermost being. Amanda's mind was constantly active, trying to sort out what might have led to these repeated displays of anger and physical assault. She thought she was secure in a relationship built on trust, but instead she found herself in a nightmare of terror. The attacks she endured could have come from a stranger—rape or assault. Painful as that would be, the anguish she felt was even greater because the attacks came from someone whom she thought she could trust.

Abusive behavior is defined as nonaccidental behavior that can include shoving, slapping, hair pulling, pinching, restraining, shaking, throwing, biting, kicking, hitting, burning, or poisoning.[35] It may involve the use of a weapon or a common object that becomes a weapon. Abuse that happens within relationships involving trust makes for a deeply emotional experience, intensifying the physical pain and deepening the emotional ache. Such trust is common among people in marriages, families, friendships, neighbors, companies, and governmental and religious organizations. The more intimate the victim's relationship is to the abuser, the greater the sense of violated trust. The victim is left thinking, *I trusted him. How could he do this? I have never felt more violated!*

Sometimes an abuser will attempt to restrict the victim from her economic resources, and isolate her from friends, family, and church. He will seek to demoralize her, to persuade her that she is crazy. Abusers are controlling people, and controlling people are fearful people. They are fearful of being exposed before man and God, and they are fearful of losing the one under their control.

Repeated abuse creates physical and emotional distance. Amanda noticed this right away. She remembered how she used to love sitting close to Justin in church, but now she kept a bit of distance between them. Her attempts at smiling and looking "normal" in public were combined with nervous glances around to see if others had noticed the changes that had taken place in their once-cozy relationship. Very honestly, she didn't trust Justin. Even though up to this point the abuse had taken place behind closed doors, Amanda wasn't sure that he wouldn't begin to mistreat her in public. That would carry a shame and embarrassment that she wasn't ready for.

More and more, Justin himself would go on unpredictable roller coaster rides of emotions. Within the space of just a few minutes he could be furious at Amanda, and then contrite and compassionate. A few times his conscience had accused him so greatly that he had come home with roses and tickets to a movie. He thought that what he and Amanda needed was to get out more—to date each other once again. He was sure this was just the thing to bring her close to him once again.

The abuser's guilt often produces displays of remorse, but when he is caught up in a cycle of abuse, this remorse is not evidence of genuine repentance. Apologies are often accompanied with elaborate excuses—some that ascribe the blame to the victim—which may include implied threats, scare tactics, or humiliation in order to further degrade her and cause her to question her own sanity. But at the end of a weak attempt to win her back, the abuse begins again. This "cycle of abuse"—anger, attack, alienation, affection, and then back to anger—seems a hopeless vortex.

Amanda was plagued by doubts and fears. Then when she discovered she was pregnant, she was hesitant to share the news with Justin. She wasn't sure how he would respond. She felt trapped because now she was carrying his child—which brought about a sense of permanence to her connection with him. She didn't trust him now; how could she trust him with their child? What would happen if he continued the abuse and she tried to end their marriage? Would she lose her job, her home, and their child? She was tempted to flee, but the potential consequences of doing that were too frightening, so she stayed. In the back of her mind she remembered vowing to love Justin during the bad times as well as the good. But how bad would it get before she could no longer endure?

• • • • •

Amanda's situation raises some good questions that need answers. Is it wrong for an abused woman to seek a place of safety away from physical violence and abuse? Absolutely not. "The prudent sees danger and *hides himself,* but the simple go on and suffer for it" (Proverbs 22:3). This is especially true if there is any reason to believe that not only you, but your children could be in danger. Children are often caught in the crossfire of spousal abuse, and can easily become unintended victims. God has compassion on those who are defenseless (Isaiah 10:1-2). In fact, one of God's most memorable accusations against the prophet Jonah was his careless disregard for the children of Nineveh, placing his own comfort above their physical welfare (Jonah 4:10-11; the "120,000 persons who do not know their right hand from their left" are presumed to be children).

The best course of action is to protect those who cannot protect themselves. In situations where child abuse has occurred, it should be reported to the appropriate civil authorities. The child abuser will suffer the consequences because the civil servant "is the servant of God, an avenger who carries out God's wrath on the wrongdoer" (Romans 13:4). Being decisive on behalf of the safety of children is imperative.

What about when a woman is seeking a place of safety for herself? Is that wrong? Again, as we saw in Proverbs 27:12, the answer is no. When evil men in the city of Damascus attempted to capture the apostle Paul in order to harm him physically and bring an end

334 · The Biblical Counseling Guide for Women

to his ministry of the gospel, he did not consider it more virtuous to remain in harm's way. Instead, he escaped over the city wall (2 Corinthians 11:32-33). Escaping evil that is coming your way is a wise and godly thing to do.

Now, you may object that Paul did not have a covenantal relationship with those evil men the way a husband and wife have in a marriage. This is true. Because marriage is the most intimate of all human relationships, carrying with it a considerable amount of trust as well as covenantal responsibilities (Mark 10:7-9; see also Proverbs 2:16-17), it is imperative that the Christian woman does everything she can to fulfill her marital vows (Malachi 2:16).

But this does not mean she cannot seek a place of safety. This is where a biblical church, one with a high view of Jesus Christ and the Scriptures, is a woman's gift of grace. Not only can such a church help a woman find a temporary home of safety in the same way the Christians of the city of Damascus assisted Paul in his flight to safety, but it can also help to compassionately counsel her through the emotionally difficult time. She will need this help!

Some women will ask, "What about divorce as a solution to abuse?" This is an important question for a Christian woman who is suffering in an abusive marriage. We have already seen that seeking a place of safety for herself and her children is biblically permissible, but may not be a permanent solution. There are only two instances in which the Bible allows divorce to take place. The first is taught by Jesus as a clear universal principle of the kingdom of God (Matthew 5:32; 19:9) and involves the unrepentant adultery of the spouse. The second involves abandonment or separation by an unbelieving spouse (1 Corinthians 7:15).

Abuse is obviously not the same thing as adultery, but what about abandonment? The original Greek text of the New Testament identifies the idea "to separate" or "to abandon" as an act of isolation by the unbelieving spouse. It is a personal act of removing oneself so that there is physical distance between spouses. Abuse can be a form of separation because violated trust creates distance, and this is especially so when the abuse is the type that is potentially maiming or life-threatening. Furthermore, the present tense of the Greek verb "to abandon" indicates an action that is relentless, determined, continual. Violent abuse of this incessant nature, producing an isolation-abandonment situation, fits the biblical category of allowable divorce by abandonment.

A woman should always seek godly counsel from her pastor or another godly leader in her church when it comes to determining whether divorce is a prudent course of action. Their biblical guidance and insights will greatly benefit her decision-making, as it is extremely easy for the strong emotions of fear and betrayal to affect an abused woman's thinking. Consider also that close family members are not always the best counselors in such situations because they often opt for *anything* to relieve their loved one of abuse. Their advice would likely be clouded by their compassion for her, and hence they might not give the best possible biblical advice.

On the other hand, there are Christian women who purposefully choose to remain in an abusive relationship for a variety of reasons. Some say they are staying for love, clinging to fond memories and attraction to their husband's positive traits, such as his reliability and capacity for affection. Others fear that if they should choose to divorce, they will be cut off from friends and financial support. Still other women resort to blaming themselves for the abuse of their husband: "If I was only a better wife, he would not be so provoked to anger." The abuser may even encourage this type of thinking and convince her that she is worthless and undesirable. She is left thinking that if she left him, no one would ever love her again.

Then there are Christian women who choose to stay in an abusive situation out of biblical conviction. Too frequently the world will unfairly malign her with a mental disease label such as *enabler* or *codependent*. They do this because they cannot comprehend her devotion to Christ and her commitment to letting her life be a testimony of the gospel, but the result is that they heap more abuse upon the already abused.

The apostle Peter addressed the woman enduring abuse at the hands of her husband. Note his careful wording in 1 Peter 3:1: "Likewise, wives, be subject to your own husbands, so that even if some do not obey the word, they may be won without a word by the conduct of their wives." The term "likewise" refers back to chapter 2 where Peter described how Jesus Christ handled personal abuse ("when he was reviled, he did not revile in return"—verses 21-25). Peter was writing to Christians enduring the early days of severe persecution by the Roman emperor Nero (AD 54-68).

Nero had falsely accused the Christians of setting fire to Rome, when it was actually his initiative to burn the slums of Rome so he could build for himself a larger palace complex. In retaliation, the populace of the Roman Empire turned against Christians. Many Christians suffered crucifixion, others were torn apart by wild dogs, and some were even covered with pitch and lit on fire as torches to light palace gardens. The example of Christ's response to suffering was a needful model for Christians facing persecution.

One of the important issues that rose among Christians during this time of distress was how a Christian wife should respond to her husband if he was not obeying the Word—whether he was a believer or not. This disobedience to the Word was presumably in the form of spousal abuse, since the term "likewise" causes the diligent student of the Bible to give attention to the examples of abuse in the previous verses:

- *1 Peter 2:18-20*—Servants were instructed to be subject to their masters, even if "suffering unjustly" by being beaten.

- *1 Peter 2:21-24*—Jesus Christ is our example, in that He did not revile in return, nor did He threaten, but continued to trust in His Father's judgment while He was wounded and killed on the cross, thereby suffering unjust abuse at the hands of sinful men.

So Peter now addresses the wife, encouraging her to remain subject to her disobedient (and perhaps abusive) husband as she seeks to win him over to righteousness as he observes her respectful and pure conduct in the midst of difficulty. As was stated above, this instruction is for "Christian women who choose to stay in an abusive situation out of biblical conviction," hoping to influence their husbands to submit themselves to the Lord. While many women choose not to follow this course of action for various sound reasons, the wife who does so by faith can be encouraged and supported that God may indeed choose to work through her gentle and quiet spirit for her husband's good. You can see this objective addressed in the surrounding context (1 Peter 2:12, 15; 3:13-17).

Peter then pointed to Sarah, a godly woman, as an example to emulate (3:6). Sarah's faith-filled husband, Abraham (Genesis 15:6), did not always obey God either, and as a result, he brought serious hardship into both of their lives (12:11-13; 16:1-4; 20:1-2).

And for what was Sarah praised? She kept her conduct respectful and pure (1 Peter 3:2); more than her outward adornment of clothing and hairstyle, she cultivated a gentle and quiet spirit, "which in God's sight is very precious" (verses 3-4); and she hoped in God by submitting to her husband by doing good and not giving way to fear (verses 5-6). The attitudes and actions of this kind of wife can have a profound and lasting testimony for Christ with her husband.

When a husband observes his wife's Christlike behavior in response, this can have a life-changing impact upon his heart. Her righteous and gracious conduct in the midst of suffering will be influential. This wife must beware, for fear will be her foremost enemy (3:6) because she is giving up all attempts to control her husband—and that feels like a recipe for disaster. Learning to trust God's sovereign work in her husband's heart requires a woman of deep trust and faith in Jesus Christ.

Contrary to what the world says, this woman is not a doormat. A doormat depicts a weak and frail woman who permits herself to be abused without cause due to a lack of moral fortitude and courage. This woman is just the opposite. She knows where she stands, and her abiding trust is strongly rooted in her love for the Lord Jesus Christ and His gospel, even if that results in ridicule or persecution (3:17; 4:19). This woman is committed to a cause greater than herself, and thus is able to rise above her fears and pain.

In fact, 1 Peter 3:4 says she has "the imperishable beauty of a gentle and quiet spirit, which in God's sight is very precious." Just because she is "gentle and quiet" does not mean she is a milquetoast or coward. Why? Because she stands in the midst of great adversity for the sake of the gospel. Truly, "in God's sight [she] is very precious." She is highly valued by God because a woman like her is so rare.

A clear word of caution is appropriate here: A woman who decides to stay in an abusive relationship with the intent of being a testimony for the gospel should never put her own children in danger (Matthew 18:2-6). It goes without saying that removal of children from the home, for their safety, also necessitates the removal of the wife (mother) so that she can continue to supervise their safety and daily needs. Indeed, if a mother believes she herself is in danger, she should consider whether staying with her husband (with or without the children) would place her life so at risk that, in the worst-case scenario, the children might be bereft of both mother and father should her abusive husband be imprisoned and she be left unable to care for them. In this case, the care and protection of her children supersede her testimony to her husband.

• • • • •

Feeling quite alone in her troubled marriage, Amanda cried out with agonizing questions: "Where is God in all this? Is He really near me? Why is He silent? Does He see what is going on?" Desperate for help, Amanda called an older woman in her church who was known for her love and faithfulness to the Lord. Mrs. Thomas had always been friendly to her, and on numerous occasions had said, "Amanda, I'm praying for you. Please let me know if I can ever be a help to you." Surely she would help her with these questions and the decisions she knew she must soon make.

Mrs. Thomas agreed to meet privately with Amanda and was relieved to know that this young wife wanted to seek help from the Bible. The questions that plagued her thoughts about God's seeming silence were ones that Mrs. Thomas was eager to help with.

During their first session together, Mrs. Thomas listened carefully as Amanda described the painful details of her life with Justin. After Amanda finished sharing, Mrs. Thomas opened God's Word to Psalm 10, which was written by someone who was familiar with the plight of a person who experiences unjust affliction from the hand of another. To him, it seemed that the Lord was standing far off in the time of trouble (verse 1), and that the abuser was getting away with his crimes against the helpless. The wicked man was arrogantly thinking in his heart, "There is no God"—and figured there wouldn't be any punishment for his wrongdoing (verses 4-6). In fact, the evil man bragged that nothing would prevent him from doing what he wanted to do; he renounced God without any apparent consequence (verse 3). It seemed like his purposes found a way to succeed all the time (verse 5).

Why does God sometimes allow a wicked person's brazen offenses to continue? Where is He when an abuser is consistently permitted to attack and destroy innocent victims with no restraint? Have you also been tempted to ask these same questions?

God's sovereign plans are too lofty to be known and understood by men (Isaiah 55:8-9). The Bible tells us that God is a God of mercy (Daniel 9:9), and the wicked person interprets this as if God is paying no attention to what he is doing (Psalm 10:5). Because of his false perception of reality, he continues to heap evil upon others, hunting down helpless individuals, seeking opportunities to degrade the poor or afflicted (verses 5-10). After he fulfills his wicked scheme, he concludes that God forgets, just like men. God doesn't have an eternal memory; that's why He does not avenge the wicked for what they have done (verse 11).

But the psalmist calls upon God to see and to not forget those who are afflicted (verse 12). He pleads for the Lord to arise and lift up His hand. Imagine a tension-filled courtroom in which the accuser has unlawfully abused and falsely accused the defendant. God, the Almighty Judge, has quietly observed all that has transpired. Finally He stands up and lifts His authoritative gavel to silence the madness and to render His judgment. This is what the psalmist calls upon God to do for the afflicted and needy. He longs for God to stand up, interrupt the violence, and defend justice in the courtroom of life.

Knowing who God is—that He defends the helpless and does not forget their trouble (Isaiah 25:4)—the psalmist wonders why the wicked have so flippantly written God off as if He does not know or care (Psalm 10:13). God has looked intently on the troubles that abuse victims face and has placed them in His own hand (verse 14). They can rest confidently in God because He is a helper of the fatherless and the unprotected (82:3-4). The psalmist is convinced that should the Lord choose to break the wicked man's arm, hardship will relentlessly pursue that person to the point that he and his wickedness will be completely eliminated from the scene. Nothing will be left (10:15).

Why can God do this? Because He is the King of the world. And He will never stop being King. Nations have already been destroyed by His hand and removed from their land (verse 16—probably a reference to the Canaanite nations that once lived in the Promised Land before God's people came in conquest). Those who stood in Israel's way were completely annihilated. If God can destroy whole nations of people, then He can remove an individual abuser from an unjust situation or even bring him to genuine repentance. In Psalm 10 we are being called to remember the past and what God has already done. Has He not been faithful to make right decisions and destroy wicked people from existence (that is, Jericho, Ai, Hazor, etc.)? Much more then will He be faithful to ultimately fulfill His justice in all situations.

God hears the cries of the afflicted, who long for safety and peace. He has not abandoned His own. Indeed, the very presence of the Lord is promised to those who trust in Him. God declared, "I will not leave you or forsake you. Be strong and courageous" to His children the Israelites, who were terrified to fight against the strong warriors who inhabited the Promised Land (Joshua 1:5-6). Israel's best warriors had seen the strength of the enemy, and by human reasoning, had every right to be shaking in their boots. Read the entire book of Joshua to see how God faithfully kept His promise to be with them during this difficult time (Joshua 21:45). God's promise of His presence is reaffirmed by Jesus Himself just before He ascended into heaven: "Behold, I am with you always, to the end of the age" (Matthew 28:20). This promise from Jesus was not just for His disciples, but for us today. Take comfort in the reality of His presence.

But take comfort even further in the truth that God sees all abuse and injustice, as we have seen in Psalm 10. Even as God strengthens our hearts with His presence, he also listens intently to the cry of the abused one with the aim to render a judgment on her behalf (verse 18). He does not promise when this judgment will take place; He does not provide a set time and place in which the abuse will end. However, He does promise a future day when "man who is of the earth may strike terror no more." This is a sure hope, because we know that God never lies and fulfills all His promises (Numbers 23:19; Titus 1:2; Hebrews 6:18; 10:30-39).

Amanda listened carefully as Mrs. Thomas taught her these truths about her God, the King of the world. She had never thought about God this way before. When Amanda was in high school, her youth group participated in a Bible memorization plan. She remembered learning Psalm 46:1-3: "God is our refuge and strength, a very present help in trouble. Therefore we will not fear though the earth gives way, though the mountains be moved into the heart of the sea, though its waters roar and foam, though the mountains tremble at its swelling."

Although Amanda believed these things to be true, she now had a very real context in which she was challenged with her belief. Did she truly believe that God was a refuge and strength for other people— for example, the people in Bible times when these verses were written? And did she believe that God was also *her* refuge and strength in *her* time of great danger and need? She had asked, "Where is God? Is He really near me? Why is He silent? Does He see what is happening?"

Those same questions were asked in Psalm 10:1—just in different words. The afflicted one in this psalm cried out, "Why, O LORD, do you stand far away? Why do you hide yourself in times of trouble?" Then after he decried the arrogance of his wicked abuser (verses

2-11), he called upon God to remember the afflicted. He affirmed that God is present; that He really is near; that He does see what is happening; that He is the King forever and ever. In other words, the writer of this psalm firmly believes what God has revealed about His character, His love for those afflicted, His power, and His rulership over all. He doesn't just believe it for someone else; he believes it for his particular situation.

And so he ends this psalm by declaring this truth: "O Lord, you hear the desire of the afflicted; you will strengthen their heart, you will incline your ear to do justice to the fatherless and the oppressed, so that man who is of the earth may strike terror no more" (verses 17-18).

Amanda was moved to tears as she realized that she had allowed her fear and despair to so overwhelm her that she had not truly believed that these promises of God were for *her*. She had, in her heart, accused God of forsaking her—of not being her refuge and strength. Mrs. Thomas encouraged her to repent of accusing God of wrongdoing and failing to believe what He had promised, which Amanda humbly did. Afterward, she began to experience the first glimmer of hope in her desperate situation as she read further about God's help for the oppressed and afflicted—and *believed* what she read. She knew that her ultimate hope was not in a change in her circumstances, but in the Living God who had promised to help her and, being King of the world, had the ability to make that help a reality.

Mrs. Thomas also explained what Amanda's options were as a Christian wife. She carefully walked through the critical questions that she would need to answer as she considered whether to stay or leave, based on the truths already mentioned:

- seeking a place of safety
- providing safety for the children

- divorce as an answer

- choosing to stay to win him over to righteousness

Amanda knew it was time to talk these things over with her parents, allowing them to help her make the decisions in front of her. She was tempted to be fearful of their response, particularly of their anger toward Justin, but she chose instead to trust that God would help them all to navigate through the turbulent waters ahead. She meditated on this truth in Psalm 10:17: "You will strengthen their heart" (the heart of the afflicted). She knew that no matter what happened to her and the little one growing inside, God would indeed be with her, for He promised, "I will never leave you nor forsake you" (Hebrews 13:5).

Mrs. Thomas encouraged Amanda with the following practical helps, which proved to be a great blessing in her difficulty.

Remain faithful to your local church.

Make it a high priority to join a local church that teaches and holds firmly to the Word of God. Even if your husband does not attend that church with you, these are the people of God who will provide the greatest help when you are seeking a place of safety. You will need them! Our God has always provided assistance for the helpless and afflicted; the psalmist describes Him as the God of refuge (Psalm 5:11; 7:1; 11:1; 17:7; 18:2). The counsel you can receive from biblically qualified Christians in the church, who know and love this same God, is the help you need.

Come under the protection of civil authorities and the local church.

The protection of civil authorities and the local church were both mentioned earlier. The police are God's agent for restraining those who would do evil against us; the church provides biblical guidance and a safe haven for those abused.

If your husband should forbid you to contact the police or to attend this kind of church, you should not be concerned that you are unsubmissive to him if you do so. Husbands do not have authority from God to forbid their wives to seek a biblical house of worship. Neither do they have authority from God to abuse you, nor to prevent you from receiving the help of the police. Although your husband may use threats and intimidation, the wisest decision will be for you to run to these two God-given means of protection.

Handle your fear.

Fear is a very real emotion for women who are being abused. Far from being an irrational fear, the reasons for it stare them in the face daily.

However, even if an abusive husband chooses to stay, God can help the wife to respond in such a way that fear does not completely take over her life, rendering her powerless to make necessary and morally sound decisions. Consider that when fear utterly overwhelms a wife, she may have lost sight of Christ's love and care for her. Similarly, when fear totally consumes her, her love for God is likely weak. "There is no fear in love, but perfect love casts out fear" (1 John 4:18).

Notice that the apostle John did not say that perfect love casts out a person's reason to fear. Perfect love may not remove the abuse from that person's life in this moment, but this perfect love can keep fear from so dominating her life that she remains able to take care of herself and her children. Her fearful and anxious thoughts need to be directed to Hebrews 2:18: "Because he [Jesus] himself has suffered when tempted, he is able to help those who are being tempted." Here the author of Hebrews is writing to Jewish Christians enduring continual suffering. It is reassuring to understand that Jesus Christ not only knows about their suffering, both the fact and personal experience of it, but He also is "able to help" them through it. Earlier verses (14-17) show that this help is in reference to the temptation to succumb to fear in the midst of suffering—for the very reason that Christ has defeated the greatest cause for fear: death (2:14-15).

Recognize that your strength comes from the living God.

Meditate on His promises to you.

> Why do you say, O Jacob, and speak, O Israel, "My way is hidden from the LORD, and my right is disregarded by my God"? Have you not known? Have you not heard? The LORD is the everlasting God, the Creator of the ends of the earth. He does not faint or grow weary; his understanding is unsearchable. He gives power to the faint, and to him who has no might he increases strength. Even youths shall faint and be weary, and young men shall fall exhausted; but they who wait for the LORD shall renew their strength; they shall mount up with wings like eagles; they shall run and not be weary; they shall walk and not faint (Isaiah 40:27-31).

Questions for Discussion

1. When Amanda was questioning God and accusing Him of forsaking her, this revealed that in her heart she did not _____ God or His promises to her. In what specific ways did this kind of heart lead her to despair and prevent her from finding hope in God?

2. Read Isaiah 40:27-31 again. Explain how these truths can bring hope to Amanda in her situation.

3. Read Genesis 16:1-16 and Genesis 21:1-21. This is a true account of a woman and her son who was abused at the hand of

another. List the ways that God was faithful to Hagar and Ishmael.

4. While it would be our hope that an abuser would repent of his abuse and begin to love the one he afflicts, this is not promised. What does God promise the afflicted one? As you answer, consider Psalm 22:24; 34:21; 119:50, 92; Isaiah 30:20; 63:9.

5. Read Lamentations 3:1-33. What is the hope of every child of God who suffers affliction?

Appendix A

What is a true Christian? What does it mean to have saving faith in Jesus Christ?

The gospel is the truth about God's redeeming love for mankind. It is a glorious truth, but because there are distortions of it in religious and nonreligious settings, it is important to make a clarifying statement that agrees wholly with the Bible.

According to the Bible, the gospel *reveals* the self-centered and wicked heart of every person ever born. This sin was brought about by Adam and Eve's original sin in the garden (see Genesis 1–3). The goal of the gospel is to *produce* genuine sorrow for that sin that leads to repentance and faith in Jesus Christ, the Son of God (2 Corinthians 7:10; Ephesians 2:8-9). The result of the gospel is to *transform* the sinner into a redeemed child of God, which means she will no longer live for herself but for the Lord Jesus, who died for her (2 Corinthians 5:15).

The basis of saving faith is not in anything a sinner can do, but in everything that God has done. "He [God] made him [Jesus] to be sin who knew no sin, so that in him we might become the righteousness of God" (5:21).

> When the goodness and loving kindness of God our Savior appeared, he saved us, not because of works done by us in righteousness, but according to his own mercy, by the washing of regeneration and renewal of the Holy Spirit, whom he poured out on us richly through Jesus

Christ our Savior, so that being justified by his grace we might become heirs according to the hope of eternal life (Titus 3:4-7).

When God saves a person, He creates in her a humble heart that recognizes her inability to stand sinless before Him. And by repentance and faith in the death, burial, and resurrection of Jesus she receives His gift of eternal life. Jesus Christ, who is Himself God the Son, humbled Himself to become man as well, and by His death and resurrection destroyed the power of death over those who believe in Him. What a glorious gospel!

The effect of God's redeeming love is that it draws the believer's interest away from herself. She is no longer living to

- affirm herself as she is,
- improve herself,
- authenticate herself,
- find her real self, or
- determine her existence based solely on her own interests.

Saving faith in Jesus Christ as Lord will drive you away from yourself to God. But first it necessitates a genuine repentance of

- living only for yourself,
- violating the law of God in multiple ways, and
- rejecting what He created you for: to bring glory to Him by serving His purpose for you.

The Bible is clear that those who reject the message of the gospel stand under the judgment of a righteous God: "He who believes in the Son has eternal life; but he who does not obey the Son will not see life, but the wrath of God abides on him" (John 3:36 NASB).

Because this is a book about helping women with difficult problems, it is important to clarify that the gospel of our Lord Jesus Christ is not a system of thought or process that is to be used to fix problems. In seeking out what a true Christian is, the goal should not be to find something from God that will give someone the best life possible on earth. Rather, the search for the truth of the gospel of Jesus Christ is for the purpose of living in complete submission and obedience to the God of the Bible, who created the perfect man and woman and who showered love and mercy on them when they sinned, sacrificing His very life to redeem them.

Appendix B

Scripture Index

Notes

1. Varner's work was consulted to verify this perspective as well as the entirety of James 1:19-21. William Varner, *The Book of James: A New Perspective: A Linguistic Commentary in Applying Discourse Analysis* (The Woodlands, TX: Kress Biblical Resources, 2010), 67-68.

2. Word document notes taken from Dr. John D. Street's "PM 769 Student Outline Spring 13" in PM 769 Advanced Biblical Counseling class at The Master's Seminary, Sun Valley, CA in the Spring 2013 semester, page 9.

3. American Psychiatric Association, *Diagnostic and Statistical Manual of Mental Disorders: DSM-5* (2013), 667. Emphasis mine.

4. In this verse, Solomon literally says, "…because childhood and the blackness are fleeting [i.e. temporary]." When he uses the word "blackness," it is a likely idiom for the typical color of the Jewish man and woman's hair, which will not stay silky black forever.

5. All three passages use "imperishable" (from the Greek root *afthartos*, ἄφθαρτος) as part of Peter's motif of things that last. He uses this theme to argue that these unfading and certain realities should be regarded with the highest significance by Christians in a world which is fading away.

6. Consider Paul's parallel admonition to the women readers in Timothy's church in 1 Timothy 2:9-10, where he adjures them not to place an emphasis on their jewelry or "expensive clothing" (2:9).

7. Dialectical behavior therapy (DBT); Schema-focused therapy; Mentalization-based therapy (MBT); Systems training for emotional predictability and problem-solving (STEPPS); Transference-focused psychotherapy (TFP).

8. See at www.biblicalcounseling.com.

9. Maia Szalavitz, "10% of the U.S. Population Has Overcome Drugs or Alcohol," *Time*, March 07, 2012.

10. "The St. John's Wort Study," *Journal of the American Medical Association*, 2002, p. 1813.

11. Excerpted and revised, from Advanced Counseling lecture notes, The Master's College & Seminary.

12. "Increased Mortality in Bulimia Nervosa and Other Eating Disorders," *The American Journal of Psychiatry*, Vol. 166, No. 12, December 2009, pp. 1342-46.

13. Elizabeth Kübler-Ross, *On Death and Dying: What the Dying Have to Teach Doctors, Nurses, Clergy and Their Own Families* (New York: Scribners, 2014).

14. Their certification organization was the Association of Certified Biblical Counselors, www.biblicalcounseling.com.

15. "A high-handed sin is one a professing believer commits boldly and defiantly, not caring about the consequences and feeling no guilt about it once committed…That an intentional sin is not always a high-handed sin is seen in God's willingness to forgive sins that were clearly intentional (2 Sam. 11–12). Only those who are unconverted may sin with a high hand, for a converted person will express sorrow and contrition after an intentional sin, thereby proving it was never high-handed in the first place. As we repent over sins both intentional and unintentional, we are assured that we belong to Jesus." "The Sin Offering," Ligonier Ministries, http://www.ligonier.org/learn/devotionals/sin-offering/.

16. American Psychiatric Association, *Diagnostic and Statistical Manual of Mental Disorders: DSM-5* (2013), 235-64.

17. Ibid., 235.

18. Ibid., 235, 238.

19. Ibid., 235.

20. Ibid., 238.

21. Ibid.

22. Ibid., 235-36.

23. Ibid., 242.

24. As cited in Steve Volk, "Rewiring the Brain to Treat OCD," *Discovery Magazine*, December 11, 2013.

25. Ibid.

26. Selective serotonin reuptake inhibitors (SSRIs) such as Paxil, Prozac, or Zoloft, or Benzodiazepines such as Ativan, Valium, or Xanax.

27. See at www.anxieties.com/20/panic-step1a.

28. According to the National Institute of Health, the United States Food and Drug Administration has approved sertraline (Zoloft) and paroxetine (Paxil), both antidepressants, for use as post-traumatic stress disorder medication. Occasionally benzodiazepines are used to aid relaxation and sleep.

29. *Schizophrenia,* publication booklet of the National Institute of Mental Health, Office of Science Policy, Planning, and Communications; Science Writing, Press, and Dissemination Branch, 6001 Executive Boulevard, Room 6200, MSC 9663, Bethesda, MD 20892-9663.

30. Ibid.

31. First-generation or conventional antipsychotics developed in the 1950s include Chlorpromazine, Haloperidol, Perphenazine, and Fluphenazine; second-generation "atypical" antipsychotics developed in the 1990s include: Risperidone, Olanzapine, Quetiapine, Ziprasidone, Aripiprazole, Paliperidone, and Lurasidone.

32. The rare number of intersex or hermaphrodites (old term) born atypically with ambiguous genitalia is estimated to be approximately 1 in 1500 to 1 in 2000 births and is nonsupportive of transgenderism. An infant may have the chromosomes of a female but have external genitals of a male (46, XX intersex) or the chromosomes of a male but the external genitals of a female (46, XY intersex). Legitimate corrective surgery can be assigned to infants with the chromosomes of one gender and external genitalia of another (disorder of sex development, DSD), although some secularists see this as a controversial human rights issue, removing one gender genitalia and leaving the other based upon chromosomal analysis. Extremely rare is undetermined intersex disorders (45, XO – only one X chromosome; 47, XXY or 47 XXX – an extra sex chromosome), but these conditions do not cause external and internal genitalia disparities.

33. Paul McHugh, "Transgender Surgery Isn't the Solution: A drastic physical change doesn't address underlying psycho-social troubles," *The Wall Street Journal,* May 13, 2016, http://www.wsj.com/articles/paul-mchugh-transgender-surgery-isnt-the-solution-1402615120 (last accessed June 3, 2016).

34. Walt Heyer, "I was a transgender woman," *Life Site* (reprinted with permission from The Witherspoon Institute), April 8, 2015, https://www.lifesitenews.com/opinion/i-was-a-transgender-woman (last accessed June 9, 2016).

35. American Psychiatric Association, *Diagnostic and Statistical Manual of Mental Disorders: DSM-5* (2013), 720.

Other Good Harvest House Reading

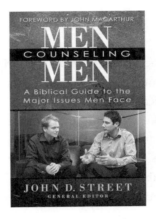

MEN COUNSELING MEN
John Street, General Editor

This is a strongly practical resource filled with the help and hope found in Scripture alone. The Bible's counsel is superior to that given by the world, addressing not just external symptoms but also the heart issues only God, our Creator, can remedy.

The trusted contributors to this volume provide tested guidance on how to effectively counsel men and real solutions for the problems they face today when it comes to these matters and more:

marriage and parenting   anger and depression
emotional extremes   conflict resolution
physical affliction   homosexuality
sexual purity   rebuilding a marriage after adultery

This book will equip all men who desire to counsel biblically—whether pastors, men's ministry leaders, or fellow brothers in Christ. And it's written with the solid assurance that when we look to God for the answers, we are building up the body of Christ in the best way possible.

The Master's University
Master of Arts in Biblical Counseling

We equip students to accurately interpret the Scriptures for insightfully understanding the thoughts and intentions of the heart, to grasp the complexity and practicality of theology, and to discern how to appropriately apply the Scriptures with truth and grace in evangelism, counseling, and discipleship. We are passionate about the sufficiency of Scripture and its unique design to comprehensively inform matters of counseling. Our training equips the whole person, building into the student biblical content, character, relationship competencies, and community.

Program Description

The Master of Arts in Biblical Counseling (MABC) is designed to be intensely practical. The content of each course emphasizes the practical skills of counseling without neglecting the solid biblical foundation upon which these skills are built. The knowledge gained from the classes and assignments can be practically implemented in each student's life and ministry immediately. Each course will enhance the student's own walk with God as well as his or her ministry.

Course instruction articulates from the biblical text both the content and methodology of counseling. This enables students to differentiate and critique various Christian and secular counseling theories and methods, comparing them with the fundamental assumptions of biblically based counseling. Students are first equipped with interpretative tools and correct hermeneutical principles to accurately exegete biblical passages for counseling purposes, while also pursuing personal progressive sanctification. This foundation yields discernment in evaluating people's character, mental processes, and behaviors from a biblical anthropology. However, because foundations and theory are still only one side of the task, the program also trains students to develop competence in the counseling and discipleship of individuals using the biblical text and effective interpersonal skills. Finally, the program develops the student as a practitioner-researcher—able to teach, train, and write in the field of biblical counseling.

Through the program, students obtain both the rigorous training of a respected master's degree and certification with the premier biblical counseling certifying agency, the Association of Certified Biblical Counselors (ACBC). That is, every student graduating from the MABC program will have completed all aspects of ACBC's certification process by nature of those requirements having been seamlessly woven into the curriculum of the required MABC courses, so as to be recognized as a certified biblical counselor upon graduation.

At the time of publication of this book, The Master's University is developing a Doctor of Ministry degree in biblical counseling. Keep checking the website for further information as it becomes available.

Contact Information

The Master's University Office of Biblical Counseling
21726 Placerita Canyon Road, Box #50
Santa Clarita, CA 91321
graduatestudies@masters.edu
Phone: (661) 362-2652; (800) 568-6248 (ext. 2652)

Association of Certified Biblical Counselors

For more than 40 years, the Association of Certified Biblical Counselors (ACBC) has been certifying biblical counselors to ensure doctrinal integrity and to promote excellence in biblical counseling. Certification is available to all pastors, professors, and other Christian servants who desire to be trained in their gospel-responsibility to be disciple-makers and provide Bible-based soul care for some of the most difficult problems Christians face. We offer a comprehensive biblical counseling certification program that is rigorous but attainable by even the busiest pastor. The biblical counseling certification phases include:

- Learning Phase: doctrinal course, outside reading, and counseling observations
- Exam and Application Phase: theological and counselor exams
- Supervision Phase: at least 50 hours of supervised counseling

We also offer annual and regional conferences as well as certification for centers desiring to become an ACBC-certified training center.

Contact Information:

www.biblicalcounseling.com
ACBC Headquarters
2825 Lexington Road
Louisville, KY 40280
(502) 410-5526